THE MURDER GUY

MIRROR BOOKS

1

Published in Great Britain and Ireland in 2026 by
Mirror Books, a Reach PLC business.

www.mirrorbooks.co.uk
@TheMirrorBooks

Print ISBN 9781917439794
eBook ISBN 9781917439800

Cover Design: Chris Collins
Editing and Production: Christine Costello, Nick Webster

Printed and bound in Great Britain by
CPI Group (UK) Ltd, Croydon, CR0 4YY

FSC www.fsc.org MIX Paper | Supporting responsible forestry FSC® C013604

THE MURDER GUY

JEFF EDWARDS

MIRROR BOOKS

For three very exceptional women;
Deborah, Victoria and Claudia.

CONTENTS

BOMBINGS, TERROR AND TRAGEDY

TERROR ON THE STREETS

CONMEN AND HITMEN

CONVERSATIONS WITH KILLERS

AUTHOR'S NOTE

I never expected to become an expert on murder. I never expected to become a leading crime reporter. In fact, I never thought I'd be any kind of journalist at all.

But, looking back, maybe it was pre-ordained that I would end up on that road. It was only because of a criminal act I was able to get a job in newspapers at all.

In the late 1960s, the area around Epping in Essex, sandwiched between east London and the sprawling post-war 'new town' of Harlow, was rarely the busiest of news patches.

So, a local reporter decided to create his own news by setting fire to a barn. Duly arrested, suddenly there was an opening at the local weekly newspaper, the *Express and Independent*, or *E&I* as everyone knew it.

However, things couldn't have had a worse start for me.

On my first official visit to a police station, aged just 18, I was well and truly roughed up when an officer thought I was looking at the arrest record over his shoulder (I wasn't).

Vaulting the counter, he launched at me before colleagues pulled him off me and, bemused, I returned to my office.

That could have been the end of my career as a crime reporter, but it was just the start.

A few hours later, a senior officer called me in for a chat and assured me that in future I could speak directly to him. I had made my first contact, in rather unusual circumstances but a contact nonetheless.

He was the first of many police officers of every rank and background who became contacts, sources and friends.

They were by my side, having a word in my ear and helping me with the inside scoop on hundreds of crime stories over the next 40 or so years as I moved from newspaper to newspaper.

From the *E&I* in the 60s to Fleet Street in the 1970s until finally ending up as Crime Editor of the *Daily Mirror* newspaper.

In what were often strange circumstances I was allowed a view from the inside as police tried to solve some of the worst crimes imaginable.

In these pages I'll take you along as I recount the inner workings of some of the biggest cases in the last 50 years and a few of the good, bad and utterly irrepressible characters I met along the way.

To all involved, thank you, but most of all to the victims and their families – I never forgot.

A CAREER IN CRIME

1967-1969: E&I

1970-1972: Newham Recorder

1972-1974: Stratford Express

1974-1981: London Evening News

1981-1986: News of the World

1986-1989: London Daily News, Daily Star, London Weekend TV

1989-1992: Sunday People.

1992-2009: Daily Mirror

PROLOGUE

I was in the office waiting to be assigned to a story when Ron, one of the detectives I had become friends with in east London, phoned me. He told me a young woman had been found murdered in Leyton, an area I knew well. The victim's name was Eve Stratford and she worked as a Bunny Girl at the famous Playboy club in Park Lane, Mayfair.

She was found by her boyfriend when he arrived home at the flat they shared late the previous day, March 18, 1975. Ron hadn't been to the scene himself, but a close colleague had, so he was able to give me a lot of important detail. Eve, who was 22, had suffered multiple knife wounds, and her throat slashed. When she was found she was wearing only a 'baby doll' nightdress and lingerie, as if she had been expecting a lover to drop by.

There were signs of her being tied up at the ankles and around her wrists, possibly as part of a sex game. I told my contact I would meet him later at a pub, and to keep his ear to the ground for further details.

I hurried over to tell George Hollingbery, my boss at the *London Evening News*. Scotland Yard had still not announced publicly a woman had been murdered, so we were ahead of the game. The details of this brutal murder were both shocking and intriguing. The Playboy Club was owned by the American entrepreneur Hugh Hefner who had also launched the pioneering soft porn magazine *Playboy* a few years before. The club and the magazine were inextricably linked.

The launch of *Playboy* magazine had caused other publishers to launch rival glamour magazines featuring spreads of beautiful young women posing naked. Two of the bestsellers were *Mayfair* and *Penthouse*. It quickly emerged that at the time Eve was murdered she had been suspended from her job as a cocktail waitress at the London Playboy Club because she had posed nude for the rival *Mayfair* magazine. Her picture had been used on the front page of that month's edition.

When police began searching the gardens of nearby houses looking for the murder weapon, a copy of the March *Mayfair*, with Eve's picture ripped and torn from it, was found in a hedge. To the police it seemed likely Eve's killer was a stalker who had seen her picture in *Mayfair*, somehow discovered where she lived, and watched her home before attacking her. The murder of this glamorous but tragic young woman dominated the front pages for days.

Initially the police had a number of possible leads, but these all turned out to be blind alleys. One of the many intriguing aspects of the case was the killer had apparently brought his own knife to the scene and taken it away afterwards. A careful check of the inventory of the rented flat told detectives no knife was missing. An inch by inch search of nearby gardens, bins, drains, coal bunkers and garages yielded nothing. The murder weapon, a crucial piece of evidence, was nowhere to be found.

I kept an eye on the Eve Stratford case, but as the days and weeks went by it became clear, despite a lot of promising information in the early stages, the police were starting to run out of leads. Several possible suspects had been traced, interviewed and eliminated.

Later that year I was tasked with dealing with the murder of another young woman. Unlike Eve, who had been a model and club hostess, 16-year-old Lynne Weedon was a quiet and studious schoolgirl. Where Eve had been murdered in Leyton, an area of east London where I had been born and grown up, Lynne was attacked and killed close to her home in Hounslow, a suburb many miles to the west of London, close to Heathrow Airport. It was an area I hardly knew at all.

On the night of September 9, 1975, Lynne was walking home from visiting a local pub with some classmates. They had been celebrating their O-level exam results. She had crossed the busy Great West Road at a pedestrian crossing and was using a shortcut through an alley, known then as 'Short Hedges' when her attacker waylaid her.

Police believed he started following her shortly before, striking her violently from behind over the head with what they thought was a heavy metal object, possibly a crowbar, tyre lever or a hammer. The blow fractured her skull and rendered her unconscious.

After knocking her to the ground her assailant lifted her body up and pushed her over the top of a nearby gate and a 6ft fence which surrounded an electricity sub station. Her killer then climbed over the fence and raped her while she lay unconscious.

When she didn't return home that evening, her parents contacted the police. The next day, a school caretaker on his way to work spotted her. She was still breathing, but in a coma. Doctors fought to keep her alive, but the damage to her brain was so severe, that after a few days she faded and died.

Everything indicated that Lynne must have been attacked by a tall man, who was unusually strong and fit. But there were no witnesses, few clues, and no suspects. Despite an intensive police search over a large area, no murder weapon was found. The killer must have taken it away with him. As part of my job it fell to me to perform the dreaded death knock – visiting her grieving parents to ask if they wanted to speak to the press. I like to think, whenever one of these awful assignments fell to me, I did all I could to be kind and empathetic.

I was always surprised how, in the majority of cases where tragedy strikes, people were prepared to invite you into their homes and engage with you. Often there were tears, sometimes anger at those who had taken their loved ones from them, or in some cases, rage at God for allowing it to happen.

In each of these encounters I suffered pangs of guilt and a feeling of intruding into the lives of people who were suffering such an unimaginable nightmare.

I still recall the Weedon family, as shocked and grief-stricken as they were, invited me in, sat me down in the living room and offered *me* tea and sympathy. I remember Lynne's mother saying to me: "It must be terrible for you to have to come and see people like us at a time like this."

They were kind and warm in the extreme, and of all the dozens of families I visited in my career, my meeting with them stands out more clearly than any other.

Lynne and Eve lived about as far apart as two people could while still being in Greater London, and thus the Metropolitan Police area. Their profiles, as victims of murder, could not have been more different. The way in which they were killed, and even the place where they were killed, was not in any way similar.

Yet, in the most extraordinary of twists, the forward march of police science and investigation was to demonstrate, 32 years later in 2007, beyond doubt they were both victims of the same murderer.

Cold case murder reviewers at Scotland Yard, a team of detectives, some of whom had not even been born when Eve and Lynne were murdered, were able to prove from minute samples of semen found on their clothing, they were both victims of the same man. Yet even now, at the time of writing in 2026, with around seven million names on the national DNA database, the culprit has still not been unmasked.

Two years to the day after Lynne was attacked, I was assigned another murder, which had astonishing similarities. Elizabeth Parravincini was a strikingly beautiful woman, aged 27, who was walking home from a tube station late at night when her killer struck from behind. She was less than a mile from the spot where Lynne had been attacked. A powerful blow with a heavy metal weapon fractured her skull and sent her sprawling on the ground. The attack took place late at night near Osterley station where Elizabeth had got off the Piccadilly Line after a night out in London with friends.

She had walked a short distance along the Great West Road and was approaching a private housing estate where she had a flat. After attacking her, the killer dragged her body into some shrubbery, but police believe he was disturbed, possibly by a car turning into a nearby side road, and fled before he had time to rape her.

As in Lynne's case, the murder weapon had been taken away from the scene by the killer and was never found. Because of the near identical circumstances I was sure her assailant was the same killer who had attacked Lynne, a view shared by detectives from Scotland Yard's murder squad. There was no sign of robbery. Elizabeth's's handbag was still on her shoulder.

In Elizabeth's case, no forensic evidence was left behind to prove a conclusive link between her murder and that of Lynne. I suspect that all three women were the victim of a serial killer who has never been found.

Throughout my career I went on to report on the still unsolved murders of over 100 girls and women, in almost every circumstance imaginable, and I have often wondered if any of them were yet more victims of the still undetected murderer who took the lives of Lynne, Linda and Eve.

My time covering those horrific crimes also marked the first use of an irreverent tag which stuck with me for the next 35 years after my boss George Hollingbery called me over to his desk and said: "Well Jeff, looks like you are the new murder guy round here now."

He turned out to be more right than he knew.

COPS AND ROBBERS

CHAPTER ONE

Arriving for my first day on the *Newham Recorder*, I had a touch of butterflies in my stomach. After three years on the smaller *Express and Independent* and *Herts* and *Essex Observer* newspapers, this was a big step up for me professionally. I was still only 21. Was I good enough? Could I cut the mustard?

About 30 minutes after settling into the desk I'd been allocated, and introducing myself to some of my new colleagues, I realised I had come out that morning without any money on me. I knew I might need some cash in order to do my job and quickly dashed to the bank.

The local branch of the Midland Bank, with an imposing late Victorian façade, was on the corner nearby. I sprinted up the three steps to the main door and hurried inside. Something was definitely wrong. Why, I asked myself, are all these people lying face down on the floor?

Right there at my feet, six or seven people, men and women, some of them smartly dressed in good suits and pricey outfits, were lying spread eagled and face down on the black and white tiled floor.

As I faltered and tried to take in the scene, I noticed the four windows usually occupied by bank clerks were empty. Then, at the window nearest to where I was standing, a woman's head, her hair looking a bit of a mess, rose up from under the counter where she had been hiding. She looked at me and in a trembling voice said: "I'm sorry for the inconvenience. We've just been robbed."

Which, I then realised, explained why there was a lot of money – green £1 notes, blue fivers, brown tens – lying about on the floor. I was quite confused, unsure if the robbery was still going on, or if it was over. But overriding my sense of fascination I knew I had to inform my colleagues.

The best way to do that was to run the 40 yards or so back to my office, and tell them personally. Mobile phones hadn't been invented then – I wouldn't get my first one for another 23 years. So I turned quickly and walked out onto the pavement and into utter pandemonium.

There, blocking the road was a 10-ton tipper truck, its engine racing, with the throttle apparently stuck open. The windscreen was shattered and inside the cab the driver was sitting bolt upright behind the steering wheel, trickles of blood running down his face.

In the gutter at my feet and on the pavement were lots more bank notes, some swirling about among fallen autumn leaves. People were picking them up. Some were stuffing them in their pockets and scarpering.

The police were not there and I realised the attack must literally have been happening as I walked the few yards towards the bank. The robbers must have escaped seconds before I arrived. If I had been there 20 seconds earlier I would have met them coming down the bank steps as I was going up.

I sprinted back and took the office stairs two at a time. Bursting in, I shouted: "Quick, there's just been a robbery at the bank on the corner." For a second or two people just looked at me. Blankly.

Then the news editor Terry Chinnery jumped to his feet, shouting instructions to other reporters and photographers.

Terry ran towards me. "Come on," he shouted. We sprinted back down to the bank. The first patrol cars were arriving, then an ambulance.

One of our photographers screeched around the corner in his little Ford Anglia, parked on a double yellow line, jumped out and started taking pictures. Terry and I started asking passers-by lots of questions. I even found two of the customers I had almost stumbled over as they lay on the floor.

In my haste I had forgotten to grab a notebook from my desk, but I still had my chequebook and a pen, so I wrote witness accounts on the back of blank cheques. Still shaking, they gave vivid descriptions of masked men with guns and coshes shouting and swearing in their faces and ordering them to lie on the floor. A local shopkeeper, who had gone to get £50 for his float was still trembling with emotion as he told me a robber had screamed at him: "Don't fucking look at us!"

The lorry driver had been shot through his windscreen. A witness had seen the robbers rush out of the bank and jump into a getaway car, a white Mark Two Ford Cortina, parked directly outside. At that moment the tipper truck had arrived on the scene travelling in the same direction and slowing for the junction.

It appeared one of the gang, fearing the truck driver was a 'have a go hero' and about to ram them, took the pre-emptive step of letting fly with a sawn-off shotgun. Fortunately, only a few lead pellets broke through the glass. The truck driver, who could have easily been blinded, received some superficial injuries to his jaw and chin. He was taken to hospital suffering from shock but allowed to go home the next day.

Several people said one of the cash bags the robbers had snatched had burst, scattering hundreds of notes on the floor of the bank and on the pavement outside. Marked police cars and two ambulances were quickly on the scene, treating people for shock and trying to make order out of the chaos.

After half an hour or so some detectives from the Criminal Investigation Depatment (CID) turned up. They started visiting shops and businesses close to the scene, looking for eyewitnesses. They were also keen to find anyone who had picked up any of the scattered money, and to make sure they handed it over.

Several years later, knowing the things some London police officers were prone to do, I did wonder how much of that money found its way back to the bank.

Although the bank knew how much was missing, who could say how much the robbers actually got away with, and how much of it was lost in the chaos of their escape?

Back at the office everyone wanted to know my account. Tom Duncan, my editor, said words to me I will never forget: "Well done. It's not just right place, right time. I think you are going to be a lucky reporter, and editors like lucky reporters."

I pulled my cheque book from my jacket pocket and started to transcribe my jottings into a proper notebook. A whimsical thought crossed my mind. Was this what they meant when they talked about 'cheque book journalism'? In the pub that night I had to borrow a fiver from a colleague to buy everyone a drink because the bank had not reopened after the robbery, so I still didn't have any cash.

It was my first big bank robbery, but not my last...

Crime did have some discernible pattern to it. On Thursdays, for instance, if the weather was dry and thus the best road conditions for getaway drivers, I could usually expect to be dealing with one or more armed robberies. These fell into two main categories, bank and security truck type attacks, and jewel heists.

The reasons for the regular cash robberies was simple. In the 1970s most working people were still paid in cash every week. Employees usually got their wages in a buff coloured envelope, mainly in green one pound notes, blue five pound notes, and brown tens (plus loose change) together with a payslip containing details of the income tax and national insurance paid, etc. And when they got their cash, they went to the supermarkets and shops and they spent it. The 'plastic revolution', the culture where people used debit and credit cards for the bulk of their outlay, was still almost a decade away.

All in all, it meant a vast quantity of money was on the streets and on the move, every week. The money needed to be physically transferred from the banks to the businesses to pay the staff and once the staff had spent it in the supermarket, it needed to be moved again, from the manager's safe back to the banks.

This gave a small army of hardcore robbers in Britain's biggest cities hundreds of opportunities every week to attack the security guards protecting the money and grab the bulging cash bags.

Most people were paid weekly on a Thursday, and some firms, particularly big construction companies for instance, had huge payrolls which became juicy targets for armed gangs. So Thursday was known to crime specialists like me as 'robbery day'.

There were variations on the usual theme, which added a bit of extra interest and variety to my life. Banks still got robbed by people, often lone raiders, who walked in and threatened the staff directly with a gun. Jewellery businesses were regularly targeted and often grabbed headlines, especially if they happened to be in one of the posh locations like Bond Street, or Knightsbridge, or in Hatton Garden, which was and remains the heart of Britain's gold and gemstones trade.

There was a kind of 'sliding scale' for how much coverage these crimes got. By the time I was working on Fleet Street at the *London Evening News*, smaller robberies, known to the police colloquially as 'blags', of say, £5,000 to £10,000, with no violence or gunshots fired, would usually rate six or eight paragraphs..

The bigger ones, in the £50,000 to £100,000 bracket, might even rate the lead story on one of the right hand main news pages. And if the crime was over £100,000 and security guards – or better still ordinary members of the public – tried to intervene, people we automatically labelled 'have a go heroes', were clubbed or even shot, it might make the front page.

Most of the hundreds of 'cash in transit' movements taking place every day were in the hands of cash moving specialist firms like Securicor, Security Express or Group Four. Their armoured vans, usually the ubiquitous early model Ford Transit, were a familiar sight on every high road. Cash in transit robbery was so common at this stage of my career I was soon on friendly first name terms with several of the directors of security companies because I was calling them to discuss the latest incident, two or three times a week. The robbers who were the scourge of the cash carrying companies were collectively known in police slang as 'blaggers' but also known to detectives as 'pavement artists', because of their technique of 'going across the pavement', in police parlance, to attack the cash guards.

Occasionally armed robberies ended in outright tragedy. One of the first murders I was called on to cover was the tragic death of an unfortunate bank clerk called Angela Woolliscroft.

In 1975 the 20-year-old was at her counter at the branch of Barclays where she worked in Richmond upon Thames, when Micky Hart, a desperate full-time, lowlife, criminal walked in, produced a sawn-off shotgun from under his coat, and told her to hand over all the money from her till. She obeyed and passed him £2,500 in used notes. But despite doing the robber's bidding, he wantonly fired at her anyway.

Angela should have been protected by the bulletproof glass screen that separated her from her customers, but the powerful gunshot from almost zero range, caused the safety glass from Angela's side of the screen to break. Several pieces of shrapnel pierced her heart, fatally wounding her. Hart was arrested a month later, tried at the Old Bailey, and jailed for 25 years.

One Thursday a year or so later, an armed robbery with an unusual detail caught my attention. Out in Lincolnshire, there was a 'pavement job' at a bank featuring two robbers; one of them was clearly identified by eyewitnesses as a young woman with long blonde hair. The hit film *Bonnie and Clyde* starring Warren Beatty and Faye Dunaway as armed robbers in 1930s America had been released in British cinemas in 1968. The temptation to describe the Lincolnshire robbers as a 'Bonnie and Clyde' style gang was irresistible, so that's how I wrote up the story.

Over the next couple of weeks this pair struck three or four more times. They were in Norwich, then Colchester, then Chelmsford in Essex. All the signs indicated they were gradually making their way towards London. One morning at about 11am I was in the office when I got a call from a detective contact in Tottenham. I knew his real name, of course, but when we were communicating we both used the name 'Harry Bailey'.

If he called me at work and I was out, he would just leave a message to say "Tell Jeff, Harry Bailey needs to speak with him". If I rang his office and someone else answered or he was out I would leave a similar message using the same alias.

'Harry' was using a payphone in a call box on a street somewhere. Many CID officers used public pay phones in preference to virtually any other form of communication.

Calls made from an office to informants, mistresses or press contacts could be eavesdropped on or even intercepted. But no one could 'earwig' a call from a 'TK' – a telephone kiosk – and the calls, which rarely cost more than a few pence, were virtually untraceable. They were the ultimate anonymous contact channel.

Harry was using one to avoid being overheard calling me from his office.

"Listen to this," he said. There was a note of urgency in his voice. "You know those 'Bonnie and Clyde' bandits you've been writing about over the last few days? Well, about an hour ago they hit us on our manor. They done a building society, a branch of the Halifax in Palmers Green. Geezer and a young Richard (Richard the Third = bird) with long blonde hair. Both armed with sawn-off shotguns.

"Descriptions from witnesses at the scene are ringers for the pair who've done the other jobs outside of London. Same MO (modus operandi) as the other jobs. They got about six grand. They made threats to shoot customers in the queue at the cash windows, but no shots were actually fired. The bank staff were good as gold, just handed them the money."

"Got anything else?" I asked. I was always looking for as much detail as possible.

"Yep," said Harry, who I guess was having a quick look at some rough notes as we spoke. They got away in a blue Vauxhall Victor. They parked right outside the branch, two wheels on the pavement."

"No getaway driver?" I asked.

"No," said Harry. "The male robber was seen to jump into the driving seat as they left. Went in the direction of the North Circular Road. Hang on," he said. I could hear him down the phone line fumbling for some more notes, probably hurriedly scribbled on the back of a cigarette packet. "I've got the index mark here – DSF 113M."

"Is it nicked?" I asked.

"Dunno," said Harry. "It's not on the system yet. It probably is a lost or stolen, but the owner probably doesn't even know it's gone yet."

Lost or stolen was formal police speak for any vehicle reported missing, probably stolen, by its owner.

"Got to go, mate," Harry said. "I'll ring you later if there's anything else. Cheers." And he hung up. I looked at my watch. We were about 25 minutes off the midday edition deadline. "Brilliant," I thought. Harry had done me proud, I had everything I needed for a late-breaking story.

I dashed over to the news desk. "The Bonnie and Clyde robbers just struck again. Right here in London. I've got the details from a mate of mine."

"Great stuff," Ken Parrish, the deputy news editor replied. "Get weaving."

I started typing: "The Bonnie and Clyde Bandits struck again today – on a London street in broad daylight. The robbery happened in Palmers Green when two outlaws, one a beautiful blonde girl, used sawn-off shotguns to terrorise customers at the Halifax Building Society. Police say they got away with £6,000. It's believed they are the same ruthless attackers who have struck four times already this month at other banks and building societies."

I added more details and included the description of the getaway car, a blue Vauxhall Victor, and its registration mark, DSF 113M.

With the story filed, I grabbed a coffee from the canteen, and was sitting back at my typewriter, looking at some other material, when I became aware of a figure standing over me in front of my desk.

I looked up, it was Ken. As soon as I looked at his face I could see he was angry about something.

"I suppose you think this is a fucking hilarious joke, do you?" Then without waiting for my reply he went on. "Well, let me tell you, if this is your idea of office humour, it's completely fucking misplaced. We're trying to get a paper out here. It's a serious job and we try to be professional about it. If you can't meet that standard, maybe you'd better think about shipping out…"

I was stunned. It was the first serious dressing down I had ever received in my career. I had no idea what I'd done to incur Ken's wrath. I began to speak, to ask what howler I had committed.

Ken thrust a sheet of my copy under my nose. It was the last page of my story. "This," he growled, stabbing at the paper with his index finger. "Blue Vauxhall Victor, DSF 113M. The getaway car. We don't have time for stupid jokes like this."

"But, but…" I stammered. "I don't understand Ken. Why are you so cross??"

"Because you know damn fucking well, this is MY car."

For a second time I was stunned. I struggled to hold on to my composure. "Ken, please, I have no idea what sort of car you drive."

I was now standing up to face him. On my desk by my left hand was my notebook, the notes I had jotted down from my contact 'Harry' were on the top page. I had carefully written down the number of the getaway car, as told to me, in bold capitals.

"Look Ken," I ventured. "Here's my original note from a detective mate who tipped me off…" I could see Ken's expression was changing. I said: "Unless he has made a mistake, this is exactly the detail my contact gave me. Do you drive a blue Vauxhall Victor?" Ken nodded. "So my contact has the correct make, model and colour…?"

There was a silence. I could see Ken's expression changing. I ventured: "When did you last see your car Ken?"

"About 6.30 this morning. I drove to work in it. It's parked in the office car park."

There was another moment of silence. Ken's stern expression softened some more. "I suppose I'd better go and have a look, hadn't I?" he said. I just nodded.

Ten minutes later I saw him breeze in through our double doors. He headed straight for me. He was smiling. "It's gone," he said.

"Fuck me," I replied. He stuck out his right hand to shake mine.

He apologised immediately. "Sorry about that, Jeff," he said. "When I saw the last part of your story, I naturally thought it was a piss-take, you were trying to wind me up."

"Bloody hell, Ken," I said with genuine astonishment. "What are the odds I'd be writing about an armed robbery, and that your car would be involved? And the first you'd know was when you read it in my copy?"

"To make it worse," he said, "today is my wife's birthday. After I parked my car I went to that posh patisserie on Fleet Street and bought the biggest chocolate gateaux they had as a treat for her. I put it on the front seat to take home. Now my car's been nicked and I'll be in the shit at home because I've lost her birthday cake."

Later that afternoon, with the last edition away, he took me to our most favoured pub, The Harrow, and bought a bottle of champagne, which we shared. I told him: "When you walked back in, I've never seen a bloke so pleased to discover his car had been stolen!"

The next day he came trotting up to me and said: "The cops have found my car. The robbers dumped it in Edmonton. Apparently there's no sign of my gateaux, but they say I've gained a sawn-off shotgun, which they found in the boot!" And from that day on we were the best of pals.

The 'Bonnie and Clyde' robbers were arrested a few weeks later. Convicted at trial in the Midlands, they were both jailed for 12 years.

CHAPTER TWO

My habit of finding myself in the middle of the crime itself continued throughout my career and one morning in 1982, when I was at the *News of the World*, was one of the most memorable. A gang of armed criminals arrived and robbed our pay offices. We were the victims.

During the 1970s and into the 1980s there had been several major armed robberies at Fleet Street newspaper offices. These were juicy targets for robbers. All the big newspaper firms had large staffs, particularly on the print side of the company. In a fairly short space of time there had been major payroll raids at the *Daily Express* and *Daily Mail* offices.

But, worst of all, a tragedy occurred during a similar attack at the *Daily Mirror*, at their offices which were then in Holborn Circus, in 1978. A security truck delivering wages to the building was ambushed and a security guard, Antonio Castro, was shot dead as the gang got away with £200,000.

In 1982 the *News of the World* HQ, which we shared with *The Sun*, just off Fleet Street, was a grubby mouse-infested warren of dingy offices and corridors.

The only security were a couple of ageing members of what was known as the 'Corps of Commissionaires', in the front door area of the building. These were former members of the armed forces, usually approaching their pensionable age. They wore impressive looking uniforms, but, in terms of a deterrent to a serious threat, were next to useless.

Our editorial office was on the second floor of the building. By some quirk of haphazard design, the entrance was down a short flight of three or four stairs from a main corridor.

On this particular day I had been nominated early reporter on our roster, which meant I was scheduled in at 9am instead of the usual starting time of 10am. I was the first editorial staff member in the office. The place was deserted and I was entirely alone.

As I was taking off my coat one of the assistant editors, Stuart Kuttner, appeared in the double doorway leading into the newsroom.

"Ah, Jeff. Good morning. Could you pop up to the wages office, please? I'm told there's a man there with a gun." And with that, he turned on his heels, and vanished the way he had come in.

Was Kuttner joking? Were we actually being robbed? I was well aware of the previous series of big cash robberies targeting Fleet Street newspaper payrolls. Cautiously, I made my way up the two flights stairs to the corridor leading to the pay office. Our wages office was two floors above the newsroom, which had earned it the nickname of 'The Bank in the Sky' because from there reporters, armed with a signed chit from our boss, could get cash advances against wages and expenses. Given the recent history of Fleet Street cash raids, it was always likely to be a vulnerable and lucrative target for criminals.

It was deathly quiet. At this time on a Saturday there were usually few people about in this part of the building. Several things were going through my mind. Was a robbery still in progress? I was loyal to my employer, but not loyal enough to die for them. I took a deep breath and padded quietly up the stairs to the pay office. Its design resembled that of a high street bank.

There were three cashier's windows, each with bulletproof glass. As I peeped through the first window a bizarre scene of chaos greeted me. One of the clerks, a man I only knew as Ron, appeared to be on his own, sitting on a wooden chair in the middle of the room. His head was down, his chin on his chest, as if he was asleep. Then I twigged why he was sitting so still, he was tied tightly to his chair with lengths of rope.

I called out: "Ron. You alright?" He raised his head and looked back at me.

"I've been robbed," he said in a flat voice. Then I saw something else, something I had never witnessed before. In view to my left, gaping open, was a huge reinforced strong room door. In normal circumstances you would not be able to see it from the cash windows, so I didn't previously know it was there.

I could see stacks of packets of new banknotes on the shelves, some ripped open, hanging half in and out of the interior, as if someone had just rifled through them, which clearly they had. The floor was awash with piles of banknotes, a profusion of fives, tens and twenties. Thousands of pounds in new and used notes were scattered under tables and desks. It was a scene of complete pandemonium.

At that moment a supervising wages clerk I knew as Charlie arrived. "What the fuck's going on, Ron?"

"We've been robbed, Charlie," said Ron, stating what was clearly obvious for a second time.

The way into the wages office was via an airlock type security door system. The second door could not be opened until the first door had been locked behind anyone entering. Charlie unlocked the first door. It was a strictly 'no go' area for anyone without authority, but as Charlie entered the airlock, I tail-gated him and got inside.

The area was strictly off limits to someone like me, but I was doing my job, and being a diligent and tenacious reporter. Charlie untied Ron, who was clearly in shock and kept saying: "There was four of them, Charlie. I never had no chance. They had guns."

I took in the scene. The robbers must have got away with a lot of money, but had clearly left a lot more behind.

"They never had nothing to take the money away in. They didn't bring no bags," volunteered Ron helpfully. "They grabbed a roll of bin liners from the cupboard and stuffed money into them, fast as they could. That's why there's so much of it all over the floor. They was in a big hurry."

From my point of view it was going well. I was an eyewitness to the immediate aftermath of a huge crime. I had forgotten to bring a notebook with me (again!), so I was drinking in the scene, trying to memorise details. Ron was talking, volunteering good information.

And then our head of security turned up. Until a few weeks before, Bert Wickstead had been an exalted Detective Chief Superintendent at Scotland Yard, where he had built a big reputation as a 'gangbuster'.

Some of my longer serving colleagues on Fleet Street had given him the nickname 'The Grey Fox'. Fleet Street was like that then, in our minds we were still living in a bygone era when top cops, and top crooks, had to be given a name tag implying mysterious cunning or infallible special powers.

Wickstead was also said to be the inspiration for the Ronnie Barker spoof detective character 'Piggy Malone' because he really did wear a belted trench coat and a Trilby hat when he was out and about.

As a young reporter on the *Newham Recorder* I had encountered him before, when he was investigating gang wars in East London. But in those days I was too insignificant for him to even acknowledge.

So Wickstead came barrelling into the wreckage of the pay office, huffing and puffing. He immediately demonstrated his detective skills by asking the pay clerks: "So, what the fuck has gone on here then?"

You definitely didn't need to be Sherlock Holmes to work it out.

Then he looked in my direction and did a double take: "And what the fuck is HE doing in here?"

"Just doing my job, Bert," I replied, but he was fuming.

"You are contaminating my crime scene. Fuck off. Now." I was swiftly shown the door.

Back in the newsroom an hour later, word about the robbery had already spread and, despite his objections, the editor insisted Wickstead gave me the details. There were four robbers, all masked, all armed with guns and ammonia sprays, which were a popular blaggers' weapon in that era.

They had entered the building through one of at least half a dozen unprotected back entrances and apparently ambushed the hapless clerk Ron as he had arrived at the office and was unlocking the door, bundling him inside at gunpoint. The estimated take was around £800,000. "An inside job?" I asked. "Got to be. They always are. Someone has to pass them the inside knowledge. But don't quote me," said Wickstead

I asked him if there were likely to be arrests. He said: "We've had one already." My ears pricked up.

"He's one of our own printers. He just nipped in to pinch a quire of this morning's *Sun* for his brother-in-law's news stand. Unfortunately for him, as he was carrying the papers through the corridors, he bumped into the robbers as they escaped running in the opposite direction. They gave him a squirt of ammonia for good measure. A PC who was responding to the shout about the wages office job found him slumped in a corner, put two and two together, and nicked him for theft."

Needless to say, none of the actual robbers were ever arrested, and none of Rupert Murdoch's cash was ever recovered.

Long after the series of raids on the Fleet Street payroll offices, it emerged a team of London robbers were in cahoots with a handful of City of London police officers, who allegedly arranged for them to have a clear run at their targets by making sure no patrols were around to interfere when the robberies took place.

One of the attacks was at a branch of Williams & Glyn's bank in the City of London in 1977 when £520,000 was taken and which I had reported on for the *London Evening News*.

Eventually, after a long running anti-corruption investigation, eight city detectives were accused of taking cash 'backhanders' for helping the robbers, but none of them were ever convicted, although several resigned while under investigation, or were sacked.

CHAPTER THREE

Throughout my Fleet Street career I was lucky to always have a good relationship with one of Scotland Yard's most legendary detective teams, the Flying Squad. Many detectives I came across wanted a posting to what was more often known as The Squad. This largely male dominated group of officers had real kudos, a mystique even, in police terms, and was perceived by many CID officers to be the pinnacle of their career.

This glamorous tag received an enormous boost in the 1970s when ITV produced the gritty and hard hitting (for its era) drama *The Sweeney*, starring John Thaw as Detective Inspector Jack Regan and Dennis Waterman as Detective Sergeant George Carter. The title was derived from cockney rhyming slang, Sweeney Todd = Flying Squad.

The Sweeney portrayed the Flying Squad as a macho band of hard drinking rough diamonds, who enjoyed a punch up with criminals and often had a tendency to be maverick characters. To be fair, a lot of Squad officers I knew fitted that profile to a tee, but a lot of it was playing up to people's expectations of them.

In a TV world full of police dramas dominated by murder investigations, it is interesting to note the Flying Squad rarely got involved in homicide cases, unless they were a spin off from their core business, which was armed robbery and the people who committed it for a living.

In the heyday of the Flying Squad, in the decades which followed the Second World War, armed robbery of banks, cash vans, wages offices, and jewellery businesses was an almost everyday occurrence, especially from the 1960s into the 1990s. Some of these were crimes which achieved worldwide notoriety. When the Great Train Robbers snatched £2.6M when they stopped a Royal Mail train in the dead of night near Leighton Buzzard, the hopelessly overwhelmed Buckinghamshire Constabulary asked the Flying Squad to find out who did it. It was also the Flying Squad that pursued and brought to book most of those thought to have been directly involved in the 1983 Brink's-Mat bullion robbery at Heathrow Airport.

Coupled with this ability to glean good information, Flying Squad teams were also top of the league at surveillance. Many of their best results came from keeping a discreet watch on the several hundred men in London and the Home Counties who were regarded as professional armed robbers.

Sometimes these surveillance operations lasted months, or even years, as they shadowed known blaggers, as they in turn did their own surveillance on security depots, armoured van routes, and other possible opportunities. I would estimate that about half the arrests the Flying Squad made, many of which I reported on, came when they ambushed robbers at the very moment they attacked a target. In the 1960s, 70s and 80s another facet of Flying Squad mystique was that they were the only Scotland Yard unit that routinely carried guns on live operations. Unfortunately, although they did sometimes fatally shoot or wound the occasional robber they caught in the act, the Flying Squad's marksmanship was generally not good.

In one celebrated incident I reported on in west London they loosed off several shots at a robber with a gun. All the shots missed, two went through the front window of a house, one narrowly missing a woman doing her laundry, lodging in her ironing board, a second smashing an upstairs bedroom window and passing through a wardrobe door and the third ricochetting off a wall and into a roadside ditch.

With typical Flying Squad humour this became known as: "The Iron, the Ditch and the Wardrobe" incident, a play on the title of the famous CS Lewis children's book. In 1987, after another incident went wrong, Scotland Yard decided they needed a radically new approach to armed operations, and from then on the Flying Squad would be supported in armed operations by today's tactically trained and properly equipped firearms teams.

It was also clear that the standard police gun, the venerable Smith and Wesson short barrel .38 calibre six shot revolver, which normally carried very low powered ammunition for fear of collateral damage, i.e. hitting innocent bystanders, was hopelessly inadequate for modern policing. All police sidearms were replaced with Glock 17 semi automatic 9mm pistols, capable of holding a 17-bullet magazine, or the improved Glock 19 which, as its names suggests, could hold two additional bullets. Flying Squad officers were no longer allowed to carry their own guns.

Over the three decades in which I had friends at the Flying Squad bases, I discovered the images portrayed by John Thaw and Dennis Waterman were by no means inaccurate. John Thaw told me himself that as part of his character research, he had invited some real members of the Flying Squad to the set of *The Sweeney* at Shepperton Studios. After filming finished they took him to a local pub and insisted he wore his usual prop, an immaculate brown sheepskin coat. In the pub this jacket was taken from him, thrown on to the spit and sawdust floor, had several pints of beer poured over it, then it was stamped on and used as a football, after which one of the Sweeney men picked it out of the dirt, put it back on the actor and said: "That's better John. Now you look like a REAL Flying Squad officer instead of an actor just pretending to be one."

Many Flying Squad officers were, out of office hours, hard drinkers, women chasers, hellraisers and revelled in their rough, tough image. But I also found them to be loyal, compassionate, dedicated to the job, and very protective of friends like me. They had a wicked sense of humour, even by the police standards of the day.

I became especially friendly with officers who served at the Squad's north London base at Finchley, which also had a strong association with Finchley Rugby Club, where I was often invited to late night beer and curry parties. Because of this link the Finchley Squad ran their own rugby tour every year to exotic locations like Hull, Blackpool, Chester and Dublin.

Not everyone on the tour was a police officer, and I was one of a select group of 'non-Old Bill' who went on the tour every year. The tour always featured a game of rugby, usually against a local police side.

It was in a bar during this annual tour in 2003 that a detective said to me: "We've got a job in the offing that you would die to be in on." He then mentioned the name of a particular criminal character who had been a thorn in the side of the Flying Squad since the 1970s when he made allegations of being framed with two sawn-off shotguns that led to a criminal trial of two Sweeney officers (at which they were acquitted) but also saw them sacked from Scotland Yard for a number of breaches of the force discipline code.

This particular villain was, with others, apparently in the advance planning stage of a huge robbery at Heathrow Airport.

I was always looking for ways to get the 'inside track' on a potential story. How could I get access to this secret and tricky police operation and get the story, without inadvertently identifying my source and getting him in trouble? The first decision I made was not to ask my friend any details of the where, what and how of the planned robbery.

My reasoning was simple, it was about self-protection. If, somewhere in the future, the job fell apart, as some ambitious police plans sometimes did, no one could point the finger at me as a possible leak whereby the bad guys had got wind of a police ambush.

Secondly, I would not mention anything about it to my bosses. I had the luxury of being able to work autonomously in a sometimes esoteric environment. They had no need to know, and again, it was a further safeguard against any accidental leak of information. But the problem of how to get authorised access to the job was vexing me. I finally decided there was a way, but it would mean doing something unconventional, going to the very top of the chain of command and drawing on some of the goodwill I had built up over many years.

By this time, I had been the Chief Crime Correspondent at the *Daily Mirror* for over 10 years. My reputation with the police for being a journalist able to negotiate my way through even the most complex of situations, was unrivalled.

I had become Chairman of the Crime Reporters' Association at Scotland Yard. Furthermore, through the backing and 'sponsorship' of a number of senior figures in British policing, I was in the extremely privileged position of being an Associate Lecturer at the prestigious National Police Leadership School, the police's own university, at Bramshill House in Hampshire.

I was part of an oversight group monitoring the performance of candidates, most of them aspiring Chief Constables, working on Strategic Command and Critical Incident Command courses. This was a unique position for a journalist and it was not lost on me the amount of trust being placed in me. Both these roles had further bolstered my reputation within Scotland Yard as a journalist who understood the often delicate relationship between law enforcement and the media. Now in the case of the expected robbery at Heathrow I decided to use some of that credit.

I went to the very top tier, to the most important and influential members of the CID and the Directorate of Public Affairs, the chief of the press officers from within Scotland Yard, and asked if I could be attached to the Flying Squad, covertly, for the duration of the operation.

I knew there were risks attached to this approach, one dissenting voice could scuttle my plan, but I was pleasantly surprised when – after a good deal of careful consideration – the superintending hierarchy at the Yard gave my request their approval.

I was officially handed over as a trusted guest of the Flying Squad at Finchley, where I already knew the majority of the team. And so, for the next seven months, I rode out to Heathrow, usually in the dead of night with teams of Flying Squad officers, waiting for the vital information from unseen forward observers to say the job was 'on' and calling in the strike.

On at least a dozen occasions, together with my colleague Roger Allen, a brilliant photographer and the only workmate I trusted enough to give a vague outline of what we were there for, we sat in Flying Squad cars in the backyard of Staines police station at midnight into the small hours, waiting for the 'off'.

The only other occupants of the police compound on those nights were about 20 crack shots from the Yard's 'SO19' firearms team. Known affectionately to Sweeney officers as 'The Ninjas', they had been called in to give the Flying Squad armed back up. We never actually saw them as they spent their entire time lurking in the back of a rented furniture van on the other side of the yard, no doubt playing cards by torchlight and dozing.

The nights came and went, through Christmas and New Year, and each time it ended in a frustrating 'stand down'. We were even out until the early hours of Christmas morning, with nothing to show. I maintained my position of not asking any of my contacts for the specifics of the job. I was happy to proceed knowing only that when (and if) the job actually came off, it would be a big one. At that time, Heathrow was getting hammered frequently with robberies of computer chips worth millions.

The microprocessors, which were mainly manufactured in Korea and Japan, were arriving daily at Heathrow in huge consignments in the cargo holds of intercontinental airliners. They were feeding Britain's own Silicon Valley industries along the M3 and M4 motorway corridors in Hampshire, Surrey and Berkshire. Dozens of large consignments were being ripped off, either in violent robberies around Heathrow, or in truck hijacks on the motorway network. The problem had got so bad that industry giants were threatening to quit the UK and go overseas. If that had happened it would have been a huge blow to Britain's 'balance of trade' and a huge loss to the treasury.

I had been told the government were putting pressure on the police to stop the crime wave. In response, Scotland Yard set up a special operation to combat the gangs under the code name 'Operation Grafton'. I formed the view that whatever it was I was part of, it had to be part of 'Grafton'.

In a conversation with one of my contacts about why microprocessors had suddenly become so valuable to organised crime, I asked: "Is it true that it's because they are more valuable than gold?" He looked at me, thought for a moment, and said: "No, Jeff. It's because microprocessors are now more valuable than cocaine."

One Saturday morning I got a call at home from the officer in charge of the Finchley squad, Detective Chief Inspector Jim Dickie. He was a larger than life character, and a proud career detective. He said to me: "Did you hear about that big blag which went off at Heathrow last night?"

I replied I had not. "That job you have been coming out with us on over the past weeks? It went down last night." I was deflated.

"Oh, well, thanks a lot for the heads up, Jim," I said, not disguising my disappointment.

He replied: "No, no. We didn't leave you out. We were not there either." As if to prove even the Flying Squad were not infallible there had been a breakdown in the police information chain and the robbers had struck unexpectedly. They had got away with it and it was cash – about £1.3M of it, not microchips.

"Don't worry," said Jim. "Keep the faith. You will have the next one." DCI Jim Dickie was transferred away on promotion to another key job at Scotland Yard and his replacement was Barry Phillips. He arrived from another crucial police operation, the investigation of shootings of young black men in London, which was known as 'Operation Trident'.

I had known and been friends with Barry, who had had a previous spell with the Flying Squad, for many years before, so he had no problem 'inheriting' me for the next upcoming heist ambush.

The next job came when some formidable armed robbers, one of whom was an ex-military special forces type, planned to rob a bullion warehouse at Enfield. I was invited to come on this job, but then uninvited when it became apparent that another elite team, in this case the then National Crime Squad, also had an interest in this job. They didn't want a reporter involved.

It was a shame because the job was a huge success. The gang was intercepted as they struck and the ex-SAS soldier put up such a tough fight as he tried to escape it took three taser shots to finally bring him down as he ran headlong from the ambush.

Back in Finchley, Barry Phillips and I drew up what we referred to clandestinely as 'The Caffreys Plan', named after a brand of beer popular with both of us. And so it was, on a Sunday in May, Barry called me at home in the evening and suggested I be at Finchley police station, with my 'snapper' Roger Allen, at 4am the next morning. An interesting scenario was unfolding. The days of the Flying Squad's much-loved Granada squad cars had passed into history along with the model, so instead Roger and I were invited into the back of a huge and powerful gun metal grey Vauxhall Senator and with squad driver Steve Ashby at the wheel and Barry Phillips in the front passenger seat, we headed off westbound on the North Circular towards Heathrow.

Sticking to my policy of not wanting to know what was in the offing until it actually happened, I didn't ask where we were going, but a few miles into the journey Barry explained.

He described how two British Airways Airbuses would be arriving at the airport in a few hours time, within minutes of each other. In the cargo hold of one, which was coming in from Switzerland, would be about two tons of gold bullion. The hold of the second, which was coming from Brussels, would be packed with boxes of banknotes being 'repatriated' for processing by the Bank of England. There would be about 20 crates of Sterling, U.S. Dollars, Japanese Yen, and other currencies which had been amassed at currency exchanges all over Europe. The cargo manifest said the weight of the cash would be over a ton, and the estimated Sterling value was about £50M. The value of the gold, also a weighty consignment, was also about £50M. A neat package of about £100M. In newspaper terms, it was like The Great Train Robbery and Brink's-Mat rolled into one.

When the planes were on the ground at Terminal Three, these cargos were to be unloaded onto nondescript lorries and rushed about a mile to a high security warehouse, operated by the airport freight moving firm Swissport, which stood alongside the airport perimeter road near the village of Stanwell.

Barry said to me: "A gang of robbers plan to attack the warehouse this morning and take the lot. When they do, we will ambush them, because we know they are coming and I have people hidden in the warehouse, ready and waiting."

"Where are the planes now?" I asked.

"They haven't taken off yet. We will know when they are about to leave so we have plenty of time. But first we have something very important to do." Which meant dropping into a traditional transport café at Hayes for a 6am Flying Squad Special Breakfast of fried eggs, bacon, sausages, tomatoes, fried bread, baked beans, black pudding, mushrooms, fried potatoes, and pint mugs of well-sugared tea.

An hour later we took up position, tucked away in a back street about half a mile from the target warehouse. Barry was equipped with two police radios, one tuned to the special Flying Squad frequency, and about three different mobile phones. Every now and then one of the phones would 'ping' with a message or a radio would crackle into life with a transmission that appeared to be mostly numbers, phonetic alphabet letters, usually followed by a terse 'yes, yes', or 'standby'.

About 7.45am Barry turned to me and said: "Plane one, the gold, is in and off loading." A few minutes later: "Plane two is on the deck. They are taking the money off now. A few minutes later, another 'ping' and: "The trucks are on the way to the warehouse."

I asked: "What about the bad guys?".

Barry shrugged: "No sign of them yet". We all started to wonder if this was going to be yet another 'stand down'.

After a while Barry looked at his watch. We were all growing a bit fidgety and restless. He said: "One of my teams has got a £25,000 security van job going down in Potters Bar at about 10am. If we put the lights and sirens on, we can get you over there for that one."

Potters Bar, right on the northern edge of London, was about 20 miles from Heathrow. I thought about it and said: "If this is a 'no show' today, how long will it be before it comes back on line again?"

Barry rubbed his chin thoughtfully, then said: "It's all dependent on an inside man being on duty. The robbers need him to tell them what's coming in. It won't all line up again for at least another two weeks."

So I said: "Fuck it. I've been riding with this job for nigh-on six months. Another two weeks is not going to hurt me." And as I finished the sentence one of Barry's phones pinged and he turned to me and said two words: "They're here."

Steve Ashby put the big Vauxhall in gear, floored the accelerator and we surged forward.

About 60 seconds later we were speeding through the entrance to the yard of the Swissport depot. The warehouse had two lanes at the entrance gate, one in and one out on each side of a gate-keeper's office. They were both protected by lifting barriers. As we approached we could see the 'out' side barrier was smashed and lying in bits in the roadway.

Something had just gone through it at speed, probably only seconds before we arrived. We swept into the marshalling yard at the back of the building. The warehouse had several steel roller shutter doors at the back. One of them had been rammed by a white Leyland Sherpa van. The van, the driver's door half open, was stuck, half in and out of the entrance, with the roller shutter crumpled against its roof. Its motor was racing because the throttle was stuck open.

Barry told Roger and I to stay put, then moving surprisingly quickly for a big man, he jumped from our car, and ducked under the shutter into the warehouse. Sixty seconds later he emerged, beaming: "Jeff, Roger. Come with me. We've got them all laid out like ham salads for you."

We shimmied past the jammed getaway van and ducked under the wrecked security shutter. We were greeted with a truly astonishing sight. The police had propped up one of the robbers sitting against a wooden crate which was full of gold bullion. As Roger started photographing the scene a detective pulled the robber's mask up over his head to reveal his identity. His face was a perfect picture of helpless resignation, later compared by one of the officers to one of the old Hamlet cigar TV adverts.

The police netted five robbers at the scene, without a shot being fired. What we didn't know at that moment was, a couple of miles away near the Staines reservoirs, there was a furious chase going on as other Flying Squad units pursued a stolen three-ton truck driven by another gang member who had fled the scene when the police sprung their trap. The truck was intended as a getaway vehicle to carry away the several tons of bullion and cash. It explained the ruined 'out' barrier we had seen as we entered the Swissport yard.

That bandit was apprehended about an hour later. After watching the Flying Squad officers handcuff and march away all the robbers I decided to phone my newsdesk at the *Daily Mirror*, to tell them what was going on.

The next day we had one of the most spectacular front pages of the decade with another four pages inside with my words and Roger's pictures right left and centre. I had been working on that story for six months and I apologised for not telling any of the *Mirror* executives what I had been doing. But at the back of my mind getting access to such a phenomenal scoop had actually taken a whole career, over 35 years of patiently building a reputation with police organisations to the point where I was trusted completely.

Later that year at the annual Press Awards, my story was put forward for the Scoop of the Year category. I finished runner-up to some very worthy investigation by the *Sunday Times*. Roger Allen, won Photographer of the Year for his picture of robber Lee Cotton being unmasked propped against a crate containing a ton of gold.

The following year at Kingston Crown Court six members of the robbery gang went on trial. They were convicted and jailed for a total of over 70 years.

MURDER MAYHEM, HEADLINES AND DEADLINES

CHAPTER FOUR

As a specialist in crime and law enforcement I was routinely being assigned stories involving tragic losses. I have often been asked by friends how I coped with a daily diary of events which frequently featured murder, and other forms of extreme violence, accidental death or suicide. I suppose the truth is I developed a kind of immunity to it, a professional detachment, perhaps, similar to that exhibited by the police themselves, or other emergency responders like paramedics or firefighters.

Just because we do not grieve or shed a tear for every tragedy we encounter does not mean we have lost our humanity, or that we have become cynics. In a profession where we witness terrible events on a near daily basis, we have to develop a psychological barrier to such events in order to keep functioning.

Over my career I reported on well over 1,000 murders and violent deaths. Some I have forgotten. A few have stayed with me forever. One involved a very unusual and sad case, which remains unresolved to this day.

Enrico Sidoli was a happy-go-lucky 15-year-old boy who came

from an Italian family resident in London since just after the Second World War.

On a hot summer afternoon in July 1976, he went with his older sister and her three young children to an open air swimming pool near Hampstead Heath known as the Parliament Hill Fields Lido. Britain was in the grip of a record-breaking heatwave, and on this school holiday afternoon the Lido was packed to capacity. At that time there was no proper check on how many people were allowed in. Figures quoted at the time varied from about 700 to over 1,000.

There is no doubt that in today's way of categorising people, Enrico would be described as 'vulnerable'. From everything I was able to glean at the time, he had something about him, something hard to define, that caused him to be picked on by other youngsters. After his death, evidence emerged that he had often been bullied at school, and I believe that what happened to him at the Lido may have been connected to what had happened to him previously at school. Whatever the circumstances were that day, there is firm evidence from witnesses that while at the Lido he was picked on by a group of boys.

Again, the accounts of how many boys, and their ages vary. Some people said a group of six. Others said it was as many as 12. They were probably a little bit older and physically stronger than Enrico who wasn't a strong swimmer.

At some point, while in the pool, he was taunted, then attacked. He was pushed and hustled out of his depth, and someone, two, three, four or maybe more teenage boys, pushed him down and held him under until he drowned. Because the pool was packed with splashing, yelling, and cavorting people, no one noticed he was being murdered. Eventually a lifeguard saw Enrico face down under the water. He was dragged out of the pool and given CPR and mouth to mouth resuscitation, but to no avail. He was rushed to hospital unconscious. He remained in a coma for 11 days, and then he died.

Officially his cause of death was oxygen starvation in his brain. But, in plain terms, he was drowned, deliberately, by others unknown. Because of the confusing circumstances, it was two weeks before the police were able to get a formal murder investigation underway. The officer in charge was Detective Chief Inspector Harry Clement and because of the murder of Enrico we became friends. Harry was a veteran of many murder investigations. He'd seen everything in a long career in CID, but he was visibly moved by the case. He told me: "I can't think of anything more sad than a schoolboy, enjoying a day out with his family, getting picked on by a gang of bullies and drowned, in front of hundreds of witnesses, and no one even noticed what was going on."

The investigation was problematic from the start. In 1976, entry to the Lido was cash only, so there was no record of who had been in on the day. Some witnesses did come forward. There were lots of people with bits of information, but all of them were confused about what they had seen, because the pool itself that afternoon was chaos, with hundreds of youngsters swimming, splashing, shouting and laughing in the water.

A group of boys splashing about holding another boy under while he struggled didn't look suspicious at the time. It just looked just like any other group of boys larking about noisily in the water.

Harry paved the way for me to speak to Enrico's parents and other members of his family. Their grief was palpable. I was moved by their sorrow and I think of them even now. All murders are unjust, but there just seemed to be something even more tragic than usual about the wicked killing of this harmless and friendly young lad.

Harry always swore he would find the culprits eventually. But he never did and the case is unsolved to this day, even though a few years ago a combined reward of £40,000 was offered jointly by Scotland Yard and the Sidoli family for information leading to the arrest of his killers. It's a sobering thought that there is a group of men, now in their mid to late 50s still out there somewhere, who know exactly who murdered Enrico Sidoli.

****

Another case that remained with me, though for other reasons, came shortly after I joined my first newspaper, the *E&I*. I started dating a young woman who worked in a local estate agents' office. Sandra was a pretty blonde and my first proper girlfriend. She lived with her mum and dad in a council house on the Debden estate at Loughton. Shortly after we started going out a young woman moved into the terraced house next door to her. Annette Wilson was a pretty, petite brunette, aged about 22. I met her a couple of times and she had an attractive, outgoing personality.

In the late 1960s the whole country was undergoing a huge programme of modernisation to its gas supply. Britain was switching from the old style of dirty 'town gas' – manufactured in countless gas works throughout the UK, to much cleaner and cheaper natural gas, which was being harvested from wells, most of which were offshore in the North Sea.

A huge network of new pipelines were being installed by a company called Sea Flame. Everywhere you went, blue and white

Sea Flame vans, each individually numbered, seemed to be there. Sandra and I noticed that there was frequently one parked outside Annette's house overnight.

As I was becoming a trained observer, I happened to notice that the vans were of various makes and models and carrying different serial numbers. Sandra's mum was a major league curtain twitcher, and she quickly reported that Annette was receiving several different Sea Flame visitors every week, and it was pretty clear they were not visiting at midnight to fix her meter.

What the attraction of gas engineers was to Annette was not known to us, and it was none of our business anyway. But as well as the gas fitters, Annette had another regular visitor who often stayed overnight. He stood out, because he drove a very flashy American car, an ice blue Chevrolet Impala, left hand drive, complete with white walled tyres. In that era the majority of tenants on the Debden estate couldn't afford to own a car of any make, so the Chevy stood out like a neon advertising sign.

Then one morning I chanced to meet Sandra and she told me some astonishing news. The police were swarming all over Annette's neighbouring house. She had been murdered. I drove to Sandra's address. Sure enough there were cops guarding the front door. And there were detectives searching the overgrown and neglected back garden. I knew one of the constables standing outside because he was a local officer.

"What's happened to Annette?" I asked.

"Why son, do you know her?" I told the cop about my relationship with the family next door, and he told me: "Wait there."

A moment or two later a CID officer, who was also someone I had met previously in the pub close to our office, came out and spoke to me. We walked to his car, which was parked further down the road. He started the motor and we drove a short distance to a car park at the Underground station.

He didn't want anyone to see us talking. This, he explained, was for my benefit.

"There are a lot of criminal 'faces' living on this estate. It might not be in your best interest for anyone to think you are the sort of person who talks to coppers." I took the point. He asked me a lot of questions, which included did I know Annette personally, and then, had I ever had sex with her on the sly?

I was a little taken aback by the bluntness of the question, but expressed the view that poor Annette seemed to have a lot of admirers, maybe even customers, but I definitely wasn't one of them.

At this stage I didn't even know what had happened to her or when. The detective looked at me and asked: "Yeah, we are getting the impression she had a lot of men friends. Do you know if she had anyone in particular?"

I told him about the bloke with the Chevy. He was suddenly interested. "Know who he is? Ever meet him?" I told him I had never seen him, only his car. He asked me to describe it, which I did. I could remember part of the registration. He wrote it down on the back of a cigarette packet, then asked me if I could remember the last time I'd seen the Chevy parked outside the house.

Now it was my turn: "So what happened to her? I don't think my girlfriend's family heard any noises that sounded like someone was attacking her." The walls of the terraced houses were thin. Loud noises were easily heard in adjoining properties.

"She was strangled with the sleeve of one of her own blouses," he said matter of factly. "But you can't report the method mate, 'cos it's something only the killer will know, and we don't want it out there. Understood?"

He told me she had been found the previous evening. She had failed to turn up for work and someone had got worried and contacted her sister who had a key to the house.

"The sister went round, let herself in," said the detective, "and that's how it all came on top. Nasty business. Sad, really. Pretty girl."

I thanked the detective and told him I would appreciate it if he let me know if there were any developments. He told me: "If you ring my office, and anyone asks whose calling, use the name Ron Brown. If I call your office and I leave a message, I'll say to ring Ron Brown. That all make sense? My guvnor doesn't like the press. I think you're alright, but best to be careful, OK?"

We splashed on the murder story. It was an exclusive. A few days later I walked into my office and there was a note on my typewriter saying "call Ron Brown". I rang the CID office and asked for my contact by his real name. I was told he was out. A woman officer said: "Can I give him a message?"

"Yes, tell him Ron Brown returned his call."

Half an hour later he called from a public phone box. He told me: "See me later in the Nightingale in Wanstead."

It was a pub I knew well. The detective was already at the bar when I walked in. I bought us both a pint of Guinness. "Got a bit of news for you," he said out of the side of his mouth.

"You know the bloke you mentioned who was a regular visitor to Annette? The one who drove an American car?"

I nodded.

"We traced him through the part of the index number you were able to give us. It was him. He did it. We nicked him last night and he coughed it right away. Even said he'd been expecting us when we called. He'll be charged later. Thought you'd want to know."

We clinked glasses. "Cheers," I said, and asked the suspect's name, where he was from, all the usual questions. Then I asked the cop what the suspect did for a living. He replied: "He's a drug dealer, son." My ears pricked up, because in the late 1960s 'drug dealer' was still a fairly rare occupation in Britain.

"How do you know?" I ventured.

"'Cos when we spun his drum [searched his home] in Leyton, we found about a monkey's worth [£500] of cannabis resin and a big bag of purple hearts."

Purple Hearts, I already knew, were one of the earliest types of amphetamine sulphate pills, later to become much more widely known as 'speed', 'whizz', or 'blue collar cocaine'.

Annette's killer was later tried at the Old Bailey and jailed for life.

CHAPTER FIVE

In 1995 I got a tip that the London police were going to fly to New Zealand to talk to a new suspect in the Rachel Nickell murder inquiry. With only three hours notice the *Daily Mirror* dispatched me for the 23-hour journey to the rural town of Napier in the back woods of New Zealand to catch up with a Scotland Yard team who arrived there on the same plane.

It was a wasted trip for everybody, the supposed suspect quickly turned out to be completely innocent. But I had become intrigued by this then unsolved case since it happened in the summer of 1992 and there was no doubt Scotland Yard were coming under extreme pressure to find the killer. There were several reasons for my interest and their urgent need to get a result.

The first was the sheer awfulness of the crime. Rachel, a 22-year-old model was walking on Wimbledon Common on a sunny morning in July with her infant son Alex and their pet dog, when she was waylaid by a stranger and stabbed to death in a sustained and prolonged attack in which her killer inflicted 49 separate knife wounds.

The fact that she was accompanied by her infant son, that the incident happened in an area usually so safe, wealthy, and middle class, and other factors, elevated the story to one of the most talked and written about murders of recent times. This was compounded by the fact that the police, aided and abetted by an eminent criminal psychologist, the use of whom had suddenly become a must-have bolt on to any sexually-driven killing at the time, zeroed in on the wrong man.

Colin Stagg, was a 'loner', a single man with a passing interest in the occult, who lived nearby and was known to walk his dog on the common.

Viewed as an 'oddball' character by his neighbours with a penchant for nude sunbathing, he immediately became a 'person of interest' to the Homicide Squad.

But because the police could not find any forensic evidence or eyewitnesses who could tie Colin Stagg to the actual murder, they came up with what they thought was a clever plan to corner him.

In investigating his background, homicide officers involved in the Rachel case discovered Stagg, their only suspect, had been placing adverts, unsuccessfully it must be said, in the 'lonely hearts' columns of local papers in his part of London.

In a world before Tinder and the numerous online dating apps which exist today, it was the only cheap option for people looking for love. With the psychologist to guide them, and knowing Stagg was a lonely man who had never had a sexual relationship (which they thought might be a reason why he would brutally and randomly murder a young woman), they contrived, via a 'lonely hearts' column in a newspaper to draw him into a 'relationship' with an undercover police woman.

The police woman was on the staff of a unit within Scotland Yard known as 'SO 10' – the 'SO' stood for 'Specialist Operations', who undertook a variety of covert jobs against various types of criminals. This team included sub teams with names made up from strange acronyms like CROPS which stood for Covert Rural Operations Police Surveillance who were SAS trained and good at pretending to be trees or living in ditches or storm drains for days on end without moving.

They set up pawnbroking businesses, second hand car businesses and purchased pubs where the landlord and all the bar tenders were undercover cops. They had another sub unit known reverentially as the 'technical people', but more commonly simply as the 'BBs' which stood for 'burglars and buggers'. Often trained by MI5, they left no trace as they broke into the homes of drug lords, terrorists, paedophiles and other people suspected of being up to no good, in order to plant secret listening devices, voice recorders, and fibre optic cameras. SO10 were always pushing the envelope of what they could legally do. There was a sign over their office door in Scotland Yard which said 'Lawfully Audacious'. These people were really good, but they were not infallible. However, I was lucky enough to have many friends among their ranks.

So very early on I learned, on the understanding of strict secrecy, about the plan to draw out Colin Stagg and into a trap. The idea was that if Stagg could be tricked into dating an undercover police woman, she might be able to get him to talk about the murder, and his supposed involvement. Much has been written about this ill-fated operation and many people have, and continue, to miss the point about it.

It was never intended to get Stagg to confess which, given he would be getting a 'come on' and the implied promise of sex, would have been of very doubtful value in court. The actual aim of the 'honey trap' plan was to get Stagg to lead a police detective using the code name 'Lizzie James' to where he had hidden the murder weapon, which had never been found.

The first date Stagg had with the undercover police officer was, at her suggestion, in the café alongside the Serpentine lake in Hyde Park. At least 60 police surveillance officers were involved in the operation to follow and watch Stagg throughout. The day started badly. A surveillance team watching him discreetly when he left his home to go to Hyde Park were thrown into panic and confusion when his first move was to get the bus going in the wrong direction. The plain clothes squad thought this indicated he was what they called 'surveillance conscious' – in other words he already suspected some sort of trap and was deliberately making a move designed to bamboozle anyone shadowing him.

But as the bus headed for Kingston on Thames instead of central London, Stagg realised his mistake, hopped off, crossed the road and caught a bus going the other way. This sent the following surveillance team into a fresh paroxysm of confusion.

When Stagg eventually reached the café, he was relieved to find 'Lizzie' had not been put off by the fact he was over half an hour late for the rendezvous. Every waiter, every cashier and every customer at every table inside, was an undercover police officer. I had several friends amongst the detail who later told me what took place. Lizzie James tried to draw Stagg out by suggesting, according to a kind of script she had been given, she was interested in sadomasochistic sex.

She introduced the subject of the Rachel murder. Stagg was discombobulated. He didn't go along with it in any way. How could he? He hadn't done it, and knew nothing about it, save what he'd read in the newspapers. At Scotland Yard, the over-eager cops and their guiding psychologist took his confusion about the conversation as a sign he was cannier than they thought and being careful not to admit anything to 'Lizzie James'. I was getting lots of discreet, and of course, unreportable, feedback from my friends in SO10.

But two days after the failed operation at the Serpentine cafe I spoke to two senior Scotland Yard friends and, on hearing details of what they were hoping to achieve, was incredulous. I said to them: "This is crazy. This can't possibly work. Even if it is him, he's not naive enough to fall for it and take her to the place where he put the knife. Surely?

"Before the next date, he might get any knife and hide it under a tree, and then take her there and say 'look, there it is, now will you let me have sex with you'. And if you arrest him and it turns out forensically not to be the murder weapon, what will you do then? You'll be up shit creek in a canoe with no paddle. Even if he does tell her it was him, he might just be agreeing to it thinking it will lead to sex, and it won't be worth a damn in court."

But my police friends remained bullish, insisting they had the right man in their sights. The code name for the operation was 'Edzell' and in the end, Stagg was arrested and charged. It was a complete fiasco. When it reached the Old Bailey, after Stagg had spent 13 months in custody, it was immediately thrown out by a furious judge who was excoriating about the police case and freed Stagg without even a trial, formally declaring him innocent there and then.

It immediately freed me to tell the whole story of the ill-fated Operation Edzell, including all the inside information I had sat on for months. Scotland Yard were later ordered to give Colin Stagg over £700,000 as compensation.

But as the police were feverishly trying to build a case against Stagg, in November 1993, and while he was in custody, another young woman was horribly murdered. Samantha Bissett was a single mum living with her four-year-old daughter Jazmine in a flat in Plumstead, south London. An intruder forced his way into their flat and murdered both of them.

Samantha, who was 27, was stabbed to death and her body mutilated in such a horrific way, some detectives compared her murder to the work of the infamous Jack the Ripper, a century before. Her toddler daughter was smothered to death in her bed using a duvet.

I noticed straight away what I considered might be links between Samantha's killing and that of Rachel. First of all, there was the sheer savagery of the attacks on both women. Both had received multiple knife wounds in what were clearly sexually-driven incidents. Both women had small children with them at the time. In the history of crime, murders of women for sexual reasons when they are accompanied by babies or young children are very rare indeed.

Then there was the geography. Growing up, living and working in London all my life meant I had a better than average knowledge of the layout of the capital, its boroughs, roads and transport routes. I knew the distance between Plumstead and Wimbledon, both south of the River Thames, was probably less than 10 miles. In a car the journey might take half an hour to 40 minutes, even on a good traffic day. On a motorbike you could perhaps halve that time. You could travel between the two areas by bus or train and only have to change once if you knew your way around.

I spoke to one of my friends on the Rachel inquiry, and they were still adamant, Stagg murdered her, Samantha had been killed by someone else. But I also knew two officers on the Samantha case. One of them was a detective I had known since the 1970s. I called him and arranged to meet him in a pub in Bromley. He knew all about the Rachel case too. And he thought his own organisation were barking up the wrong tree with their pursuit of Colin Stagg.

He said: "I have little doubt the man who murdered Samantha is the same man who murdered Rachel in July last year. There definitely are strong similarities in my opinion and the opinion of many of my colleagues.

"Now they have Stagg in custody awaiting trial, he can't be the perpetrator in the Samantha and Jazmine cases."

I said to him: "If this was any other police area, Norfolk, or Dorset, or North Wales, those forces would automatically be drawing parallels between these two cases. Why are they not treating two cases just a few miles apart in London in the same way?"

His response was: "They have put all their eggs in one basket with Stagg. They are so heavily invested in him as the Rachel killer, they've put in so much effort, tried dangerously ill-advised and unconventional techniques, like the Lizzie James honey trap nonsense, they have, to use a metaphor, painted themselves into a corner. They now can't find their way back without important people losing face and credibility."

He and I turned out to be right, though it was to take another 10 years or more to prove it. A man called Robert Napper was tracked down and convicted for the murder of Samantha Bissett and her infant daughter. He was also a serial rapist who had attacked a number of women at knifepoint over a period of years in south London. Several of his victims had been walking with young children in woods and parkland when he struck. Already known to the police for previous matters, one of his fingerprints was found in Samantha's flat, and he lived within walking distance of her apartment.

He was charged and in 2004 he appeared at the Old Bailey where he was found to be psychiatrically ill and sent to Broadmoor, never to be released. Continuous steps forward in forensic science allowed police to link him to Rachel's murder, but it wasn't until 2008 he was finally put on trial for her killing where he pleaded guilty but denied criminal responsibility through his mental illness, and he was sent back to Broadmoor where he is expected to spend the rest of his life.

***

Another crime which left the nation scarred occurred in August 1988 when a loner named Michael Ryan, who had somehow been able to acquire several powerful guns, including a military style 'Type 56' semi-automatic rifle, and a Beretta automatic 9mm pistol, went on the rampage in the market town of Hungerford in Berkshire.

During the worst mass shooting incident of its kind in Britain, 27-year-old Ryan began the day by visiting nearby Savernake Forest where he found a young mother picnicking with her children.

After forcing her at gunpoint to put the children in her car, he walked her to a clearing and shot her nine times with the Beretta, killing her instantly. He then drove back to Hungerford, where he lived with his elderly mother, and began walking around the town shooting at random at anyone he met. Over several hours he killed 16 men and women, including an unarmed police officer, and his own mother, and severely wounded several more.

For at least four hours there was no one able to challenge him as the entire Thames Valley specialist firearms response team was on a training course about 50 miles away. Eventually he was cornered while hiding in a school, which was closed for the summer.

With the school surrounded and police negotiators trying to set up a dialogue with him to persuade him to surrender peacefully, his final action was to shoot himself dead with one of his own guns. I think I was the only reporter on the London staff of the *Daily Star* that day who was not deployed to Berkshire.

Instead, my editor Brian Hitchen, decided to keep me back in Fleet Street to act as 'anchor' at the centre of the unfolding story, and to weave together the dozens of tranches of 'copy' which were coming in from our own staff and agency reporters at the scene.

I was also kept back so I could tap into my various police contacts, particularly those with knowledge of firearms tactics and operations.

The Hungerford Massacre profoundly changed the way that all British police forces train, equip, and deploy gun teams. It is possible that on that fateful day, had Thames Valley police had more armed officers in fast response vehicles available, fewer people would have died, but some things are simply unknowable and hindsight is always perfect.

Theories abounded, but it was never discovered why on that particular day Ryan decided to become a mass murderer.

CHAPTER SIX

Some murders stay in the memory not just of the police, family and reporters, but of the nation itself and the killing of Jill Dando is one of those everyone recalls.

On the day the TV presenter was killed I was sitting at my desk in the *Daily Mirror* newsroom in Canary Wharf. It was, in my terms, a routine day. No big immediate stories to be getting on with, so I was catching up with other tasks and writing up some background work on a forthcoming Old Bailey murder trial.

About 1pm, I was thinking of going out to buy a lunchtime sandwich when my line manager Eugene Duffy walked over to me from his chair on the newsdesk. He was straight to the point. "Jill Dando's been murdered. She's been stabbed. Over to you."

"Where? When?" I asked.

"Fulham, outside her house," he replied. "Last half hour or so I am told." Then he walked away. At times like this, we kept words to a minimum.

I didn't need to be told what to do. I hit the phones. I knew several detectives on the Homicide Team that covered west London and I had their personal mobile phone numbers.

The first two I called didn't pick up. The third one did.

"Can you speak? " I asked. This was always my first question because the contact might be in their office, or in a car with someone else, and when it was business, I always wanted to be sure not to put anyone in an awkward spot which might embarrass them.

"Yes," he replied. "Go ahead."

"Jill Dando," I said. "You know about it? Are you on that one?"

"No," he said. "But I know what's happened."

"She's been stabbed, is that correct?" I asked.

"No, not stabbed," came the reply. "She's been shot. In the head."

"Shot?" I could not contain my surprise at this news. "Yes. Once. In the head at very close range. On her own front path. She was just going in through the front door and someone walked up to her and shot her. There's a nine millimetre cartridge lying in her front garden."

"So it was a semi-automatic," I said. It wasn't a question. I had learned enough about guns over the years to know that a revolver when fired retained the empty cartridge cases in its revolving chambers. But an automatic weapon was, mechanically, completely different.

The ammunition was stored in a magazine, sometimes referred to as a 'clip' housed in the butt of the weapon, and as it fired it ejected the spent cartridges.

"Yes mate, an automatic. Look, I've got to go. Message me later. I'll know more later today."

So Jill Dando had been shot, not stabbed. I knew that would put a different complexion on things. I went over to Eugene and told him what I'd found out.

By that time the office had sent every available reporter, probably about 15 in total plus six or seven photographers out on the story.

My job, as usual, was to sit at the centre of the operation, working my own contacts, attending any press briefings by the police, and collating an avalanche of other information I knew would be coming in from my colleagues and other sources.

I didn't leave the office until close to midnight that day by which time we had produced the front page and at least seven other pages inside the next day's *Mirror*. I had met Jill Dando several times in the past at functions hosted by Scotland Yard and the BBC *Crimewatch* team. We had become well-acquainted over the years, and spoke often on the phone about cases her programme was highlighting. She was a genuine enthusiast about the subject, and I liked her outgoing and open personality. Despite her fame there was nothing 'showbiz' about her and I was very sad about what had happened to her.

In the aftermath of Jill's death and for months and even years afterwards, the demand for stories about her and who killed her and why was insatiable.

There have been thousands of newspaper and magazine articles, a dozen television documentaries, and at least two books. I can say for sure that about 75% of the news stories and most of the theories I've heard put forward for the motive for her killing are pure hokum – absolute nonsense.

Among the theories I would describe as absolute garbage are the suggestions repeated many times, she was killed by a criminal in revenge for something she had reported on *Crimewatch*.

Her role on the well-watched programme was purely as a presenter. She didn't solve crimes, or produce evidence that put people behind bars. She was merely a mouthpiece for law enforcement, reporting what the police asked her to report. The suggestion that anyone would take the enormous step of hunting her down and killing her as revenge for something *Crimewatch* had done is absurd.

Likewise, I don't believe she was killed by a professional killer working for a Serbian crime lord she had snubbed during one of her holiday programmes. This also strikes me as stupid and naïve. Many intelligent people, including a number of journalists with whom I have debated her murder have said to me: "But, all the signs are, she was killed by a professional hitman."

Actually, on the contrary, many of the signs, to my mind, show that she was killed by a rank amateur. In a 40-year career I have reported on at least 1,000 shootings, many of them in Northern Ireland during The Troubles, others clearly linked to organised crime, where the shooter falls into the category of professional assassin.

I have read about hundreds more in America, Russia, Mexico and many other parts of the world.

There are only a very few I can recall where the intended target was shot only once. The hallmark of gangland or political killers, some of whom were previously in the special forces, is they kill with multiple shots.

Classically, army and police firearms types talk about the 'double tap' – ideally two bullets in the head and two in the upper body, as the perfect way of killing.

There is a good reason for this.

If an assassin sets out to kill someone, they need to be certain of one thing and one thing only; and that is the outcome. And to be certain of the outcome, you need several shots. People frequently survive one bullet wound, even to the head. So what happened in Jill's case?

Here's what I think. In 1999 when she was murdered, Britain, particularly London, Liverpool, Manchester and Birmingham had become flooded with so called 'reactivated' or 'converted' guns.

These were mainly handguns, both revolvers and semi-automatic pistols, which fell into two main categories. The first were real firearms which had been rendered unusable by either removing critical components from the firing mechanism, welding key parts to stop them moving, or filling the barrels with liquid metal which, when it cooled and solidified made the gun permanently unusable. These guns can then be legitimately sold on the open market as ornaments or to gun collectors.

The second category were replica guns and starting pistols, which looked and felt exactly like the real thing, but were actually gas or air weapons which were designed to fire a .22 air gun pellet, or in some cases a BB pellet,

At the time of Jill's murder, this category of gun was legal because it was not covered by the Firearms Act which outlawed real guns in Britain. But in the 1990s a number of criminals with excellent engineering skills and good equipment – which was small enough to set up in a garden shed or spare room – began to take deactivated weapons and return them to partial working order.

It was usually a relatively simple job that involved drilling out the blocked barrel and inserting a new inner sleeve made from special high tensile steel. In all cases the reactivated weapons were only capable of firing one bullet. They were not even very reliable.

Getting ammunition for them was the next problem for buyers, and running alongside the gun conversion business was another specialising in making 'homemade' ammo for them. But there was still a ready market for them, particularly with teenage street gang and estate drug gang members vying for territory.

One of the most favoured types has traditionally been the

'Brocock', a pistol manufactured to use air pressure or a small CO2 gas cylinder to shoot. Hundreds of them are known by police to have been re-engineered to fire a real bullet. Dozens of them have been seized by police tackling drug dealers and street gangs in our major cities.

These guns could easily be obtained in the 1990s, but they were used mainly by what the police, often half-jokingly, referred to as 'disorganised crime' characters. Real 'top drawer' criminals, or politically-motivated killers, do not use them because they are not reliable or robust enough, and critically, they can only fire one shot. True professionals, people who kill people as part of their living, know how to get and use the real thing – guns of devastating power which could fire multiple shots in the blink of an eye.

My conclusion has always been Jill was shot by a stalker type obsessive.

I believe she was shot only once, albeit with fatal consequences, because her killer only had the type of converted or reactivated weapon which could fire one shot.

To bolster this view, police ballistic experts who examined the single cartridge case left at the scene by the gunman under the microscope could see clear signs the ammunition was of the homemade type.

There was strong scientific evidence to say the case had been held in a vice and 'crimping' carried out, probably with a hammer and screwdriver blade, to make sure the bullet fit snugly. In plain terms, the bullet that killed Jill was not manufactured in an industrial arms factory, but probably in someone's kitchen or garage.

A local man, Barry George, was arrested some months after the murder. There was good evidence that he was interested in guns and shooting. There were inconsistencies in his story about his movements the day Jill was shot and he was charged with murder.

He was convicted of murder at the Old Bailey, on what was frankly far from conclusive evidence and jailed for life, but later, defence lawyers challenged the conviction, there was a retrial and this time he was acquitted and set free.

George, who had a criminal record for attacks on women, was a disorganised character who lived in the same area as Jill and had historically belonged to a shooting club and had some guns which were believed by those who saw them to be replicas.

I can't put my hand on my heart and say I know who shot Jill Dando or why it happened and now I don't think we will ever find out.

SEEING THE FUNNY SIDE AND ANIMAL CRACKERS

CHAPTER SEVEN

One of the joys I quickly discovered of working in newspapers is speaking to people, finding out their stories and the extraordinary things that have happened in their lives.

But not all interactions with the public go according to expectation…

At my first ever newspaper I remember Lily Buckley, our receptionist at the main entrance to the building, looked into our office one day, saw me, and said: "Jeff, there is a lady at the front desk who I think has a story."

In those days, most newspaper offices had a 'front office' the public could simply stroll into and ask to speak to a journalist, even the big national titles, and quite a few important stories began with what we called 'walk ins'.

So, I went through to the front counter. My heart was racing. This was my first 'walk in'. What was I about to find out? The answer to an unsolved murder perhaps? Or how her daughter had been abducted by a religious cult? You never knew.

There stood a formidable looking old lady. She was wearing a heavy black coat, with a black felt hat and black horn-rimmed glasses. She was carrying a black umbrella with a hefty cane handle. Before I was able to introduce myself she looked at me earnestly and demanded: "Young man. Are you a reporter?"

I replied affirmatively.

"Right," said the lady. "Now tell me. Is there anywhere round here where I can buy a nice bit of fish?"

I was nonplussed. "A piece of fish?" I managed to ask.

"Yes," said the old lady: "Not just any old bit of fish. It's got to be a nice bit of fish. Do you understand me? Now, come on, tell me. Where can I get a nice bit of fish?"

Tentatively, I half turned towards where Lily was sitting, her head buried in a big accounts book. She didn't meet my look, but I could sense that under her auburn tresses her shoulders were heaving with laughter. I looked back at the old dear.

"Have you tried the fishmonger, over the other side of the road?" I ventured.

The old lady erupted: "Young man, do not disrespect your elders. The fish they sell is horrible. Everyone knows that. It's rotten. They don't sell nice fish. Now, for the last time, tell me, where can I get a NICE bit of fish?" And to reinforce the urgency of the situation, she slammed her umbrella on the counter, causing me to flinch and step back.

Pathetically, voice trembling, I whispered: "I don't know. I am new here." The old battleaxe stared at me as if I was the devil himself.

"I can see I am wasting my time here," she growled. "I'll go to the Fire Station. They are bound to know." And with that, she marched out. I turned to Lily, she had her face turned away from me, but I could see she was dabbing her eyes with a handkerchief trying to stop the tears of laughter.

"Don't worry, Jeff," she said kindly, "all sorts of strange people turn up here. Some of them just want someone to chat to. You will get used to it."

She was right, I did get used to it, and some of the funniest moments of my career came courtesy of some very strange individuals, often in a courtroom.

I once witnessed a chap charged with breaking the 40mph speed limit on the edge of town plead guilty but ask the magistrates for clemency. He explained: "I was one of the organisers of a Church fete. My job was to deliver several boxes of ice creams. It was a hot day and I was hurrying to try and get to the fete before they melted." The beaks absolutely fell about at this one, but they fined him £5 and endorsed his driving license anyway.

The following Friday the normally sleepy courtroom at Epping Magistrates exploded in drama and I was there to see it. A lanky youth, by the name of Stephen Watkins, appeared, charged with stealing a car, an offence known then as 'TDA' or 'Taking and Driving Away'. He stood in the well of the court, head bowed as a rotund sergeant read out details of the offence to the Bench. Without warning, the lad got to his feet as if he urgently wanted to say something. The Chief Magistrate, an affable local farmer, peered over his bi-focals and said: "Yes, Watkins. What is it?" But there were no words.

Instead, with the speed of an Olympic sprinter, Watkins bounded forward and leapt, gazelle-like, onto the Clerk of the Court's table which was in front of the Magistrates' bench. From my position in the press bench, set at a right angle to the well of the court, I had the perfect view as the lad then clambered athletically from the Clerk's table up onto the Magistrates' bench itself.

Fearing they were being attacked, the Chairman and his two assistants ducked sideways, but the youth was not attempting an assault. He was escaping. Behind the Magistrates' chairs was a door leading to their deliberating room, where the beaks would sometimes adjourn to discuss a case and have a crafty cup of tea and a laugh about some pathetic excuse which had just been offered up by an accused. The fugitive opened the door and vanished from view. Inside the court there was pandemonium. Police officers, ushers, solicitors and members of the public were on their feet shouting and pointing.

A constable ran through to the Magistrates' room. Seconds later he was back and I heard him say to one of the JPs: "He's escaped. He's legged it out of the back door." I knew there was a rear door to the court building, leading to a small car park. It had obviously been left unlocked. The court was adjourned. I went out of the front door to call my office from a public phone box outside the adjoining police station.

Two cops ran down the front steps of the 'nick' and ran towards the right. I followed them to see what they were going to do. At the end of the block was a side street and a small triangular area of green space with three or four large trees on it. The cops I had seen running had joined two other officers, including the sergeant who had been giving evidence. They were all standing at the base of the largest tree. And there, about 30ft from the ground, nearly at the top of the tree, was the fugitive, clinging on to the trunk for dear life.

He had sprinted about 40 yards from the court. And then,

because he had acted spontaneously and without a plan, he had sought refuge, like a cornered squirrel, up a tree. A crowd soon gathered. The sergeant was calling to his prisoner: "Don't be a twat, Steve. Come down. You are surrounded."

"Fuck off," said Steve. "I can't come down. I'm scared of heights. I can't get down."

The adrenaline rush of the escape had given him enough strength and courage to shin up the tree like a cat. But fear had taken over and he had realised his predicament. About six coppers had gathered at the base of the tree. One suggested they should all shake the tree until the fugitive fell out. The sergeant countermanded him, but not for fear of injuring the fugitive. "No, no," he said to his colleagues. "He might fall on top of me and break my neck."

There was laughter from the crowd. I slipped back to the phone box, called my office, told them what was going on, and asked them to get a photographer there as fast as possible. The town fire engine, manned by a crew of local volunteers, arrived. There was now a crowd of about 100 onlookers. The firemen and the cops all scratched their heads. Someone tried to tempt him down with a mug of tea, a very British gesture.

Eventually the fire brigade put a long ladder up the tree and one strapping fire fighter, who was also a useful amateur heavyweight boxer, clambered up, grabbed the boy, slung him over his shoulder and carried him down. From the crowd there were cheers, clapping, and from some of Watkins' mates who had come to support him, hoots of derision and verbal abuse aimed at the police.

Once he was on the ground two PCs rushed forward and one slapped handcuffs on him. Watkins was in no shape to resist. He was shaking like a leaf, there were tears dribbling down his cheeks, and his nose was running. He had scared himself half to death. As the cops grabbed him, one of Watkins' mates shouted from the back of the crowd: "Oi, you're all bleedin' brave now he's back on the ground, ain't yer?" Which I thought was fair comment.

Most of my professional life did feature murder, mayhem and violence. It was just nice, from time to time to write about something criminal that still put a smile on the face of most people.

Another instance came when I discovered that in a suburb of south west London a Neighbourhood Watch co-ordinator had spotted two men removing furniture from a neighbour's house. Convinced they were burglars, the nosy amateur spy called the cops, telling the police operator he was a proud Neighbourhood Watch representative proving the value of the 'citizen crimefighter' programme. The cops arrived and detained the removal men as they loaded a valuable mahogany dining room table and chairs onto their van. But when challenged by the cops, they produced documents which showed they were genuine house moving professionals hired to help with exactly that, a house move. The police apologised and went on their way, as did the removal men. Then the householder came home and discovered his house had been burgled and all his furniture stolen. The cops had been conned.

I wrote up the story, but the headline, put on by a clever sub-editor, contained only two words but it was witty and memorable. It read simply: 'Neighbourhood Botch'.

CHAPTER EIGHT

The British obsession with pets meant animals were always good for stories, so when a mate happened to mention that his brother Mike had a collection of exotic pets – snakes, big spiders, parrots – I asked if he would do an interview with me. It was a 'yes' so the next afternoon I visited and sure enough, it was a menagerie.

Mike greeted me at the door with a large pure white Sulphur Crested Cockatoo sitting on his arm. His wife, Gloria, was sporting a huge Amethystine Python, draped around her shoulders like a chiffon scarf. Dotted about on shelves and tables, there were several glass vivariums in which cavorted a Mexican Red Kneed Tarantula and other huge hairy spiders.

There was a large fish tank, and in the shallow water, sitting on a rock, was a small Cayman alligator. You could not move for critters, and they all had interesting 'back stories', about where they had been acquired from, what they ate, etc. My pencil was skittering across my notebook, jotting down all the information. Gloria invited me to hold the snake, which I did, because snakes don't bother me. I was surprised at how heavy it was, and how dry to the touch, not slimy as many people assume. I baulked at handling a tarantula, because snakes are one thing, but I am not keen on spiders.

Then Mike said to Gloria: "Shall we show him Barry?" Gloria went to the airing cupboard and sitting on a pile of blankets, was Barry, a Frilled Lizard, nearly 3ft long. He looked like some kind of miniature prehistoric monster. She carefully lifted him out and offered him to me to hold. "Don't worry. He doesn't bite," she said reassuringly.

And then I noticed something very odd about Barry. From just behind his front legs, to just in front of his rear legs, he was swathed in thick silver tape. "What's this wrapped all around him?" I inquired innocently.

"Ah," said Mike, "That's gaffer tape."

Gloria interjected: "You see Jeff, lizards like to be kept warm. So Barry sleeps in the airing cupboard. Unfortunately he has taken to sleeping on top of the hot water cylinder, which gets really hot sometimes.

"A couple of days ago we noticed the heat had caused him to…. well, erm… he had split."

"Yes," said Mike helpfully. "I opened the door and I noticed all his insides were hanging out."

"Really?" I said, fighting back a sudden wave of nausea.

"Yes," added Mike. "I repair fibre glass bodywork on things like sports cars and speed boats. So I nipped back to my workshop, got some fibre glass material, and I've fixed Barry with it to stop his insides falling out.

"I used two rolls of gaffer tape to fix it firmly in position until it all set nicely. He seems perfectly fine now, well and comfortable with the arrangement."

Now I may have been a sprog reporter at the time, but I knew an 'angle', a key component of any news story, when I saw one. "So Mike," I said thoughtfully. "Your exotic pet is now half lizard, half speed boat, is that right? "

And Mike nodded and smiled enthusiastically and said: "Yes, you could say I am at the cutting edge of veterinarian medicine, I suppose."

I telephoned one of our photographers who arrived a little later and took some nice pictures of Barry, the half lizard who was, in some respects, also half a Lotus Elan – a revolutionary sports car of that era with a fibre glass body. So when I wrote my story, I didn't spend much time describing the parrots and snakes and hairy spiders. It was all about Barry, the very rare lizard, who was held together with fibre glass panels and gaffer tape. And, as invited, I quoted Mike as he had described his innovation as being at the cutting edge of pet medicine.

If I remember correctly, the story, which was prominently positioned on a right hand news page, was headlined by a witty sub editor: "Meet Barry. Half Lizard. Half Speed Boat."

And everyone seemed happy. Until a few days later when Mike phoned me in a high state of anxiety, and said the local RSPCA inspectors had read my story. They had descended on Mike and Gloria and confiscated Barry and had warned his owners they were likely to be prosecuted for animal cruelty.

It was another valuable lesson for me in journalism. Think carefully about what you disclose when you are writing, because there could be consequences.

It also wasn't the last encounter I had with a very large reptile… Twice a week, after I joined the *Newham Recorder*, on Tuesdays and Fridays, I went into the five police stations in our area, gathering as much information as I was allowed (and often stuff I wasn't really allowed) to work up into a story.

There were a lot of grim events. In that part of East London murders happened on average about once a fortnight and fatal accidents, whether on the roads, or in a factory or a house fire, were common. There were stabbings, shootings, armed robberies, rapes, arsons – you name it, it was going on.

At the time Newham, which on Scotland Yard's map of London was known as 'Inner K Division' had the highest crime rate of not just all 32 London boroughs, but the country as a whole. For a young reporter I could not have been in a better, or more exciting place.

I rarely finished my police calls without a notebook bulging with a broad outline of a serious crime. I learned that what was contained in those hefty leather bound police station log books – known in turn as the Major Crime Book, The Minor Crime Book, The Motor Vehicle Crime Book and the Occurrence Book, was usually just a brief outline of the event.

I also learned to ask for the name of the officer assigned to the case, especially in those heavy duty entries about robberies, rapes, murders and other violent assaults.

Back at my office I would telephone the police station and ask to speak to the officer in the case. This was not just to try and elicit more information, it was also, I thought, a matter of courtesy to let the officer know I was interested in their case and details would probably appear in the local press.

The reactions could go either way. Much of the time the detective involved was forthcoming and often an invitation to meet later at one of several favoured pubs was extended. This was how I started to build trusting relationships with a number of CID officers, many of which have lasted a lifetime. Most of them were relaxed, easy-going by nature, and good company.

There were also a minority of CID men (there were hardly any female police detectives then) who didn't like 'the press' and would give me short shrift. In one or two extreme cases even a polite and friendly approach resulted in a curt 'fuck off' and the phone being hung up, but this was rare. And so, meetings were held and usually the detail of the real story turned out to be far more interesting than the rough outline scribbled in longhand in the crime book.

By recent standards, the amount of information journalists like me were allowed to see and have back then, was quite staggering.

But it wasn't always the most dramatic 'Major Crimes' entries, with their tales of criminal mayhem, which produced the most interesting and off beat stories. The 'Occurrence Book' – the 'OB' was where officers wrote up every other occurrence reported by the public, or themselves.

It ranged from accounts of 'officer injured on duty' to even UFO reports, and it was a mine of interesting and sometimes very funny stories for an inquisitive reporter like me. An account of 'police called to gain entry' turned out to yield the following; A man living in a second floor flat in Forest Gate had two hobbies. The first was keeping tropical fish in a huge 200 gallon glass tank, the second was making his own wine. According to the 'OB' report the police had been called to force the door of his flat after a downstairs neighbour reported his ceiling had collapsed and two hundred gallons of water, plus several dozen tropical fish, had poured into his apartment, wrecking it.

The owner could get no reply from the flat upstairs, so had called police because he feared a mains water pipe had burst causing the deluge. The police investigation discovered the owner of the upstairs apartment had gone away for a few days. While he was away, one of his glass carboys full of fermenting wine had blown its cork, causing it to ricochet around his living room with such force it had smashed the reinforced underside of the fish tank sending water cascading through the downstairs neighbour's ceiling.

I visited the owners of the ruined flat, and then the guy upstairs who was heartbroken about the loss of his pet fish, and even more distraught about the loss of his home brewed 'Chateau East Ham'. For a local paper like the *Recorder*, it was a terrific off beat story.

Another report I saw one day listed an officer being injured on duty. Thinking this must have been the result of a high speed car chase or a violent arrest I asked for more details only to discover the officer had been driving his patrol car along a local side street when a woman ran into the road in front of him, frantically flagging him to stop. The terrified lady explained there was a mouse in her bath. Could he remove it? The officer, a man I knew personally, obliged, but when he tried to catch the tiny rodent, it savagely turned on him, biting his index finger.

He was required to go to hospital for a tetanus jab and was off sick for several days. His account of how he had chivalrously attempted to protect the member of the public from this frightening beast and had suffered a finger injury as a result made a page lead for me that week.

Animals were always good for a news story and again the police occurrence book often delivered. In the early 1970s the laws governing the selling and keeping of exotic pets, some of them, like crocodiles and pumas, very dangerous beasts, were very loose. In the area where I worked we had two pet shops selling rare and sometimes dangerously unpredictable critters.

One of them, at Manor Park, was called 'Alexander's Pet Boutique' run by a man called Alexander Duncan. If you were short of a light touch story and an off beat picture Alexander would always help out with something, be it a porcupine or a penguin. One day the police OB showed officers with tranquilizer dart guns had been sent in a hurry from Scotland Yard to Alexander's Pet Boutique after a full-grown chimpanzee had gone berserk. The chimp, which London Zoo had told the cops would be several times stronger than a grown man, had to be shot with tranquilizer darts after it wrecked the shop on a Saturday afternoon.

I spoke to the distraught Alexander who told me the chimp had inexplicably and unexpectedly gone on the rampage, terrifying customers and other more mild-mannered pets alike. In the end, armed only with a stout yard broom, he had managed to force it back through a door leading down some stairs to a basement, where he had had to then nail lengths of strong timber across the door and the frame to stop the enraged simian battering its way out.

The police marksmen had to smash a hole in the basement door in order to poke a torch and a dart gun through to suppress the beast. One of the cops who had attended said: "I've fought with a dozen drunken Irish navvies in a pub brawl and I would rather do that again than take on a chimp that's lost its mind."

The chimp was finally loaded into the 'prisoner cage' of a police paddy wagon and driven at speed with blue lights and blaring sirens to London Zoo in Regents Park, where they had people who knew how to calm it down. It was a great story.

About two weeks after the chimp went loopy I was visiting Forest Gate police station when a PC leant across the front desk and in a conspiratorial manner whispered: "Do you want to see my snake"? Naturally I was wary because, based on my experience of the local police, a remark like this could come before some awful practical joke involving a huge plastic penis or something similar.

But no. The officer went to a cupboard in a corner of the front office and returned staggering under the weight of an enormous python which, sadly, was very dead. "This is Monty," said the policeman, while several of his colleagues grinned inanely at me from over his shoulder.

I was astonished and keen to know by what means such an exotic creature had come into their possession. "We ran it over. In the Area Car," came the reply. The 'Area Car' was the sector patrol car for Forest Gate. It was a powerful dark blue Rover V8.

I pressed for a further explanation. The PC, who now had the 12ft snake corpse looped around his neck and waist said: "I was late turn driver on the Area Car last night with Jim [another PC]. It was a rainy night.

"As we cruised along Upton Lane I heard and felt a 'ker-donk, ker-donk' noise from under the wheels. I hadn't seen anything in the road, so I stopped to see what we had run over, and there was Monty. Sadly, it was a fatal accident, as you can see. Look, you can see where our wheels went over him." Indeed, there were four very obvious flat spots on Monty where the tyres of the patrol car had squashed it.

"So who does it belong to?" I asked."Dunno, mate, haven't a clue. No one has reported it missing." And no one ever did. No one ever inquired if anyone had come across a huge rare and undoubtedly very expensive python slithering about the darkened streets of East London. The dead snake sat in the cupboard at Forest Gate nick for days, before someone noticed it was starting to stink and it was eventually unceremoniously dumped in a bin in the back yard of the police station until the dustmen took it away.

I thought that a deranged chimp and fugitive python might have been the end of the exotic animal stories filling my notebook at this time. But I was wrong. Just a few days later I was telling another PC friend of mine, based at neighbouring East Ham, about the python when he looked at me straight faced and exclaimed: "That's nothing, mate. PC Potter has got a crocodile! And he keeps it in his room in the Section House!"

The 'Section House' was a residential block of rooms for usually young, single officers, provided by the Metropolitan Police. There were a number of them, usually attached to police stations all over London. Once again, I looked sideways at my informant, in full expectation of this being just another police 'wind-up' at my expense.

My friend caught onto my scepticism, and said: "No. It's really true. Potter HAS got a crocodile. He's got it in his room in a big fish tank, you can see it if you want." So a day or two later I was led, surreptitiously, through the yard of East Ham nick, and up the back stairs of the Section House to the room belonging to PC Potter. Now, it's important to say here, that in light of subsequent events, PC Potter is not his real name.

Living conditions in a police 'Section House' at the time were spartan.

Usually, the furnishings were no more than a grey painted metal framed single bed, a wardrobe, a desk and chair, a cast iron radiator, and that was it. Apart from a small hand basin, there were no washing or lavatory facilities in the room. All the lavatories and bathrooms were communal. But Potter had installed one additional item in his abode. It was a plate glass fish tank, about 4ft long on top of a wooden table he'd bought from a junk shop.

In the tank, lying motionless in murky green water was, as described to me, a real live crocodile. Potter was grinning from ear to ear. As were several of his colleagues, crammed into his room with us. The croc was obviously a big draw among the Section House community.

"It's brilliant, isn't it," he said. It was a statement, not a question.

"What sort is it?" I asked.

"It's a crocodile," said Potter, clearly oblivious to the fact nature produced several different species of the carnivorous reptile.

"Is it a male or a female?" I enquired.

"Not sure mate," replied Potter, "but if you want, you can stick your hand in the water and check for yourself". Loud guffaws all around the room.

"How big will it get?" I ventured to ask, making a mental observation the animal already looked suspiciously jammed in, with no room to even turn around.

"Not sure," said Potter, "but it has doubled in size since I bought it a few weeks ago."

Finally, I asked: "Do you have a name for it?"

"Yes, I call it Kevin." Some of the PCs visiting Potter's croc were now feeding it. Pieces of Mars Bar were dropped in the tank, along with some Hula Hoops.

"Is it supposed to have things like that?" I ventured, not wishing to sound censorial. "I thought they were strictly meat-eaters."

"Course they are allowed chocolate," said one of the visiting coppers. "This stuff won't do it any harm. Crocodiles will eat ANYTHING."

Everyone laughed. I had little doubt where this already formidable looking reptile had come from. About two miles from East Ham police station, along the Barking Road in Plaistow, was another pet shop selling exotic and highly dangerous animals.

I had done a story on the place just a few months before, when the owner told me he allowed two 8ft alligators to roam the store loose at night, to deter burglars. "This beastie will probably grow to 10ft long, maybe more," I told Potter. "What will you do with it then?"

He just laughed: "If it does, I'll give it to the London Zoo. They will be happy to take it." Before I left I told Potter I'd like to do a story about his exotic croc, but he put his finger to his lips in a 'hush' gesture and said: "No story please Jeff. You see the Section House rules mean we are not allowed to keep pets in our rooms. I could be in a bit of bother if the guvnors find out." I nodded agreement. I knew enough to know that sometimes it was better professionally to keep on the right side of potential contacts.

A few weeks passed. Then one day the PC who had introduced me to Potter told me, in hushed tones: "There's been a bit of a row about the crocodile." It turned out the croc had, as predicted, rapidly outgrown its tank.

Potter had phoned the London Zoo and offered them the crocodile, only to be told: "Sorry, we've already got plenty." Rebuffed, he tried Whipsnade Zoo in Bedfordshire, only to be told: "We are up to our armpits in crocodiles. No thanks." It was the same everywhere. And then things got worse. At the police Section House where PC Potter lived there was a communal bathroom which contained three baths. They stood in a line on the floor, with no partition between them. So, telling everyone it was just a temporary measure, Potter transferred his pet croc Kevin into one of the bath tubs. And everything would have been fine, until the morning the cleaner, a lady called Joyce, came in to mop the floors. She hadn't been told about the new bathroom arrangements and

Potter's croc, probably fed up with a diet of salt and vinegar crisps and Cadbury's Fruit and Nut, and fancying some fresh meat, launched itself at her. Joyce was agile enough to jump out of the way unscathed, but according to my informant, her scream of terror was heard all over East London. Now, to mix metaphors, Potter and his crocodile were in the doghouse.

Potter had been summoned in front of his boss, a Superintendent who was much lampooned secretly by his staff for his attempts to disguise his East End roots by trying to speak 'posh' English. Due to his misunderstanding some basic rules he was prone to inserting the letter 'H' in front of words beginning with vowels.

So he told Potter: "It's come to my hattention that are you are keeping a prohibited hanimal, namely a halligator or crocodile on police premises. Get rid of it, Potter. Now."

PC Potter had tried to explain that he had explored every means possible to offload the now muscular and ferocious beast, without success, but his boss was having no truck with him. He was given a week to get rid of it, or a Scotland Yard gun team would be brought in to deal with it.

And then something happened which has remained a mystery ever since. On a Saturday, about a week after Potter's predicament was told to me, I turned on a local London radio station hoping to catch the football results, when I heard a news bulletin.

The announcer said: "And finally… police divers are searching a lake in East London after reports that a crocodile had been spotted in Wanstead Park….."

After a couple of days the fruitless hunt for the Wanstead Park crocodile was called off. There were no more sightings. There were even doubts it was ever there in the first place. If asked, PC Potter always insisted he had sold the crocodile to a stranger called 'John' he had met by chance in a pub. Whatever the truth was, no more was ever heard of Kevin the crocodile.

POLITICAL AND FOREIGN AFFAIRS

CHAPTER NINE

There were, of course, times when the great and the good – and the not so good – found themselves tangled with the police, and thus me as well.

By the spring of 1975 I had my first contract at the *London Evening News* when I got a good tip off.

One of my old policeman friends, Jim, called and asked me to meet him at the pub. He asked me if I knew Ray who was a PC and specialist dog handler in East London.

My friend said: "Late last night Ray was out in his van. He parked up near the Wanstead Flats, to exercise his dog." The Wanstead Flats are a large area of open flat land, covering some 460 acres. At night they have always been a popular spot with courting couples.

"Last night while Ray was exercising his dog, he saw a bloke acting a bit strangely. It was a warm night, but the bloke was wearing a heavy raincoat, and he was sort of creeping about.

"So very discreetly, Ray kept an eye on him. The bloke was completely unaware a policeman was keeping him under observation. Then Ray twigged there were two or three courting couples having sex in the long grass, and this bloke was creeping about watching them. He was getting his rocks off watching people having sex."

This was not unusual in an area popular with lovers who liked the great outdoors. It was a practice which later became known as 'dogging'. My police chum broke off and checked around the bar to make sure our conversation wasn't being earwigged.

He continued: "So Ray pounced on him and nicked him for a breach of the peace. He cuffed him up and put him in the van and drove into the backyard of the nick and the prisoner, who's a well dressed, nicely-spoken bloke, starts giving it 'do you know who I am?' and all that, and Ray says 'I don't give a fuck who you are mate, and…'."

Now Jim really had my complete attention. "Who was it?" I said, now intrigued.

"He was only a fucking Member of Parliament Jeff, the dirty sod. He's Michael Ward, the Labour MP for Romford. He was watching people screwing in the long grass.

"Anyway, when Ray got him in the charge room, he really came on strong. He demanded to speak to the Commander." I knew the local police commander was a man called Cornelius 'Con' Mulvihill. He had a reputation for being a tough man to work for, who didn't suffer fools and spoke his mind. Jim continued: "So whoever was duty skipper last night decided to bite the bullet. It was after midnight but he rang Commander Mulvihill at his home, woke him up, because he was in bed fast asleep.

"And Commander Mulvihill, who lives out in Essex somewhere, put his clothes on and drove straight down here." I had never met Con Mulvihill, but I knew about his reputation as a hardline boss.

"Mulvihill arrived and said to the skipper and to Ray, 'So this bloke is a local MP is he?' What's he been nicked for?' And when they told him he said: 'Where is the evidence of a fucking breach of the peace then?"

"So, Ray replied, 'Well Guv, I was working on the basis that if someone having a shag in the grass in the dark with a woman suddenly catches someone watching them then in my view there's going to be a fucking great breach of the peace.' Mulvihill then said to Ray and the sergeant: 'Release this man. There's no offence here.' So the MP walked out, and Mulvihill fucked off back home to bed."

My mind was racing. This was a terrific story for the *London Evening News* but if there was no prosecution, and Ward had been allowed to go, officially there would be no record of anything happening at all. Difficult to write if Ward and Mulvihill both refused to confirm it or comment at all. I told Jim my concerns. He looked at me and said: "I thought that's what you'd say. So I brought you this."

And he reached inside his jacket pocket and pulled out a photocopy of a page from an official police record book.

"There," he said. "That's from the 'Book 58' from last night."

I knew what the 'Book 58' was. It was a kind of an 'occurrence record' a formal log of everyone who had been arrested and brought into a police station, whether they were charged or not. The copied page was absolute proof. It was dated, timed, and signed by the arresting officer. It recorded the name, age, occupation, address etc. of the prisoner, and a brief summary of why the arrest had been made and for what offence. It was there in black and white; Michael Ward, Member of Parliament.

But perhaps best of all was what Commander Mulvihill had done before leaving that police station. He'd taken a thick blue pencil and in huge capital letters scrawled across the whole log entry: 'NOT FOR THE PRESS'.

Thus he had ensured that any officer thumbing through the book would stop and carefully read what had been noted there. Con Mulvihill retired and died before I got a chance to ask him, but I like to think the wily old police chief knew exactly what he was doing.

The next morning in the office at the crack of dawn, I hurried over to my boss George and excitedly told him what I had found out. Before he had a chance to ask how, in the face of a certain denial, we were going to stand the story up, I whipped out the copy of the police log and put it under his nose.

I started to write up the story while he detailed one of our Parliamentary reporters to speak to the MP and ask him his version of events. Ward at first denied anything had taken place. Then he changed his story and said: "I was driving home from Westminster after a late debate. I had a headache and needed some air. I stopped and went for a walk to clear my head. I was detained by the police, but it was all a terrible misunderstanding."

My copy was checked by our lawyers. A few careful amendments had to be made. Then it appeared prominently on the second main news page under the headline: "Night an MP Went For a Walk and Ended Up in the Cells".

My boss George took me to the bar and bought me a bottle of champagne.

***

Political machinations didn't stop at the British borders, as I discovered on my very first day as the Chief Crime Correspondent for the *Daily Mirror* in February 1993.

In the early 1990s the newspaper was selling well over three and half million copies every day. Perhaps more importantly, throughout my career I had wanted to work for the *Daily Mirror*. I admired its style, professionalism and history of great journalism. For me it was the thinking person's 'Red Top'. It dealt with serious issues and made them accessible to all levels of readership through excellent reporting, writing and presentation.

It had been a quiet day and as I headed home, I felt my pager vibrate on my trouser belt. Usually the message was brief and succinct, 'Call the office' or 'Ring Harry' for instance. But this message was a bit longer and certainly more intriguing. It said: "If you want to learn something to your advantage, give me a call." It was from a friend of mine, a Metropolitan Police detective. I turned round and went back up the stairs to the *Mirror* newsroom to call him.

"Listen to this," he said. "I've just accompanied some Homicide Squad officers to a semi-detached house in Harrow.

"In the garage we found the bodies of two men stuffed in big cardboard boxes. They've both been shot in the head several times. I am told they are Russians." I was stunned. It was a sensational tip off.

My friend added: "It's not my investigation, you need to speak to…" and he gave me the name of someone on the Homicide Command who luckily I was on good terms with. I called this friend and he answered. I told him what I just heard. His first response was: "Blimey, you must have radar controlled ear holes." Then he said: "Ever heard of a place called Chechnya"? I confessed I had not. "It's a little obscure place somewhere near Russia. It was a part of the USSR until Communism collapsed a few years ago.

Now it's independent. Our victims are Chechen nationals. They were part of a delegation of four diplomats sent to the UK to set up an Embassy. It looks like there's been a falling out and two of them have murdered the other two. I've got to go. I'll call you tomorrow morning."

It wasn't the whole story, I could see that, but it was enough. It was a great start to what turned out to be the most exciting part of my entire career.

The murders became the opening act in a series of events over three years which led to the shooting of an innocent woman in Surrey by a hired assassin, snake venom being smuggled into a maximum security prison in the UK, and a KGB assassination in Russia…

After the collapse of the USSR the state of Chechnya had declared independence. In 1993 few people in the UK had even heard of the place.

My pal from the homicide team was as good as his word. To avoid any suspicion falling on him as my source he called me from a pay phone in central London. His colleagues had been working hard throughout the night. He explained the dead men had been identified as brothers Ruslan and Nazarbek Outsiev. They had both been shot in the head multiple times with a 9mm Beretta semi-automatic pistol.

After the murders the killers had placed the dead men in cardboard boxes which had been used to deliver new white goods to a flat where the men had been living in Bickenhall Mansions, in Marylebone, a very upmarket and grand district of London. The killers had then hired a removal company to shift the boxes out to Harrow. But the removal men had noticed a suspicious smell and what appeared to be trickles of blood coming from the boxes and contacted the police. After the police found the bodies in the garage they searched the Harrow house and found links to the flat in Marylebone. Discreet inquiries about the Bickenhall Mansions apartment revealed that at the same address were two men who had now been identified, not as Chechens, but as Armenians. They were Gagic Ter-Ogannisyan and Mkrtitch Martirossian.

Police lay in wait for them and intercepted them coming back to the garage with saws, bottles of acid and plastic bags which were to be used to cut up and get rid of their victims. Detectives then discovered the four men had come to the UK as part of a delegation to set up an embassy for the embryonic new country of Chechnya and to arrange secure printing of banknotes, stamps and passports. They had paid £750,000 cash for the flat and rented a semi-detached house in suburban Harrow as a diplomatic residence. They also had wads of cash totalling over $500,000 US.

One theory behind the murders was that the Outsiev brothers, instead of behaving like true diplomats, were instead spending every day drunk on vodka, high on cocaine, and hiring expensive prostitutes. It was claimed that Ter-Ogannisyan and Martirossian, frustrated by their colleagues' behaviour, complained to their masters back in the Chechen capital, Grozny, who gave the order: 'Kill them and dispose of the bodies. Nobody in the UK will notice they are missing'.

However the true story was far more nuanced and steeped in a background of espionage, secret missile deals, double agents and all the intrigue we have come to expect from a Russian-influenced, gangster-run state.

When he was arrested, Martirossian first claimed to the police to be a KGB officer. Then a substance found in his possessions in Bickenhall Mansions turned out to be a phial of deadly snake venom with which to commit suicide if captured. He never got a chance to use it.

Through my contacts, I uncovered the first big twist. Ter-Ogannisyan was married to a British woman. Alison Ponting was a fellow journalist who ran the Russian desk of the BBC World Service. They had met in Armenia when she was a student learning Russian. Initially Alison was arrested as a suspect for assisting in the murders. But then she was released. I tried to contact her, but no joy.

She had effectively vanished off the face of the earth. I wondered if she had been spirited away by the Special Branch. After all, I reasoned, if she was co-operating her life could be in mortal danger. And if that was the case, I also knew there was no way I could find out about it.

After a few days of questioning, her husband and Martirossian were charged with murder. The pair went on trial a few months later at the Old Bailey. They were found guilty and sentenced to life imprisonment. But then came another unexpected chicane in the chain of events. I became aware that MI5 and Special Branch had discovered that associates of the dead men in Chechnya had sworn vengeance on the killers, even though they had been jailed in the UK.

The police decided that, unable to get to Ter-Ogannisyan, his enemies might try and get to his wife. My early instincts had been right, she was now under the wing of the security services.

Unbeknown to us all, she was sent to live with her sister, Karen Reed, an ordinary woman with an ordinary job, who lived in Woking in Surrey.

Of course, none of this was known to journalists like me at the time. It was, and had to be, a closely guarded secret. Although I tried to keep track of the switchback ride of events of this story, which had followed the shootings uncovered on my first day, I had a huge basket of other crimes – murders, robberies, drug busts, the whole panoply of police matters to deal with.

For the next 12 months or so I had not thought much about the affair. But on Sunday May 1, 1994 I received a phone call at home early in the morning from a contact on the Regional Crime Squad in south west London which caused the hair on the back of my neck to stand on end.

He told me there had been a spectacular shooting murder overnight in Woking, Surrey, a place where extreme violence was rare. My contact only had a brief outline of what had happened, but then he said something that stopped me in my tracks. "It looks like a very professional 'hit'. Apparently it's linked to the case of the Chechen murders you reported on last year."

It quickly emerged Karen Reed had been shot dead on her doorstep the previous evening. Of course, until that morning I had not heard of Karen Reed, and had no idea of what a sensational case her murder was about to become.

There was a press conference called at Woking police station. I drove down from London as soon as I heard.

They declared from the outset they believed the intended target was a woman called Alison Ponting, who had been under protection from the Metropolitan Police following her husband's involvement in a double shooting murder in London in 1993. The revelation hit me like an electric shock.

There were many other journalists in the room that day who

still didn't know who Alison Ponting was, but I did. On the advice of Scotland Yard's Special Branch, who had told her directly they were worried her life was at risk, she had moved from the home in London she had shared with her husband and gone to stay with her sister Karen in Surrey.

The Surrey police explained, on the night of the shooting Alison had gone out. She had left Karen enjoying a night in with a friend who was visiting. Karen was married but separated from her husband and her house in Woking was on a pleasant estate of three and four bedroom detached executive homes.

It was an unlikely place for such a dramatic sequence of events. At about 8pm there was a ring at the doorbell and Karen answered. On her doorstep was a man holding a flat cardboard box. In perfect English he asked if she'd ordered pizzas.

As she answered 'no' he pulled out a semi-automatic pistol and shot her five times in the head and body, killing her instantly. Her friend, who was in the kitchen preparing some supper didn't see what happened but heard the verbal exchange at the front door and later told police the killer spoke perfect English.

It was clear from the outset Karen had been shot in mistake for her sister. The police were supposed to be keeping watch on the house. Alison and Karen had received advice about what to look out for and what to do if they felt threatened. Panic button alarms, linked directly to Woking police station, had been fitted in several rooms in the house. But it looked like the police, and the unfortunate Karen, had dropped their guard.

More astonishing facts emerged over the next few days. To reinforce the belief the shooting was the work of an expert assassin, the ammunition used was of a rare and sinister design. The 9mm bullets were 'mercury-tipped' rounds, designed to explode as they entered the body, causing internal injuries impossible to survive.

I spoke to a military firearms expert who explained the nose of each bullet had been drilled out, mercury inserted, and the hole sealed with wax. He described the ammunition as "an absolute Cold War classic. The hallmark of a professionally trained and equipped killer."

Then it emerged that three weeks prior to the murder, a routine police patrol had become suspicious about a red Vauxhall Cavalier parked nearby. As they approached the car it sped off. There was a chase but the driver abandoned the car near Woking football club and escaped on foot.

Police searched the car. Under the driver's seat they found a loaded Hungarian made PA 63 semi-automatic pistol fitted with a silencer and loaded with mercury tipped ammunition. There was also an SAS-type dagger, and a map of the area with the house belonging to Karen Reed marked on it. The car, which had been abandoned a mile away, had been stolen in London.

There were a number of burning questions. Did the police have any idea who had done it, and who had arranged it? How did the killer know how to find where Alison was living? Clearly it should have been a closely-guarded secret known only to a few operatives at MI5, Special Branch and a few carefully selected Surrey officers. Was there a secret double agent in one of those organisations?

And suddenly, Surry police went from from being happy to talk to reporters like me, to clamming up. They were saying absolutely nothing and it was clear they had been warned to say nothing, probably from Home Secretary level. I spoke to all my best contacts at Scotland Yard. But in all the top crime fighting units, even those who specialised in tracking hit men, the answer was the same: "We know nothing. We are being excluded. It's an MI5 job."

It goes without saying, Alison was immediately taken into hiding by the police and remains in hiding to this day. I have no doubt at all she was taken out of the UK immediately and is probably now living in a place thousands of miles away on a different continent under a new identity.

The intrigue didn't stop even after Karen was murdered. Several years later in early 1997, Mkritch Martirossian was visited in Belmarsh Prison, London by an Armenian compatriot, Ashot Sarkissian. He had links to both the KGB and the Russian mafia. After the visitor left, Martirossian was searched by prison officers who found a small glass phial of snake venom hidden in a bandage on his arm. Tests showed it was from a Gaboon Viper, one of the world's most deadly snakes. It was an invitation to commit suicide.

The poison was confiscated, But Martirossian was not to be thwarted and committed suicide by hanging himself a few days later. Ashot Sarkissian was mysteriously shot dead in Moscow the following year.

The gunman who shot Karen has never been traced. I remember the officer in charge saying that according to Karen's friend, who heard the front door conversation before the killer opened fire, the hitman had a British accent.

This raised another intriguing question: If the murder was ordered from Chechnya or Moscow, by what chain of connections did they end up contracting a British hitman?

I don't think we will ever find the answers. Needless to say, the murder of Karen Reed remains unsolved.

CHAPTER TEN

In the world of crime there's the dark side, and then there's the very dark side. Something I learned very early in my career.

Entering the Duke of Fife pub in Forest Gate, I could see the bar was crammed with a noisy bunch of burly men. At first glance you might have thought they were car dealers, market traders, or even local criminals. No one could have denied, at first sight they were a motley looking crew. But I knew these people were actually all police officers, detectives from the local CID.

As I pushed my way towards the bar the air was thick with tobacco smoke and the pungent mixture of beer and Scotch whisky. It was 1971, and at that time, virtually everyone was a smoker. I was quite an exception, I didn't smoke tobacco, but I did enjoy a drink. And in my line of work, as an aspiring young crime reporter it was an absolute necessity to be a drinker.

A thick set man with broad shoulders, long hair and a 'gunfighter' moustache, a member of Scotland Yard's elite Flying Squad, slapped me on the back, pressed a pint of beer into my hand, and introduced me to someone I hadn't met before.

Over the previous 12 months I had made a whole load of new friends in the police. And, one way or another, I had picked up some great stories, some of which I could even report in the *Newham Recorder*. I was a quick learner, and one of the things I cottoned onto fast was that for every story I was able to write, I was hearing several others I could not report from my new pals in the CID. There were many reasons for this. Sometimes it would have been too dangerous to my friends and a story coming out in the press at a particular time might have exposed one of my sources, an absolute 'no, no'.

In many cases there was intriguing information about who had committed a particular crime. But for the police there was often a big gulf between 'knowing it and showing it'. In plain terms, we often shared a similar problem; there was a world of difference, both for the police and journalists like me, between knowing who had done it, and proving who had done it. But I was grateful for the intelligence, even if it didn't amount to something I could actually print.

Another lesson I was quick to understand came from the mouth of one wily old detective who, speaking out of the side of his mouth, in a grubby back street bar told me: "I'll tell you anything son, just as long as it never comes back to my door."

I understood. Another one, a barrel chested Glaswegian, put it another way, telling me: "Trust is like virginity, son. You only lose it once." My growing band of detective contacts featured a disparate group. There were wily old detective sergeants, and detective inspectors coming up to the end of their service, who had seen everything you can possibly imagine about the dark side of the world. Some of them had even worked on the Great Train Robbery investigation. Others on the Kray Brothers saga.

There was a detective constable with 30 years service who had worked the West End when the clip joints and prostitutes were controlled by legendary gangsters like Jack Spot, Billy Hill and the Maltese Caruana brothers.

I was spellbound by their stories. This was truly authentic. I felt privileged to be in their company. I became known and trusted.

And as a result, here I was, walking into a back street pub and a large knot of hard-drinking, hard-bitten CID men who knew they could tell me almost anything and it wouldn't end up in print... Unless they said: "Go on mate, fill your boots, put it in the local rag," which meant it was OK to write about it.

As long as it was all unattributable, of course. And walking into the Duke of Fife led me to one of the most amazing exclusive stories I ever got to NOT write about.

The chatter spontaneously died down as, a very handsome man came in through the door with a stunning young blonde woman on his arm. The debonaire man, beautifully turned out in an immaculate silver grey hand tailored Saville Row Mohair suit, carefully steered the woman through the throng.

She was wearing a crocheted white mini dress, the height of fashion for young women in 1971. It would not be an exaggeration to say she looked like a model. Several people greeted the man. He was a detective who had just been transferred to East London from the West End.

His name was Steve. He introduced me to his girlfriend, Michelle. I didn't say much to her. I couldn't. Like every other man in the room I was suddenly bashful and struck dumb by her beauty.

At the end of an entertaining evening, I left making a mental note to contact Steve in the hope of making a new friend. I also thought his girlfriend might have a similarly beautiful pal I could be introduced to. About a month later I arranged to meet some detective friends at another well-known local pub, The Spotted Dog. But when I arrived there was no sign of Steve.

I asked where he was and was greeted with an awkward silence. Then one of the officers lowered his voice and said: "Steve's got a bit of a problem. Actually, it's a fucking big problem." The other chipped in: "We won't be seeing him again Jeff. He's finished. And when I say finished, I mean properly fucking finished." And they told me the following story.

It seemed there was a bit more to the woman I had met with Steve. In fact, she was one of the highest paid prostitutes in London with a number of extremely wealthy clients. But she was romantically involved with Steve, who seemed not to be bothered by his lover's profession.

One of her clients was a wealthy member of the Saudi royal family. He came to London about four times a year. And he had three vices. The first was good looking blonde women. The second was he liked to play roulette in high-end casinos. And the third was he liked to smoke dope – cannabis resin. These were all things forbidden in his strictly Muslim home country.

This prince's favourite blonde was Michelle. He always called her when he was on his way to London to ask her to come to his suite at the Dorchester Hotel. He also wanted another favour and asked her to get him a small block of cannabis resin, just a few grams, but enough to last him for his trip. All of this information she had disclosed to her detective boyfriend. And there was more.

She told the cop that after having sex with her on his first night in town he always rolled a cannabis joint from the block of resin she had brought to him, which they shared. Then, after getting high, he paid her from a bulging roll of banknotes he kept in his hotel bedside drawer. This wad was his gambling and hookers cash reserve. She said she thought it was about £25,000, huge money in the early 1970s.

But the information that caused the detective's ears to prick up was this; not only was her dope smoking client a member of the Saudi royal family. He was also a Colonel in the Saudi Air Force where he flew a supersonic Phantom jet fighter. Steve, the calculating and cunning detective, could see the perfect blackmail plot unfolding. He told his girlfriend to inform him immediately when her Saudi client was coming to London. He would then go to a magistrate and get a drugs search warrant for the Dorchester Hotel.

Unlike an ordinary search warrant, which was only valid for 24 hours, a drugs warrant in this era was good for seven days. Steve told his girlfriend she should buy the cannabis for the prince and take it to the hotel. She should ascertain for certain her Saudi pilot had the big wad of cash with him. And after she had sex with him she should leave, go straight to one of the pay phone booths in the hotel lobby, and call her policeman lover and tell him the prince, the dope and the money, were all in the one place, in his suite at the hotel.

The cop would then go and knock on the door and when the prince answered, he would show him his ID and the search warrant. He would search the room, find the cannabis and the big wedge of money and would tell the compromised prince: "This is very bad news for you. Because you are a member of your Royal household, and an Air Force Colonel to boot. Furthermore, when the Air Force hear what you have been up to and caught with, they will be very displeased. And in a Draconian country like yours, you might find it hard to sustain a career flying a jet fighter when they have cut off your right hand." Because it was well known then that the Saudis favoured severe corporal punishment for people who had brought shame on their nation.

But in the detective's plan, he would then show the big bank roll he had just found to the now badly rattled and anxious prince and say to him: "On the other hand, if you allow me to keep this money, which I am sure is a mere trifle to you, then no more will be heard about it. No one will ever know."

It was an outrageous blackmail plot.

Steve had thought this was an absolute foolproof plan. And he went and persuaded a magistrate at Marlborough Street Court to grant him the drugs search warrant, even though by now he had been assigned away from the money soaked and glamourous West End to the dog-eared and dirt poor east of London.

But, as my friends told me over pints in the Spotted Dog, something had gone awry to spoil Steve's corrupt get rich quick plan. They did not know exactly what it was. But the counter-corruption branch, the 'rubber heels', so called because it was said you could not hear them creeping up on you, had arrived, unannounced, a few days previously, when Steve wasn't there. They had searched his desk and discovered a drugs search warrant for the Dorchester Hotel.

Steve had been summarily suspended and placed under investigation. But within a few days he had thrown in the towel. He'd resigned his job and left the organisation. In the early 1970s a series of corruption scandals rocked the Metropolitan Police and caused severe damage to their reputation. Rather than face more embarrassing trials, however, the powers that then governed Scotland Yard allowed a number of officers caught taking bribes or stealing money from suspects to quit, with no more being said. Steve was allowed just such a way out, and he disappeared and would never be heard of again.

None of my friends knew for sure how he had been found out. I knew it was a good story, but somehow I knew it was one I would have trouble progressing. After all, I wasn't supposed to know any of this. And officially now, none of this had ever happened. If I started making waves, by asking probing questions, there would likely be an investigation into how it was I knew about these things. My friends had been very forthcoming. I was conscious of not wanting to drop them in trouble.

On the other hand, I also knew that if I rang the *News of the World*, they would probably give me £100 just for the tip. That was more money than I earned in a month. After all, the story had everything, didn't it? A beautiful blonde hooker, a bent cop, a Saudi prince, the Dorchester Hotel. It was a royal flush.

But I had second thoughts. Headlines in the *News of the World* might bring the pains on at Scotland Yard. There was a lot to consider. If there was a full investigation my friends, now emerging as excellent contacts, might end up in a world of trouble. I decided it was best to play the 'long game'. If people knew they could trust me, more good stories would come my way, further down the line. So I walked away, never told a soul, and I have never written about this story until now.

The sudden disappearance of the new detective and the explanation for it was a real eye-opener for me. It was the most serious case of police corruption I had come across. It was a stunning story, even if I couldn't write it.

CHAPTER ELEVEN

My Scotland Yard contacts meant I could bring in big stories that the rest of Fleet Street didn't have a sniff of.

One of the best examples happened just before Christmas 1990. Earlier that year Iraq, a relatively poor Arab nation, had unexpectedly invaded the neighbouring state of Kuwait which although territory-wise was much smaller, because of its huge oil reserves, was much richer.

The reaction from the US, the UK, and some other allies was unyielding. Iraq's leader Saddam Hussein was told by Presidents and Prime Ministers to pull his troops out immediately. When he refused, plans were made to liberate Kuwait by force. But this was a huge undertaking. Iraq, in Middle East terms at least, was described as a 'superpower' with a well-equipped army of over a million soldiers, and a powerful air force equipped with a large number of modern and potent combat jets.

For several months before the war, which everyone knew was inevitable, America and Britain carefully put a huge task force of armoured regiments, jet fighter squadrons, and tens of thousands of soldiers into place in Saudi Arabia and Bahrain.

The operation was code named 'Desert Shield' and we soon learned the forthcoming war would be known as 'Desert Storm'.

Like all other Fleet Street papers, Mirror Group Newspapers put a huge team of reporters into the region in several strategic locations. Because I was the only member of *The People* staff with a significant background as a daily paper reporter, my editor Richard

Stott, a first-class journalist who had been a fine *Daily Mirror* reporter in his own right, co-opted me into a joint reporting team with colleagues from the *Daily Mirror*. At virtually zero notice I was dispatched first to Cyprus, where the RAF was positioning fighters and transport planes at Akrotiri, then to Abu Dhabi for a few days, and finally I was told I was being posted to Amman, the capital of Jordan. At that stage no one knew which way Jordan would jump in the forthcoming war. Even though it had a King educated in Britain and a military where most commanding officers had been trained by the British army at Sandhurst or the RAF at Cranwell, about 70 per cent of its population were Palestinian, with a fervent wish for Iraq to kick out the Americans and the British.

My flight there was memorable and a little unnerving. My office booked me, Business Class as was the custom for reporters then, on a Middle East Airways flight for the 90-minute journey. At the boarding gate I thought things looked strangely quiet. The jet was a Boeing with over 200 seats. But I was the only passenger. Well, the only paying passenger that is.

There were actually four other people travelling with me and they were all well-armed security guards. All of them were dressed identically in dark suits and shades and making a show of the fact that under their jackets on the left side, they were packing shoulder holsters with 9mm automatic pistols.

They never spoke or looked directly at me. But, as if to emphasise who they were, when we took our seats, one sat next to me, on the aisle seat, one sat directly behind me, one sat directly in front of me, and the fourth sat on the floor with his back against the cockpit door.

I was literally surrounded. I didn't need any explanation. I was the only passenger on the flight because every sensible person in the Middle East thought Jordan would be dragged into an imminent war, and if they were travelling at all it was AWAY from that country.

The flight was uneventful. but I couldn't say the same about my time in Jordan. After a few days I was joined by several Mirror Group colleagues. We hired taxis with English-speaking drivers on permanent wages. Most days they drove us to the border with Iraq. If we tried to cross we would have been arrested. Coming in the other direction we met many families, some of them Kuwaiti, who were fleeing to Jordan via Iraq, braving hundreds of miles of desert.

Many of them worked for British companies based in Kuwait City. They told harrowing stories of being forced from their homes by Iraqi troops at gunpoint. Others had their cars stolen when they were hijacked by armed Iraqis. One even told me, after stealing his car from his driveway, the uniformed thieves came back 15 minutes later and demanded money from him at gunpoint so they could fill it with petrol.

In Amman there was a tense atmosphere, and you needed to be careful where you went. Together with other British journalists we decided if anyone challenged us about where we were from, we would say we were from Scandinavia.

One afternoon, together with a couple of Fleet Street friends, we ventured into the central Soukh, the biggest street market in the city. All the stallholders were flying Palestinian flags or had large pictures of the Iraqi leader Saddam Hussein on display. Three westerners would have stuck out like a sore thumb at any time, but in this moment of conflict, looking back, we were taking a risk.

In a corner of the market we saw a small crowd gathered round a man sitting on the floor. When we got closer I could see he was peeling vegetables with a large knife, but he also had some sort of hawk or other species of raptor sitting on a perch. Falconry is a popular sport in some parts of the Middle East. As I looked at the bird, the guy peeling vegetables caught my eye and greeted me in English.

I could see in his eyes he was stoned on some sort of narcotic. He asked where I was from. I lied and told him I was from Norway. I asked him what sort of falcon it was. He replied it was a Merlin, which I knew was a very fast flying bird of prey. By now a crowd had gathered and some were showing more interest in us than the hawk seller. By now we were all feeling a little nervous, there were no other Europeans anywhere to be seen in this crowded market, so we decided to move off.

There was a side street that led to a busy main road where some of the big hotels were. So we figured we might be safer heading that way and we left the Soukh picking up the pace a bit, thinking we would seek refuge at the first big hotel we came across. Three or four minutes later, as we walked away from the Soukh, I heard a commotion behind us and saw a man running furiously through the shopping crowds. It was the hawk salesman.

He was running so fast he was barging people who got in his way out of his path. As he got closer I could see the knife he had been paring vegetables with was still in his right hand. I warned my colleagues and we all turned to face him. We had nowhere to run.

As he got within striking distance of us, he suddenly stopped. He was out of breath, panting with exertion. Then he said to me: "Hey mister… are you going to buy my fucking Merlin or not?"

Back at our hotel that evening I found a colleague from *The Sun* at the bar with two young men I didn't recognise. They were both in their early twenties, fit and tanned, dressed in t-shirts and jeans. They clearly were not Fleet Street hacks. We got into conversation. They were British soldiers. I was slightly taken aback. I asked, straight out what they were doing in Jordan and one of them said: "We're on a hiking holiday." Which sounded very unlikely.

We talked a little more and one revealed he was a lieutenant, the other a corporal. A commissioned officer and a man from the ranks, on a hiking holiday together in Jordan? Just as the region was about to descend into a cataclysmic war? Something didn't add up. So semi-jokingly I asked them what it said in their passports under 'occupation' and one promptly volunteered: "It says 'student'," I was getting worried about how quickly they appeared to be giving in to my questioning, so I changed the subject.

They had a few beers, and a steak dinner paid for by us. They later borrowed a double room from one of my colleagues who rented another room for the night, so they could get a good night's rest and the next day, before any of us was about, they'd gone.

It was obvious to me they were British special forces. At a time when the 'Coalition Powers' couldn't be sure which side the Jordanians would pick when the shooting started they had probably been out in the hinterland counting tanks and troop deployments, assessing the strength of a potential enemy.

Why were they in Amman hobnobbing with reporters from the 'red top' press? To me the answer was clear. Working undercover in a potentially hostile country, what better place to lie low for a while than in a big hotel surrounded by Westerners? At that time hotels like the Sheraton, Marriott, Hilton and Hyatt were full to the brim with print reporters, photographers and camera crews from all over the world.

If you didn't want to stand out as a non-Arab, the big hotels were the places to be. For my new special forces friends it was the best definition of the phrase 'hide in plain sight' I've ever come across. A couple of days later I had another strange encounter when a delegation of British women, all wives of high ranking Jordanian military officers, besieged and beseeched me and several other Fleet Street reporters.

Their message: "Tell your Government to send its troops back home. Saddam Hussein is a good man, you should not be going to war against him."

These women, all in Laura Ashley dresses and sling back Jimmy Choo shoes, had been wooed by their husbands while they were undergoing officer training at Sandhurst or Cranwell. They had all been born or brought up in genteel Conservative strongholds like Tunbridge Wells, Weybridge or The Cotswolds, yet here they were, stridently berating us to "Tell Mrs.Thatcher" (PM at the time) to send 'her boys' home before their husbands were forced to get in their tanks and kill them all.

A colleague from the *Daily Mail* described it as "like being on the set of 'Beau Geste' and suddenly being harangued by the Guildford Women's Institute." A few days later I got a personal call from my editor Richard Stott. He asked me: "Is your partner expecting a baby soon?" She was due to give birth to our first daughter a few weeks later. He told me he was bringing me home.

He told me: "Robert Maxwell has directed he wants to bring out anyone who has children or a partner who is expecting." I protested. I didn't want to miss my first proper war, but Stott was adamant. He explained: "Maxwell doesn't like the insurance implications of having family people at the front. Personally, I don't care if you get blown up, but the Chairman says the pay outs would be too expensive."

Three days later, at the beginning of December 1990, I was on my way home. I was glum, but I should not have been, because within days the forthcoming Gulf War was to hand me one of the biggest scoops I ever had.

It was the Saturday after I had got back from the Middle East. I was in the office, about three in the afternoon. I can't remember what I was doing, but as far as I knew, the contents of the next edition of the *Sunday People* had already been decided, even the front page 'splash', so I was just killing time until about 6.30pm when I would head home. It would take something seismic to change the situation. And then something seismic happened.

A simple phone call from a police contact. A car had just been broken into in West London. A laptop computer and some briefcases had been stolen. This was not unusual, and I said so. But my contact had the perfect riposte: "Yes. But THIS laptop belongs to the Royal Air Force. And it contains all the RAF's top secret plans for the forthcoming Gulf War."

It was being looked after by a Wing Commander. The material on the computer was classified 'Top Secret'. It was so sensitive he was ordered to have it in his physical custody at all times. He had been instructed never to let it out of his sight.

The high-ranking RAF man was on his way back from an emergency meeting at the Ministry of Defence. The computer contained every detail about the forthcoming air war you can think of. How many planes Britain was going to send, how many bombs and missiles they were going to need, how much fuel they would need to stockpile for the campaign, where they will all be based.

"If it has fallen into the hands of the Iraqis, it will be absolute gold dust. If they've got it, it means they will know everything and be able to plan accordingly," said my contact. "It literally could cost British lives and it is hugely embarrassing because they are going to have to tell the Americans what's happened and a lot of their plans will be compromised as a result. It's an absolute disaster."

I asked if he knew more about what had happened. It turned out the RAF officer had been into Whitehall that day to present these plans to the Prime Minister, then John Major, and to most of the Cabinet.

On the way home to RAF headquarters at High Wycombe in a shiny RAF Austin Princess staff car, he had asked his driver to pull over to the side of the A40 main road in Acton so he could visit a car showroom to look at a Range Rover he was thinking of buying for his wife.

His driver, an RAF corporal had gone in with him. The pair were only absent for 10 minutes, but when they got back they discovered a thief had broken into the car and the laptop and the briefcases had been stolen. I walked over to my news editor, Phil Hall, who was sitting at his desk. I told him what had happened, and what it might mean.

He sat bolt upright. It was a huge story, and I had brought it in in that most coveted category of 'exclusive'. Five minutes later we were with editor Richard Stott in his office. Stott was a great news man, a former Chief Reporter and Editor of the *Daily Mirror*.

He asked me outright: "Are you sure?"

"100 per cent. I've got lots of detail."

"Where from? " snapped Stott.

"An impeccable source," I replied. "And better than that. No one else knows. It's not going to anyone else. We've got it to ourselves, it's absolutely exclusive."

"Right," said Stott "Start writing. We'll have to change the whole front end of the paper." But that was not the end of the drama. As a protocol I decided to put in a call to the 'Press Bureau' at Scotland Yard. I did this as a 'private inquiry – if asked only basis' which meant they would not put out the information unless another news organisation called and asked about it.

They had no knowledge of the incident. Good. But I knew they would ring the police at Acton, who I knew were investigating, to tie up any loose ends. About 90 minutes later, having filed my story, Stott called me in again. He was beaming: "Well, there's no doubt your story is a belter, Jeff. Because I've just been having a telephone argument with a fucking Admiral at the Ministry of Defence, who wants to slap a 'D' notice on us to stop us publishing it."

I knew that a 'D' notice was a Draconian 'last line of defence' the government could invoke if they thought national security was about to be compromised. "Fuck me, boss," I replied: "So what did you say?"

"I told him they should 'D' notice themselves. It's the RAF who have breached national security by losing the fucking thing, not us for writing about it. He thinks we know more than we actually do. I have told him we will run the fact the computer and briefcases have been stolen, but not the details of what they contain." Then Stott looked at me and said: "Do you actually know any of the details contained inside that laptop?"

"Unfortunately not Richard. Only the sort of subject headings.

How many squadrons? How many bombs? etc," I replied. "You can tell him I only know the hardware has been stolen. But not the detail of what's in the software."

So we splashed the story under my byline, and the whole of the news media raced to follow it up as soon as the first edition of *The People* dropped. The story made world headlines and even reached US military headquarters in The Pentagon in Washington, a great embarrassment to the British Ministry of Defence. The briefcases were actually found by the police, dumped behind some derelict garages, about four hours after they were stolen, but we didn't know that when the paper went to press.

But the laptop was missing for over a fortnight until it was mysteriously posted anonymously to Scotland Yard in January 1991, a few days before the first Gulf War went from steady build-up to furious assault. This included waves of RAF combat planes, when 'Operation Desert Storm' began with a series of huge air attacks on Iraq.

The police view was the theft had not been by an Iraqi spy, but by an opportunist thief, who then got cold feet when he read the headlines his crime had caused. Nevertheless, the following year, the Wing Commander who had been in charge of the material faced a court martial and was convicted of 'Conduct Prejudicial to Good Order'. He escaped jail but was demoted and later left the Air Force.

The police view of the crime at the time was not far from the truth.

Thirty five years later, in a remarkable coincidence, I met two experienced organised crime characters while making a TV documentary about the Brink's-Mat gold robbery. Neither had any idea of my involvement in the story of the RAF computer, but in a coffee break during filming, they were reminiscing and one said: "I was offered this stolen RAF computer once, way back in 1990. It was just prior to the first Gulf War and it contained the full list of everything the Air Force, and the US Air Force would need. Even down to the number of Tomahawk cruise missiles they would need.

"The thief wanted £500 for it, but it was too hot to handle, so he was told to dump it – quick."

I knew this tale must be true, because my contact who had tipped me off had specifically mentioned Tomahawk missiles to me, but part of the negotiation between Richard Stott and the MoD that enabled us to publish, was not to use that detail. Sometimes it is a small world.

GANGSTERS AND GOING UNDERCOVER

CHAPTER TWELVE

Around about the time I became a journalist, the infamous Kray brothers were arrested by Scotland Yard and jailed for life for murder. It was a sensational story and a wake-up call to British society to the fact that organised crime, the sort most people had only previously seen in American gangster movies, was thriving right here in our midst.

There were Maltese gangs who controlled prostitution in the West End, British gangs who controlled the burger and ice cream vans that set up in central London, using extreme violence and intimidation to neutralise rival operators, and Essex gangs which controlled and fought with shotguns over the burgeoning minicab business of the 60s and 70s.

But organised crime was continually shifting its shape with changing social patterns. In my career witnessed how Turkish organised crime seized control of the heroin trade, how West African gangs cornered the market in fraud and how first Chinese 'Triad' groups and 'Snakeheads' took over people smuggling only to be pushed aside by groups from Albania and Romania.

I learned the world of organised crime was highly adaptable and able to exploit every opportunity.

The jailing of the Krays at the end of the 1960s left a vacuum in the London underworld, and as my career progressed the wars between the rival groups intent on filling that void provided me with big stories, many featuring murders and violent retribution.

The fact was, working and living on the borders of East London and Essex, you were never far from a person, pub or street with a solid connection to Britain's gangland. Which is exactly how I stumbled across one of my first big 'organised crime' stories, when I was just a teenage apprentice.

A few months before I got my first job as a junior reporter on the Leytonstone *Express and Independent* there was a spectacular robbery in East London. Over a bank holiday weekend in 1967 a group of men broke into the security vaults of the Co-Operative Society in Stratford.

The robbery made national headlines because the gang used a thermic lance to cut their way through the massive steel doors which protected the strong room. It was also the first time criminals had broken into such a strongly defended vaults company.

A thermic lance was a rare and exotic piece of high tech equipment. It was a cutting device which generated a super hot flame using pressurised oxygen. In the 1960s it was considered a highly specialised tool used only in industries like ship dismantling and for cutting up old railway steam engines for scrap. Whoever masterminded the Co-op vaults robbery must have known a lot about the technology because as the police were to discover, the gang who attacked the vaults had cleverly constructed their own equipment using copper tubes and a supply of pressurised oxygen.

When the gas was concentrated over the end of the copper tubes and ignited it developed an astonishing white hot temperature of 2,500C. Even so, engineering experts called to the scene later by Scotland Yard estimated it had taken the gang about eight hours to burn through the vault doors, which were made of slabs of steel two feet thick. It was the first time such a piece of kit had been used in a crime anywhere in the world.

Inside the vault there were 600 locked security boxes. Once inside, the gang used crowbars, cold chisels and sledgehammers to break open 120 of the security boxes containing cash, diamonds, gold coins and ingots, valuable jewellery, and expensive works of art. Why didn't the gang break open all the boxes? It was impossible to say. Perhaps it had taken longer to break open the main doors than they had anticipated. Perhaps the gang hadn't brought enough bags to carry away all their loot. But I was soon to hear an interesting alternative explanation.

No one knew exactly what had been stolen, because the owners of the boxes were never asked to declare what they were keeping in them. There was speculation the gang had got away with money and goods worth over £1M and around the pubs of East London, which I frequented, the word was, many of the boxes were rented by some of London's most feared and revered criminal faces. The names being mentioned included the Kray twins, who in 1967 were still at liberty and the dominating force in protection rackets and other criminality across East London.

The name of one man was mentioned for several reasons. It's hard to believe, but absolutely true, that a man with the name of Tony Maffia, really was a big time underworld figure. He was widely known throughout the London underworld as a fence

– a man who dealt in stolen goods, particularly jewellery and antiques.

In the previous few months I had become friendly with a second-hand car dealer called Terry. We had been introduced because I had been at school with his brother. Terry was a mine of information. He knew every dodgy trick in the book in the used car business, and he seemed to know a lot of people who were full-time criminals, including Tony Maffia. A few days after the Co-op vaults job happened, I was in the pub when Terry sidled up to me and quietly said: "What do you hear about the Stratford Vaults job?"

I told him, truthfully, that all I knew was what had been in the Fleet Street papers. He took a sip of his pint of lager and lime. Every man who regarded himself as cool in the 1960s drank lager and lime. Terry looked furtively up and down the bar to make sure he wasn't being overheard, took a drag on his Benson and Hedges cigarette and said to me: "Tony Maffia set it up."

Terry had told me a bit about Maffia before, even offered to introduce me and had warned me Maffia was a big time criminal. He said he fenced stolen goods for criminal firms but also set up burglaries on the homes of the wealthy – bookmakers were one of his favourite targets – then sold on the stolen property to contacts in Hatton Garden, the epicentre of Britain's jewellery and antique trade, both of which were then riddled with crooked characters. He had said to me: "I'll introduce him to you sometime if you want. He's a nice geezer. But don't ask him questions about what he does for a living. He wouldn't like that."

Now Terry was telling me Maffia had set up the most notorious crime since the Great Train Robbery. "Tony has five or six boxes in there himself, where he keeps loads of money, and all the stuff he receives from various jobs until he can place it," he said. "It's ideal see, 'cos not many people know he has them. Especially Old Bill and the tax man, if you follow me?

"And here's a funny thing, OK? Whoever done the job didn't touch any of Tony's boxes. Strange that, innit?"

I was 18, young and naïve, but not so young and naïve as to think I could nip round to Tony Maffia's house the next day and ask him if he was behind the Stratford Vaults job.

A few weeks later I walked into The Royal Standard, and saw Terry standing at the bar. He was with a man in his 30s. The stranger was dressed in a Saville Row tailor-made Mohair suit, and expensive handmade shoes. He had neatly trimmed brown hair fixed in position with pomade. He looked like a real smoothie.

Terry waved me over: "Hello, Jeff. Meet Tony." The stranger and I shook hands and he asked me what I wanted to drink. He was an affable man, with a sharp sense of humour. Fairly quickly it became apparent to me this man was in the car trade, the same as Terry.

Soon the penny dropped. This easy going character I was drinking with was the underworld villain Tony Maffia. A few minutes later Tony finished his lager and lime, and said he was off home. He shook my hand and said: "Don't forget, Jeff, if you are ever looking for a good motor, come to me first. Don't waste your time with this bloke here," pointing at Terry. "He's a right dodgy fucker." We all laughed.

I never met Tony Maffia again. Because a few months later he was murdered, shot dead by a gangland hitman. The news broke on Sunday June 2, 1968 when it emerged the body of a man had been found dead in the rear footwell of his own Jaguar at a restaurant car park on the A127 Southend road at a place called East Horndon in Essex. A couple of days later the man was named as Tony Maffia from Buckhurst Hill.

I was stunned. I rang Terry. When I mentioned the conversation we had had about Maffia being the architect of the Stratford Vaults job, Terry said: "Don't ever fucking tell anyone I told you that, OK? I never told that to you, right?"

I muttered: "OK."

Then I said: "So, who do you reckon has topped him then? What's it all about?" Terry was clearly not comfortable being asked that kind of question. "How the fuck would I know, Jeff? I hardly knew the guy. I don't have a clue who done him or what the fuck it's all about. OK?" I took the hint and backed off.

A few days later I met Terry's younger brother, my schoolmate, and we fell to talking about the Maffia murder when he said: "My brother Terry knew Tony Maffia had been murdered three or four days before his body was even found. He told me so himself."

I was torn about what to do. The next day I saw Terry again and while I didn't want to drop anyone in it, the budding news reporter within me compelled me to ask. "Word is Tel, you knew Tony Maffia had been topped several days before they found him?"

I wasn't prepared for what happened next. He looked at me and his eyes were like lasers. He moved in close to me, until his face was about an inch from mine and whispered: "If you tell anyone that, I will fucking have you killed. I mean it. Understand? Got it? You tell fucking no one."

I nodded my understanding. I was shaken and a bit frightened. In that instant our relationship changed forever. We never spoke again. I didn't tell anyone else, at least not for many years. In 1968

I didn't know any police officers well and, looking back, even if I had done, I don't think I would have told them. I don't know what Terry knew, but something told me he knew a lot, and maybe he knew stuff he wished he didn't.

Over the next few days startling details of how Tony Maffia met his end started to emerge. He had been found in the footwell of his own Mark 10 Jaguar. He had been shot in the head twice with a calibre .22 pistol.

The gun was small, but the killer had drilled out the head of each of the bullets, effectively creating a 'dum dum' round which would explode into fragments as it entered a victim's body. The entry wounds were tiny, the diameter only of a pencil, but the bullets had exploded inside their victim's skull, causing massive damage.

Maffia had been missing for five days when his body was found. According to his wife, he had gone out to meet with a man who was interested in purchasing his luxury motor yacht, which was moored at a marina near Burnham-on-Crouch, in Essex. When he failed to come home she had phoned around a number of his criminal friends. One of them, the famous jail escaper Alfie Hinds, even drove out to Burnham to check to see if he was on the boat, but it was locked and empty. A witness came forward to say he had seen a man wiping down the outside of a parked bottle green Jaguar in a lane in Essex as if trying to eradicate any fingerprints.

He took police to the spot and they found an expensive dark blue Crombie overcoat in a hedge. In one of the pockets was a .22 bullet with its nose drilled out. While all this was going on, a man contacted a detective in Manchester and told him he wanted to talk about a murder in Essex. Stephen Jewell, a professional criminal from Lancashire, told the detective he had met Maffia in prison, and after their release they had stayed in touch.

This was the man who had gone to meet Maffia shortly before he was killed, but he insisted he wasn't the killer. By now the case was in the hands of Scotland Yard. Ken Drury, a Detective Chief Superintendent, went to Manchester, arrested Jewell on suspicion of murder, and brought him to London for further inquiries. Drury was already working on the theory that Maffia's murder was connected to the Stratford Vaults job the previous year.

When he asked Jewell why he had contacted Maffia and come to Essex to see him, the Mancunian said he was in possession of over £30,000 in forged banknotes and knew Maffia was a man with the right contacts to sell them on at a profit. While they were there Maffia had asked him if he was interested in buying his boat, and they had driven out to the coast to have a look at it.

Jewell let drop that while they were at the marina, Maffia had said he had £200,000 of stolen gold bullion to sell and was planning to sail it over to Holland where he would sell it to a contact in Amsterdam. Drury thought this was closer to the truth than anything else. He thought Maffia had set up the Stratford Vaults job and the gold bullion had been stolen from one of the burgled boxes. He thought the gold belonged to another organised crime figure who wanted revenge on Maffia and had paid Stephen Jewell to shoot him. Jewell gave a different version, telling Drury that on the drive back from the coast they had been forced to stop by four men in another Jaguar who had kidnapped Maffia and driven off, taking his car as well.

Drury didn't believe him. The Crombie coat with the bullet in the pocket could be forensically linked to him. Jewell was charged with murder. He went on trial in November 1968 at the Old Bailey. He stuck to his story, that Maffia had been murdered because he had double crossed London villains who had put a contract out on him. Jewell insisted he was not the killer, he was just unfortunate enough to be in the wrong place at the wrong time when Maffia was abducted and murdered.

The jury didn't believe him and he was convicted and jailed for life. He served 11 years. In 1981, when I was on the staff of the *News of the World*, in connection with another matter, I was introduced to Jewell who had been released from jail. He was happy to talk about Tony Maffia, but he still insisted he wasn't his assassin.

Jewell told me Maffia was killed over £500,000 in gold bullion which was stolen from a Royal Mint van which was hijacked by an armed gang in Clerkenwell, London, in May 1967. One of the robbers had a security box in the Co-op vaults in Stratford, and the bullion was hidden there two days after the raid. Maffia was then asked to fence the gold bars. Instead, knowing the number of the box containing the gold, and also knowing there was likely to be at least £1M of other valuables stashed there, he organised the thermic lance job. It cost him his life.

When detectives eventually got authority to open Maffia's own boxes in the vault they found a mountain of valuables.

There were 3,000 gold sovereigns, and another 3,000 Anglo Saxon gold coins, stolen from a burglary in Maidenhead. There were three briefcases containing 27 17th century miniature paintings, plus hundreds of diamond rings and necklaces. One box was filled with rare Dresden porcelain figures, jewellery, cash, gold coins, counterfeit currency and antiques, with an estimated value of £175,000. There was around £100,000 in mixed currencies including Swiss Francs, Sterling, US Dollars and Dutch Gilders.

Perhaps the most interesting find of all, they discovered a gold ingot worth £20,000 which could be traced to the previous year's Clerkenwell job. Maffia had delicately sawn it into eight equal pieces to try to disguise its origins.

Stephen Jewell died of cancer, aged 68, in 1991. still insisting he didn't kill Tony Maffia.

CHAPTER THIRTEEN

Initially, after the Kray brothers got their just desserts, I really had no idea about how bad the problem of gangs and violence really was in London. In short, hard men, gangsters and assorted underworld figures were locked in a bloody struggle to control East London.

There were three groups, known as the Jacobs, the Nichols and the Tibbs. These 'firms' were, in the most part, based around family groups, but they also included several dozen affiliates and hangers-on, all of whom revelled in violence. There had been a whole sequence of attacks in which various characters had been shot, stabbed, slashed, bludgeoned, run down with cars, and generally beaten up.

Many of these incidents had been reported to the police, many more, at least officially, had not. A supposedly secret detective squad, under the leadership of Detective Chief Superintendent Bert Wickstead, was set up by Scotland Yard to tackle the problem.

But Wickstead's squad believed, with some justification, that these various criminal groups had corrupted a number of local officers.

It was with this background that I arrived at work one morning at the *Newham Recorder* in the autumn of 1970 to learn there had just been a violent explosion outside the home of Jimmy Tibbs, a successful professional boxer, whose family were well known in the following spheres of great local interest; fighting, scrap metal, and protection rackets.

The explosion had happened at about 8am, in a residential street of Victorian era terraced houses not far from our office. I hurried round there and the sight that greeted me was truly extraordinary. In the middle of the road, parked at an angle to the kerb was a little Ford Anglia van. The back half was pristine and intact. The front half, forward of the passenger compartment, was completely missing. The two front wings were splayed outwards. The bonnet was about 20 yards further down the road in someone's front garden. Where the engine compartment was supposed to be was just a smoke-blackened hole.

There was a small crowd milling about, mostly middle aged women still with their obligatory curlers in, gawping and gossiping. Several houses had their front windows blown in by the blast. I moved closer to the van for a better look. Thin wisps of black and grey smoke were still drifting up from the empty engine compartment.

There were a couple of uniformed constables standing around. I knew one of them and sidled up to him. "Where's the engine"? I asked out of the corner of my mouth, trying to be discreet. The PC looked at me and chuckled: "It's in the fucking back garden of that house."

I was uncomprehending. How did a Ford 997cc engine, weighing about 250lbs, get to be in the back garden of a terraced house? The PC laughed again: "Put it this way, son, it was a fucking big bang. Lifted the engine clean over the house! It's half buried in the back lawn."

It was an early lesson for me in the power and unpredictable nature of home improvised explosives.

I wondered whether it was worth me approaching Jimmy Tibbs, who, unsurprisingly, was not at home.

Not only was he the son of a legendary East End underworld figure, but he was also the nephew of another feared London gangster, who had been a mate of the Kray twins.

He had become embroiled in his family's dispute with minicab operator, Albert Nichols and his assorted gangster clan. One low point of this ongoing feud took place in December 1968, when Albert received a visit at his office from some men, one of whom was armed with a sawn-off shotgun. In the ensuing fracas, which involved other members of the Tibbs firm, there was an attempt to blow off Nichols' testicles with the shotgun.

His testicles survived the attack, thanks to a roll of fat around his lower stomach getting in the way of the downward blast of the first barrel, and the shot from the second barrel passing to one side of his scrotum but blowing away a large portion of his right leg. For good measure, one of the attacking group hit Nichols over the head with the edge of a spade, splitting his scalp and fracturing his skull.

When one of the main protagonists was arrested later, his defence was he had not known the gun was loaded and was only attempting to hit Nichols with the butt end of it, when it accidentally went off severely wounding him – twice.

Three men were charged with attempted murder and attempted wounding. At the Old Bailey a few months later Jimmy, John and George Tibbs all pleaded not guilty. But after hearing the prosecution lay out their damning case to the jury, all three changed their pleas.

It was an unexpectedly good decision, because after hearing their change of heart the judge sentenced all of them to two years in jail (suspended for three years) for the attempted murder of the severely wounded Albert Nichols and fined them each £100 for possessing an illegal shotgun in a public place.

The worst part for Jimmy Tibbs was, as a criminal convicted for violence, the Boxing Board of Control took away his professional license.

Of course, it was not the end of the war between the Tibbs' and their rivals. Which was why I was now standing next to the smouldering wreck of a Ford van. The full facts emerged later. Jimmy Tibbs had come out that morning to take his four-year-old son, also called Jimmy, to school. They got in the van and when the former boxer turned the ignition there was an almighty explosion.

'Miracle escape' was one of those expressions much overused by young reporters like me. But in this case, I would argue, the phrase was fully justified. A bomb featuring the powerful explosive nitroglycerine, had been expertly wired into the van's ignition system during the dead of night. But when it detonated, the blast was diverted forwards and up by a stout steel bulkhead that separated the engine and passenger compartments.

As a result, the bonnet had been blown down the street like a crisp packet, and the chunky engine block, with its weighty cylinder head, carburettor, and exhaust manifold still attached, hurled 30ft in the air, clearing the intended victim's house and landing in his own back garden.

By sheer luck the intended murder target and his son escaped with barely a scratch on them. It was a big story. That evening I went into a pub frequented by detectives from the CID office at East Ham police station.

I spied three or four of them at the bar. One was a jovial Devon-born sergeant, Dave Brinham. He was a larger than life character with a shaggy permed hairdo which was sometimes dyed jet black, and a gunfighter moustache.

I asked if he'd been involved but Brinham recoiled in mock horror: "Not us, mate. No, no, no. Far too heavy duty for us. We aren't trusted with jobs like that."

Then he leant in conspiratorially and said: "There's a special team from the Yard working on it. It's all top secret, very hush, hush. Why don't you ask them what it's all about. I bet, if you do, they will deny anything happened at all. It's all smoke and mirrors, my friend. Nothing is ever what it seems at first. Remember that."

And that's pretty much what did happen. Because when I found out who was investigating the incident I was given very short shrift. In effect, Superintendent Wickstead sent the message that I shouldn't ask too many questions about things I did not understand.

In that era, cops like Wickstead had God-like status and power. The police could hold a person they had arrested for as long as they liked. There was no time limit. Solicitors who represented serious criminals often found their clients had been mysteriously moved from one London police station to another, and then yet another, making it almost impossible for them to actually find them, let alone represent them. And another CID friend told me Wickstead's favourite expression then was "Let's nick them first and get some evidence later".

Although we didn't know it at the time, a few days before the attempt to kill Jimmy Tibbs, there had been an explosion at a scrapyard in Canning Town. It had been written off as 'no crime' by the police after the fire brigade conveniently concluded the blast, which broke windows in houses all around, had been caused by an exploding gas cylinder.

But when, the following week, another blast demolished a café owned by the Tibbs family, the police were unable to write it off as yet another gas explosion. Knowing I would get nothing from Wickstead on these matters, I decided to be brave, visit the scrapyard, which was now back in business, and see if I could find someone who might talk to me. Before I went out I told my boss Tom Duncan where I was going and why, he rocked back in his chair and laughed: "They will probably stick you through the car crusher. Good luck."

I hoped they wouldn't.

The yard was smaller than I expected. At the back I spied a very large man, stripped to the waist, swinging a 14 pound hammer as if it was a fly swatter. I realised I was in the company of George of 'Bogey' Tibbs, one of the godfathers of East End crime. He was busy breaking lorry batteries to extract the lead plates from within. It needed a strong man to break batteries, and I could see from the sweating frame 'Bogey' Tibbs was a very strong man.

Bogey didn't look up as I approached, he just kept swinging that mighty hammer. He was wearing hob-nailed boots, probably size 12 at least, with soles an inch thick, which was just as well as he was standing in a large pool of battery acid.

As I got a few feet from him he turned and looked at me. "What do you fucking want?"

"Hello," I said, trying to sound confident. I introduced myself.

He eyed me up and down: "I said, what do you fucking want, son?" So I asked him if he knew who had bombed the Tibbs family's yard and café and who had tried to blow up his nephew Jimmy.

And to my surprise he looked thoughtful for a moment. Then

he hoisted the big dirty hammer in his meaty right fist, stepped forward, and placed it under my chin, with just enough restraint not to knock me spark out. He spoke quietly but he was to the point: "I don't have a fucking clue what you're on about, son."

He towered over me, by at least eight inches and exuded menace.

Then he added: "So, why don't you fuck off before I mistake your head for one them fucking batteries I'm busy breaking."

"Sorry to trouble you, Mr.Tibbs," I said bravely and scurried away.

Back at the office Tom looked up from his typewriter and said: "They didn't kill you, then?"

I explained how I had just had a memorable meeting with 'Bogey' Tibbs.

"What did he have to say?" asked Tom. "He threatened to do me with a sledgehammer, then told me to fuck off." My boss roared with laughter. "Well done, sounds to me like you got what we call a full and frank interview."

Working in East London, I got to experience a few of those. But I also realised the importance of weighing up a situation before making an approach to dangerous people. There was no story worth dying for – or losing your teeth over.

We didn't run a story about my meeting with 'Bogey'. To be fair, he hadn't told me anything useful. I pondered the situation. There was a violent gang war going on right in the middle of our patch, and neither the police dealing with it, nor the hard men involved, would give us the time of day. I was learning fast that sometimes there were situations you just couldn't do anything about.

Five or six weeks later there was another incident which demonstrated how violent the post-Kray scene was in East London and how much of a 'hall of mirrors' the way the police were handling it had become. I arrived at work on a Monday morning and phoned round some police contacts to check if anything interesting had happened at the weekend.

One detective told me: "We've had a really bad knife attack overnight. The victim got chopped across the back of his neck with a machete, he was lucky not to be killed."

Then he mentioned the name of the victim. Billy Williams was a well known professional boxer and hard man, closely associated with the Tibbs family. This was a big story for us. "Give me a ring later. I'll have a look in the Major Crimes log. There will be more detail there." Then he hung up.

The attack happened at a small hotel in Manor Park where there was an over-21s nightclub on a Sunday night. I drove directly to the hotel to see what I could find out.

The 'Courtney Hotel' was closed – locked up completely. No one at home. It had three wide, light coloured, concrete steps leading up to the front door. And on those steps was the biggest quantity of still tacky, slowly congealing blood I had ever seen. It was everywhere, the aftermath of a savage incident.

Because the place was closed, there was no one to try and get information from. I went back to my office and rang my detective contact. I told him what I had seen at the hotel.

"Got some bad news for you," he said. "I know the night duty CID put a report about the attack in the Major Crimes log before they booked off early this morning. But when I looked just now, there was nothing there. I spoke to one of my colleagues, he told me Superintendent Wickstead dropped in early this morning. He tore out the page with the entry about the attack written up on it, put it in his pocket, and walked out. I am sorry mate, but officially now, that incident at the hotel, it never actually took place."

I was staggered: "But I've just been up there. There's about four pints of blood congealing on the front step."

My contact laughed: "Well mate, officially at least, it must have been down to someone having a nose bleed." And as far as any story went, well, that was that.

Williams was in a local hospital recovering from the attempt to decapitate him. I thought about dropping in there to see if I could get a word. But my boss Tom Duncan thought it wasn't a good idea. He said: "Do that and you will probably end up as a patient on the same ward. Let's leave this one alone for now." Sometimes discretion is definitely better than valour, as the saying goes.

A few weeks later I heard Williams had recovered and, after advice about his future safety, had gone to continue his career in America and was in Florida training at the world famous boxing gym owned by Angelo Dundee who was Muhammed Ali's manager at the time.

Apparently it was thought he would be safer in Florida than in East London, and I later learned Superintendent Wickstead also wanted him out of harm's way, for his own reasons.

As it turned out, he put himself in an even more dangerous situation. I later heard he had taken up with a young American woman and had got her pregnant. Apparently her father was very well-connected to one of the big New York mafia families, and he thought the boxer should do the right thing and make an honest woman of his daughter by marrying her. The fighter said he didn't want to be tied down by family commitments but was then sent a message from New York that it would be better to be tied down by a new wife and child than tied up and dumped in an Everglades swamp wearing concrete boots.

He was spirited away back to Britain where he went into hiding, emerging only after the heat had died down both over the Scotland Yard gang investigation and the mafia man's daughter terminated her pregnancy.

Several members of the Tibbs family were later jailed for long stretches for various serious crimes. Williams, the man attacked at the Courtney Hotel wasn't among them, but about three years later, after he had quit the ring, he was jailed for 11 years for attempted murder in an unrelated matter. This involved two men holding down the victim while the ex-fighter reversed a Ford Cortina estate car over him. Not once, but three times. The estate version of the popular family car was notoriously light at the back, making it prone to skid in wet conditions, which explains why the man who was supposed to die escaped relatively unscathed with merely a few broken ribs and three parallel sets of tyre marks across his chest.

The legacy of the Kray brothers, even though they were serving huge prison sentences, continued to reverberate across East London. Shortly after the boxer was attacked outside the hotel disco, there was another incident on our patch that linked back to the Kray family. George Ince was another notorious East London criminal character. A well-known armed robber, he was also the secret lover of Dolly, the wife of the eldest of the Kray brothers, Charlie. After the Krays were jailed Ince and Dolly were able to be open about their relationship. Clearly this was humiliating for Charlie.

One evening in 1971 Ince, then aged 30, opened the door of his flat and a man forced his way inside and produced a sawn-off shotgun. There was a violent struggle as the gunman tried to shove the weapon down the front of Ince's trousers. The gunman's intentions were clear.

In the struggle the gun did go off, but although Ince's scrotum was singed by the blast, the shot missed its intended target and instead tore away a chunk of his left calf muscle. The gunman, believing his work to be successful, fled the scene, leaving Ince bleeding on the floor. Neighbours who heard the commotion called the police. Ince was taken to hospital and placed under guard where he told officers he had no idea of the identity of the man who had attacked him.

But one seasoned CID officer told me they believed Charlie Kray had ordered the shooting as revenge on Ince for daring to have an affair with his wife. He was banged up in jail and now his wife's affair with Ince was out in the open.

It must have been humiliating for him and he probably felt he had lost face and needed to do something to restore his reputation. As the detective told me: "The gunman nearly succeeded in his mission. He was obviously trying to shoot Ince's bollocks off and the blast actually singed his scrotum without doing real damage in that area."

After Ince left hospital I visited him at his home. He was on crutches when he opened the door. I told him who I was and he replied cheerily: "Thank fuck. I thought you might be someone else come to shoot me." He was more friendly and cheerful than I had expected him to be, so I asked him outright if he knew why he'd been shot and who had done it. He looked thoughtful for a moment and said: "No, mate. No idea. I think it was probably just a case of mistaken identity." Then he thanked me for my interest and closed the door. Needless to say the police never found the gunman. They probably knew it would be a pointless task and concentrated instead on crimes they could solve.

The damage to his leg didn't slow Ince down. The next year he was arrested both for his part in a huge silver bullion robbery at Mountnessing in Essex, and for the murder of a woman called Muriel Patience in the infamous 'Barn' murder case a few miles away at Braintree. Ince was jailed for 15 years for the robbery, but acquitted of the murder.

Two other men were later convicted of shooting Muriel Patience and for shooting and wounding her husband Bob and their daughter Beverley. Many detectives of my acquaintance, both in London and Essex, were to tell me over the years of their suspicions around the Barn shootings, which happened during an attempted robbery where they took about £900 from a safe they forced Bob Patience to open. The main rumour was the incident had been triggered by the belief that Patience had organised the disposal of the stolen silver for the Mountnessing robbers and they thought his safe would therefore be stuffed with cash.

Several years later I interviewed Bob Patience. He steadfastly denied any involvement in the Mountnessing robbery, a position he held until the day he died.

CHAPTER FOURTEEN

Jimmy Rodriguez was a mainly small-time criminal in his late 40s, though he did have a couple of convictions for being a getaway driver on payroll robberies when he was a teenager in the 1950s. His career stealing and driving cars had come to an end when, pursued by the police after one of the cash grabs, he had crashed a stolen Jaguar into a bus, somewhere in West London. The fire brigade had to cut him from the wreckage and a broken pelvis and a smashed leg incurred in the crash had left him with a permanent limp.

Jimmy had been born and raised in Gibraltar and his heavily-accented English meant he was known to everyone around Soho, where he worked casually as a doorman at various strip joints, as 'Spanish Jimmy'.

He became one of my boss George's best informants and someone he passed onto me. It was soon clear to me Jimmy knew a lot of cops around the West End and at Scotland Yard's vice squad. It didn't take much to figure out that Jimmy was also a police informant, a 'snout' in the cop speak of the time, but he was sharp enough to make a little money as a strip club doorman, a little money from the cops for information, a little money from people like George and me for information, and a little money from working as a 'minder' to a couple of Maltese Soho brothel keepers.

Jimmy was certainly well plugged into the Soho vice scene, and he knew most of London's top gangsters, so if Jimmy dropped by to see me, I knew he was always worth listening to. One of Jimmy's friends was a former Scotland Yard Flying Squad man who had retired and was, in the 1970s, head of security for the freight handling part of British Airways at Heathrow Airport. The air freight business was beginning to boom at the time and BA had moved into the international cargo handling business in a big way. But they, and all the major airlines using Britain's busiest airport, were being plagued continually by theft of cargo at the airport itself. The phrase 'Thief Row' soon came into regular use for Heathrow, and it was reckoned that airlines using the famous hub were losing about two per cent of all the cargo they were handling to theft. It was out and out organised crime.

The airport freight handlers at that time were highly unionised. Early attempts by the airlines to crack down on the theft problem, which included the arrest of some freight handlers, led immediately to costly industrial action. The airlines were losing a fortune to the thieves, but trying to stop them by prosecuting those responsible, was proving even more expensive, because the airlines lost more revenue to strikes than they did to theft. Any attempt to infiltrate the freight handlers, using undercover police officers, were doomed to fail. The freight handling business at Heathrow was effectively a closed shop, much like the London docks had been in earlier times.

People could only get a job there if they knew someone, and were personally recommended by someone already working there. But somehow, Jimmy Rodriguez, put forward by his former Scotland Yard pal, managed to get taken on with a team working, not for British Airways, but for the German national airline Lufthansa, and the Italian Alitalia national carrier, both of whom had freight handling businesses at Heathrow. Perhaps, with his gammy leg and 'Spanglish' accent, his new co-workers figured he couldn't be a secret police agent.

Jimmy ingratiated himself to his new workmates by stealing everything he could get his hands on. What he couldn't sell immediately to his contacts he would bring to the *Evening News* editorial office to give to me and my friends, whether we wanted it or not.

One day he turned up with several micro cameras, rare items in that era. Another day it was bottles of expensive French perfume. Then it was fine German porcelain. This was embarrassing because I did not want to be involved in handling stolen goods, even if, bizarrely, its theft had actually been sanctioned. One day he turned up with a sheaf of what appeared to be Russian bond certificates. They were banknote quality, obviously the product of a highly secure printing process.

He told me he had grabbed a handful of them when a packet, produced under contract by the Bank of England's own printing works, 'accidentally' burst open while being loaded into the hold of a Lufthansa jet bound for Moscow. I told him to take them away although they were rather beautiful objects.

But I kept Jimmy sweet. Because I knew, once he had compiled enough evidence the airlines would call in the police, there would be a huge swoop on dozens of Heathrow staff early in the morning, Jimmy would tip me off and I would have a front page exclusive story. Week after week he told me to be ready, the raid was imminent. But the raid never happened. Because when Lufthansa and Alitalia saw Jimmy's list of thieves they were allegedly employing, they ran a mile. There were so many names, so many addresses for the police to hit, the airlines knew their lucrative business would immediately be crippled by a lack of staff. And that was before the unions got involved and brought everyone else out on strike.

They scotched the whole operation. Jimmy stopped working at Heathrow, the thieves carried on thieving unmolested and I was able to tell my contact to stop bombarding me with stolen goods. And in the middle of all this, Jimmy gave me a story about one of the cleverest and most audacious criminals I encountered in my whole career.

Stephen Raymond was in a league of his own as a criminal. He reputedly had an IQ of close to 140, which put him well over the threshold to become a member of MENSA. People I knew who had dealings with him all said the same thing. Raymond was originally just an ordinary back street boy from Highbury, North London. He was considered so bright by his school teachers and others who knew him, he could have risen to the top in any profession, if he'd chosen to.

But instead he chose a life of crime. By the end of the 1960s he had convictions and jail sentences for robbery, burglary, theft and fraud. By the early 1970s he was out and looking for new criminal opportunities.

In the mid-1970s a number of airlines using Heathrow Airport suffered a sudden rash of unexplained high-value thefts. According to my informant Jimmy, these totalled well over £3M, a huge sum of money at the time.

The missing items included bags of uncut diamonds and other gemstones, on their way to European jewellers in the UK, Belgium and Switzerland, large quantities of American Express traveller's cheques, and even pouches of cash in diplomatic bags. The cash in US dollars was in transit from Washington DC to London to pay staff at the US Embassy, and for forward shipment to other US embassies across Europe.

American Express were one of the best known suppliers of traveller cheques, issued in denominations ranging from $10 to $100. Loved by criminals, and known in their lingo merely as 'TCs', blank traveller cheques were a favourite target for theft, because they were almost as good as cash. They could be converted into money at virtually any bank in the world and the only security requirement was the production of a passport or other form of ID. With identification documents easy to forge, it was a fraudster's dream.

These airport crimes were causing consternation among airline security staff, the banks, and even in diplomatic circles, because no one could figure out how they were being committed. The consignments were being 'signed on' to transatlantic flights in New York and were supposedly being placed in a special 'high value' security safe on the aircraft. But when the planes arrived in London and the safes were opened – many of the most valuable packages were missing. The investigation process was chaotic and arguably non-existent. Airport authorities in New York were adamant the goods had gone on board. They claimed the valuables must be being stolen after the plane touched down in London.

Their counterparts in the UK denied responsibility, saying the goods must have been stolen in New York, and documents showing they had gone on the flight were fraudulent. Jimmy had heard about these crimes from his handlers who were employing him to work undercover in the freight handling crews.

He passed this information onto me and I made inquiries with the police at Heathrow, at Scotland Yard, and in New York. On the record, no one knew anything. But off the record a friend in the CID at Heathrow told me it was true. Neither the Metropolitan Police in London, or the NYPD, wanted the hassle of taking responsibility for investigating. It best suited everyone to put the blame, and the problem, on others 3,000 miles away. So the thefts continued.

Then Jimmy, who was well-connected in criminal circles, told me what was really happening. When Boeing launched the Boeing 747 Jumbo Jet at the beginning of the 1970s there was a huge fanfare. It was the biggest and most glamorous airliner that had ever flown at the time, more than twice as large as its predecessor the Boeing 707. It was the veritable Queen of the Skies.

When he heard about the launch of the new giant passenger plane, Stephen Raymond was intrigued. Could this new sky giant offer criminal possibilities? Raymond already knew that dozens of consignments of valuable items, particularly jewellery and large sums of cash, were being transported on commercial aircraft everyday. Pretending to be a model aeroplane enthusiast he contacted Boeing and obtained a set of design plans for a 747. He quickly discovered the high value security cabinet abutted the First Class lavatories. A panel held in place by just 16 small rivets was all that separated them.

Raymond devised a clever plan. He flew to New York then booked himself, first class, on a return flight to Europe with Pan American, which was one of the first to use the new 747. For his plan to work the flight needed only two requirements. It had to be overnight, and it had to make a stop, as many long haul flights did, at Shannon Airport in the Republic of Ireland.

When Raymond boarded he took with him only one piece of

hand luggage, a brown briefcase. In the briefcase he placed a small battery powered electric drill, with special drill bits for penetrating metal, and a small bag of rivets identical to the ones used by Boeing on cabinet fittings. He knew he would not arouse suspicion. In the 1970s, there were far fewer security checks on airline passengers than there are today, especially on First Class travellers.

Once on board, Raymond waited for the other passengers in First Class to settle down to sleep, then he went to the lavatory. Locking himself in, he swiftly drilled out the rivets in the panel separating the cubicle from the locked cabinet. He then took out any packages which looked like they might contain valuables or money. He put the items in his pocket or under his clothing, replaced the panel using the spare rivet kit he had brought onboard, then returned to his seat.

At Shannon, where he knew there was little chance of a customs search, he got off, returning later by ferry to Britain. Meanwhile the plane took off again for London, Paris, Amsterdam or Geneva. Raymond correctly calculated that it would be at least another two hours before the missing packages were noticed. It would then be many more hours of international phone calls to establish whether the stolen items had actually been loaded on the flight in the first place. By then, even on the off chance he was suspected, he would be untraceable.

Raymond, who was also a master forger, used many aliases and many different passports or false IDs and is thought to have got away with this trick at least a dozen times. There were estimates his 'take' from these crimes exceeded $15M and it's likely he would have committed more had he not come up with an even more audacious criminal plan at Heathrow.

Raymond got himself a back office job with the Heathrow-based security firm Purolator Services. How did a man with a long criminal record manage to land a job with a company whose core business was to safely transport large quantities of cash between the offices of various airlines at Heathrow? Simple. He forged references on letter headed note paper from another well-known security firm saying he had been a trusted and reliable employee. Purolator managers accepted the references at face value.

Once at Purolator, Raymond went to work studying their procedures and secretly copying dozens of important documents to enable him to make forgeries. One detective later told me: "Raymond being given a job at Purolator was like giving Dracula a job at the blood bank." The American owned company had a number of contracts for the safe transport of large quantities of cash which were moving everyday between different airlines using terminals One, Two and Three. In the 1970s Heathrow was smaller than today and terminals Four and Five were yet to be built.

In June 1976, two men, one smartly dressed in a business suit, the other wearing a Purolator Services uniform, turned up at the offices of the Long Haul division of British Airways.

A little earlier that morning some real Purolator guards had delivered three holdalls of cash to the office for onward shipment to America, Canada, Japan and the Middle East. This was in the days before Europe had accepted the 'Euro' as currency and the holdalls contained money from half a dozen different countries. The new visitors presented Purolator ID and documents, later described by police as 'impeccable', to the BA staff saying the consignments needed to be handed back because the sums they contained had been miscalculated.

Convinced by the documents, the airline handed them the three packages. These contained $1.2M U.S, £1.04M sterling , 430,000 Lebanese Lira, 2.25M French Francs, and 50M Italian Lira. The estimated total amounted in Sterling to about £1.75M.

The pair then moved on to the offices of the European division of BA where, using more expertly forged documents, they reclaimed another six million French Francs. Their final stop was at the Belgian airline Sabena. Real Purolator guards had been in about half an hour before and dropped off a consignment bound for Brussels and Paris containing another 700,000 French Francs, 25,000 Norwegian Krona, and another £2,000 in UK currency. The two bogus guards, one of whom was Stephen Raymond, the other a well known London villain called Tony Franciosi, presented authentic-looking documents purporting to be from their company saying the cash urgently needed to be handed back. The Sabena staff complied without question.

I later learned that the $1M US taken from British Airways belonged to the CIA. It was on its way to the Middle East to pay a top level informer in Syria. The total amount stolen was put at a value of somewhere between £3.5 and £4M. It was a bigger cash take than even the Great Train Robbery.

Raymond and Franciosi then left the airport in a Ford Granada that had been hired using more forged ID documents. It was found abandoned two days later in one of the airport's long term car parks.

As often happens in complex cases, much of the most interesting detail didn't emerge until much later, partly because they were not even known to the authorities until days or weeks after the crime, and partly because embarrassed losers like Purolator tried to keep their mistakes well-hidden or put pressure on the police not to reveal them either.

Gradually, through working my contacts at Scotland Yard, I managed to flesh out all the details. Months after the crime took place, I discovered Raymond was so confident he would pull off this most audacious of thefts, the previous week he had flown to Dublin where he had entered the Allied Irish Bank on O'Connell Street, opened an account using the alias Colin Dunne, and even booked in a deposit he told staff would be "about $4M in various currencies".

Just three hours after the crime, and with the stolen cash stuffed in a holdall, Raymond, using another fake ID, boarded an Aer Lingus flight from Heathrow to Dublin. But even the cleverest of criminals sometimes suffer unexpected setbacks. Taking a taxi from the airport to Dublin city centre he arrived at the bank to find it was closed. The staff had gone on strike and placard waving demonstrators were picketing the place.

Resourceful as ever, Raymond backtracked to Dublin Airport and booked on a Swiss Air flight bound for Zurich, paying for his ticket with stolen US dollars. Arriving at Zurich Airport he breezed through Swiss customs without a hitch, rented a car, drove into the city centre, and booked a hotel room at the $500 a night Baur au Lac hotel. But he was too late to catch the banks which were already closing. Bright and early on Monday he started touring the city's commercial banks setting up special numbered private accounts. Incredible as it may now seem, in 1978 Switzerland's lax banking rules allowed a stranger to do this with no questions asked.

The only restriction on depositing money was a recently introduced law which made it an offence to bring more than £4,500 into the country without reporting it. By the end of the day Raymond had managed to deposit over £500,000. When the banks closed he made his way back to his hotel, but as he did so he made a serious mistake. Passing an upmarket menswear shop, a suit displayed in the window took his fancy. It was priced at 600 Swiss Francs, a huge sum in 1978. But he tried it on and it fitted perfectly, so he bought it there and then and paid in cash.

The woman assistant who served him could hardly fail to notice the free spending Englishman, who paid from a fat roll of 100 Franc notes, and with a flourish gave her a 100 Franc tip.

What Raymond didn't know was the shop assistant was the wife of a top Swiss police detective. As he left, she discreetly noted down the number of the car he was driving. When she got home she told her husband about how the cocky Englishman appeared to be rolling in money. Raymond had also failed to take into account that back in the UK, all hell was breaking loose in the wake of the robbery. At Scotland Yard detectives in the criminal intelligence branch drew up a list of characters they thought might be capable of such a crime. There were not many, but one was Stephen Raymond.

Details of the crime were in the headlines and a huge reward of £125,000 was offered. And just that afternoon the Swiss detective had seen a teleprinter message from Europol informing all police forces in Europe about the Heathrow raid, adding Scotland Yard believed the culprits were already out of the UK. They added details of some possible suspects, including Stephen Raymond, The Zurich cop wasted no time. He alerted colleagues who began searching airport and car hire records.

Within hours they had discovered the car that had been hired by a man calling himself Colin Dunne and he was staying at the Baur au Lac hotel. In the early hours they raided 'Mr Dunne' at gunpoint. In his room, in a briefcase, was £250,000 in mixed currencies, plus the deposit slips from all the accounts he had opened that day. He was arrested and the next day Scotland Yard flew out. In follow-up inquiries another £250,000 was found in a case in a hotel room he was renting in Dublin. He was later returned to the UK to face a four week Old Bailey trial, at the end of which he was sentenced to 10 years.

But jail was never going to slow Raymond down. He was too much in love with the criminal life and was immediately making new plans and contacts to use when he was released. I knew I would be hearing about him again, but it was not until several years later in the 1980s, when he resurfaced. One of Raymond's favourite sayings, according to people who knew him, was: "It's the documents that slaughter them." Meaning if you have convincing paperwork and identification documents, most people will believe you.

This time he had posed as a buying executive from the Department of Education to swindle the TV rental company Granada out of video recorders worth £500,000 which were delivered to a warehouse he had rented near Witney in Oxfordshire. By the time the TV firm realised they were missing several thousand recording machines, both Raymond and the goods had vanished. In police parlance, it was a classic 'LF' or 'Long Firm' fraud.

He was eventually arrested and jailed for that crime, but allowed home leave from Wayland prison in Norfolk, and went on the run for several months during which he set up more frauds.

Recaptured, he again demonstrated his amazing ability to

beguile and manipulate people. To represent him at a forthcoming trial he hired a top London lawyer, John Blackburn-Gittings. He sent his daughter, 25-year-old Emma, a trainee solicitor, to talk to Raymond who was in Aylesbury jail. He promptly swept her off her feet and seduced her.

After several more visits from Emma, Raymond broke out of Aylesbury jail by sawing through the window bars in his cell with a smuggled hacksaw. It was never established who provided him with the saw. The couple then had a series of clandestine dates in London during which he schooled her in how to get a phoney passport and other fake ID and to fly to Luxembourg and open a bank account in the name of a wealthy American heiress called Susan Krimholtz.

The couple then went to a London bank, where Emma pretended to be the American millionairess by using two letters forged for her by Raymond, and tried to persuade the bank to transfer £428,000 to the bogus account she had set up in Luxembourg. But bank officials smelt a rat and called the police. Emma Gittings was arrested, but Raymond, with his uncanny ability to sense danger, had already strolled out of the building and vanished. His gullible female co-conspirator was convicted of conspiracy to steal and forgery and jailed for nine months. But her jail term was later quashed by the Court of Appeal who accepted she had been victim of "threats, influence, and manipulation" by a man they described as one of her father's "most dangerous and glamorous clients".

In the meantime Raymond was hiding under a raft of aliases and fake identities abroad. I did not hear about him again until 2004 when a contact at the Customs Investigation Division told me about an interesting case. They had arrested a British man for a huge importation of cocaine, three quarters of a ton of it, with a street value (then) of £35M. The man was living under the identity of Simon Price, but his real name was Stephen Raymond.

He had set up a smuggling conduit from Colombia to Europe by creating a sugar and molasses importing business with himself as the Chief Executive.

The cocaine, hermetically sealed in plastic, was hidden inside steel drums containing liquid molasses. Raymond's operation was being run from a 15-bedroom French chateau he had paid two million euros in cash for in the late 1990s. Officers who searched the house in Charance, in Provence, discovered he had been running a 'cordon bleu' chef school and had even set up a brandy distilling business.

In 2005 he was returned to the UK to face trial for the cocaine smuggling operation. He was convicted at London's Snaresbrook Crown Court and jailed for 28 years.

CHAPTER FIFTEEN

While the moniker of 'the murder guy' stuck with me throughout my career, there was much more to my job.

On the face of it, the murder of a young drug dealer in 1983 was interesting, but in my world as a crime specialist, it didn't seem exceptional. I was soon proved wrong.

Gary Collins was a 25-year-old, low-level dope dealer from Hastings, in Sussex. In December 1983 his immaculate green BMW 2002 Alpina sports saloon was found abandoned in the car park of the railway station at the historic market town of Battle, on the main line from Hastings to London. It was unlocked and had apparently been left with its lights on because the battery was flat.

Collins, who was known to the police, had been reported missing by his longtime girlfriend. To add to the mystery his dog Trudie, an Alsatian cross who he took almost everywhere with him, was also missing. It wasn't until three months later his body was found in undergrowth by a wooded track near a gypsum quarry close to the village of Brightling a few miles away. He had suffered multiple stab wounds, including having his throat cut. Poignantly, the remains of his beloved dog were found nearby. She had also been stabbed to death.

Sussex police set up an 'incident room' at Hastings police station and took a team of detectives from other inquiries to form a murder squad. I decided to go to Hastings to see if I could find a new angle to the story. In a local pub I came across a group of detectives who were working the case, enjoying a late night drink. We got talking.

They were a congenial bunch, and over the next few weeks I made time to return to Hastings on a couple of occasions to meet with them and find out what the latest was with their investigation.

To begin with they had a number of intriguing leads. One suggested that Gary might have been the victim of a hitman sent from London after he had double crossed another dope dealer. But gradually, as these lines of inquiry failed to unmask a suspect, the case ran out of steam and the investigation and my interest in it, was wound down. The world of crime never stopped and I simply moved on to new stories.

But some months later, in the spring of 1984, and completely out of the blue, I got a call from one of the officers I'd met in Hastings asking me to meet him at a pub in Brighton.

When I got there he was with some other detectives I had not met before. They turned out to be drug squad officers from various places along the south coast of England and they had an unusual proposition for me. Would I like to meet a person they obliquely only referred to as 'one of their friends', an outlaw biker who had information about how a Hells Angels gang in Holland were planning to flood England with the drug 'LSD' in the coming months?

Naturally, I was intrigued and I agreed to the suggestion. The following week I went, at their invitation, this time to a pub near Eastbourne where they introduced me to a very unlikely character. Ivan arrived on a customised Harley Davidson motorbike. A few years before I had read the book *Hell's Angels: A Strange and Terrible Saga*, by the American author Hunter S Thompson, so I was well briefed on the cult of the Harley.

I'd had a long interest in powerful motorbikes, so I admired his 'hog', as he referred to it, and told him I liked his special ape hanger handlebars and teardrop fuel tank. He was impressed by my knowledge and I could see we were going to get along.

Ivan, who was bearded with unkempt shoulder length black hair, was dressed in a sleeveless denim jacket, ripped and grubby jeans and oil stained motorcycle boots. These he called his 'originals' and were very important in outlaw biker folklore. But my fears that he would be a surly roughneck were quickly dispelled. He was an affable man with a beaming smile and a gruff rumbling laugh.

We got down to business and one of the cops outlined the plan. Ivan, who was a member of the All England chapter of the Hells Angels, was well connected in Amsterdam. He had lived and worked there in the recent past. He explained to me there was a strong brotherhood type friendship between the Dutch and the British Hells Angels.

Would my paper (I was Crime Correspondent at the *News of the World* at the time) be interested in arranging for him and me to go over there, meet some of his biker gang contacts, and get them to talk about their plan to flood Britain's summer music festivals with LSD? That sounded good. I could already see how and why this was shaping up.

It was clear to me Ivan was a key police informant. What was also clear to me was that the drug squad guys needed Ivan out in Amsterdam to scope the situation, and gather intelligence for them. But my guess was there was no money in the police budget to fund the operation, so the detectives had decided to think laterally. Why not get the *News of the World* to bankroll the job? Very smart, very cool. The cops would get what they wanted. I would get a good story. Everybody wins. But what was in it for Ivan?

If he was a police informant he would also need to be an active drug dealer. Otherwise, I reasoned, he wouldn't have any information for his handlers and would be of no value. So, if we went to Holland, he would probably want to do a few side deals of his own. Which, as far as I was concerned and in order to let the job run smoothly, was none of my business.

We talked a bit about how it would all work. Ivan said he had good contacts with biker gangs in Holland. I couldn't carry off being an outlaw biker, we both agreed I didn't look right. But I had learned to dress and act like a convincing underworld 'buyer' – of drugs, stolen goods, guns – and with my East London roots I had learned how to talk the talk and act the part.

The best plan was for me to pretend to be an investor, someone perhaps 'fronting' for a London criminal 'firm' who were interested in making a big purchase of LSD from the Dutch Angels. Ivan said it would be no problem for him to introduce me to some powerful underworld figures when we got to Holland.

I ran the situation past my bosses at the *News of the World* and they liked the sound of it, so I was told to go ahead. I asked our secretary to book me and Ivan an early flight to Amsterdam.

As was the custom we were booked Business Class on British Airways out of Heathrow. When we boarded the plane we looked incongruous to say the least. The 7am flight was full. Everyone sitting around us was an industry boss, corporate lawyer or high flying city banker. I was dressed in jeans and a pricey brown leather bomber jacket. My hair was shoulder length but neatly styled. Ivan looked like he'd slept in a rubbish skip.

We arrived at Schipol Airport and headed for our hotel, a Hilton, in the centre of Amsterdam. Over a breakfast of bacon, eggs, pancakes and beer, I asked Ivan to tell me his background. How was it he knew Holland so well?

He explained: "A few years ago I worked here. I was a 'roadie' working with well known rock bands on tour. I also worked for a big recording studio as a fixer. One of my jobs was to get whatever 'gear' (drugs) whatever band we were recording with at the time wanted. To grease the wheels, the studio always kept a fat stash of cash, about 15 or 20,000 US dollars, in a safe on the premises. The money was to pay for the drugs.

"A few years ago, I was a bit bored. I knew where the key to the safe was kept. So I nicked all the money. I went straight to the airport and bought a one way flight to Australia. Over there I hung out in Sydney and at Bondi beach, I bought a few nice motorbikes, had a few blonde Aussie surfer-type girlfriends. And then, after a few months, I was skint. I'd spent the lot."

"So what did you do then?" I asked. He shrugged and laughed: "I used the last of it to buy a plane ticket back to Amsterdam. I walked into the studio I'd robbed, said 'hi, I'm back'. Waited while they called the cops to come and arrest me, got sentenced to three years, and did my time in the Scheveningen jail, in The Hague."

Ivan explained that while he was in Scheveningen penitentiary, which I knew was Holland's foremost maximum security prison, he had met and befriended several Dutch Hells Angels who were also doing time for various crimes. They had kept in touch. Ivan explained all we needed to do was hook up with one in particular, a man he referred to only as 'The Bear', who would introduce us to the big suppliers. "I don't have a phone number for him. But I know where to find him," Ivan said. "There is a café here which belongs to the Hells Angels. It's called Angel Place, that's where he hangs out. That's where we will find him."

Ivan sounded confident. What could possibly go wrong? So later that day, after a few more beers, we went to Angel Place. It was in a busy urban area, fronting onto one of the city's famous network of canals. It was a rainy late afternoon and as Ivan and I approached in a taxi he mentioned it was a pity it was wet, because if it had been a dry evening, we'd see an impressive array of Harley 'hogs' parked outside. Instead, the small contingent of bikers who were already in the place, were using their 'alternative' method of transport and there were several American made pickup trucks or flashy Chevrolet Camaro and Corvette sports cars drawn up to the kerb.

We strolled in. I admit I was feeling slightly apprehensive. I knew the Hells Angels had a reputation for extreme violence. How would they react to strangers in their camp, especially when one of them – me – was so obviously not an outlaw biker?

But once inside my fears subsided. The place was fairly small and unremarkable, a long bar with tall stools along the right hand side and towards the rear a number of café type tables and chairs where, here and there, Bohemian-looking student and hipster types sat drinking beer or coffee. One or two were smoking cannabis 'joints' – even in the 80s in liberal Holland this was within the law.

Dotted around at intervals TV sets hung from the walls or from ceiling mounts. They were switched on and showing video episodes of the British comedy hit *The Benny Hill Show*. The place felt friendly and not at all intimidating.

We sat up at the bar. The lone barman, a young guy in his 20s came over. He had long hair and was sporting a sleeveless denim waistcoat with a Hells Angels 'Death's Head' skull design embroidered on the back. When we ordered our first two beers we discovered he was English.

Ivan struck up a conversation with him as the barman polished pint beer glasses with a tea cloth. After passing a bit of small talk together I heard Ivan ask: "Will The Bear be in later?".

The barman stopped polishing the glass and put it down. "Man, you must have been well out of the loop." He pointed with his index finger to the wall of the bar directly behind us.

There was a framed picture of a burly bearded man sitting on a kerb in front of an immaculately burnished Harley Davidson. The picture was lined out in black. It bore the simple inscription 'The Bear: 1950 – 1984. He Lived Like a Loser. He Died Like a Loser.' We had come all the way to Amsterdam to meet a dead man.

I stared into my beer glass, then turned to Ivan and said quietly: "What the fuck do we do now?"

In the background, on the TV, Benny Hill was chasing after several scantily dressed girls accompanied by saxophonist Boots Randolph belting out 'Yakkety Sax'.

"OK, leave it to me," said Ivan. "I've got a back up plan." He hoisted himself off his stool and walked down the length of the bar to where the British bartender was unpacking crates of bottled beer into a cooler cabinet.

After about five minutes, Ivan sidled back to my side and said: "It's being taken care of. I'm starving. Let's go and get steak and chips."

Over huge T-bones and French fries, Ivan told me what his new plan was. "I told the barman why we are here. He's cool, he understands. I told him you are fronting for an organised crime firm back in the UK who want to purchase a big parcel of acid (LSD), to flood this summer's music festivals. I told him The Bear was my best connection, but now that's fucked, was he connected to anyone who could make that happen? We need to meet someone high up in the food chain, someone plugged into the manufacture and supply business. He told me to come back on Wednesday. On my own. He will try and sort it."

It was only Monday but Ivan was calling the shots. "Relax," he said. "We will get there, it just might take a day or two."

Sure enough, by Thursday Ivan had arranged for us to meet a man called Willem back at Angel Place.

"When we get there, let me do the talking," Ivan said. "You are just the investor, but I know how this business works."

When we got to the club the same barman picked up a house phone from its wall mount and had a brief conversation with someone while looking at us the whole time.

A few minutes later a tall slim good looking man dressed in jeans, a black leather coat and sporting a red bandana round his throat appeared. In most ways he looked unremarkable, except on a very short lead he held a huge and ferocious looking Dobermann Pinscher. The dog had on one of those collars which was covered in half inch long metal spikes.

There was no preamble, no hand shakes, no 'pleased to meet you'. Willem gave us the visual once over and said in English: "Follow me, gentlemen."

We walked with him to the back of the club where we approached a security door protected by three robust looking mortice locks. Willem took a big bunch of keys from his pocket which were connected to his leather trouser belt by a chain. He undid all the locks carefully in turn and ushered us inside. We were in a small windowless office with a desk and a couple of chairs. He was straight down to business.

"OK," he said. "Here is the deal. We are going to produce one million panes of acid in this year's production run. Minimum buy is 250,000 panes at three US dollars a pane. So that's $750,000. Are you doing your own transport to England? Or do you want us to do it? If you are making your own transport arrangements I can give you a three per cent discount."

He looked at me hard. I said: "No decision on that yet, I'll have to talk to my people back in England."

He was straight back into his sales pitch. "OK, tell your people this. If they want to buy the whole batch, the entire one million units, I can give them a six per cent discount, plus another three if they want to do their own shipping." He opened a desk drawer and took out an electronic calculator and tapped away at the keys.

"So, for the whole batch, etc. I can do it for you at… let's call it a total of 10 per cent, so that's $2.7M. Does that sound acceptable?"

I must have been feeling brave because I suddenly said: "Yes. That's the kind of figure we had in mind. I think we can do that." Verbally we had a deal and we shook on it.

Then, just as we were about to leave, Willem said jovially, "but you will not want to go without sampling the goods."

He pulled a large leather pocket book from a drawer and opened it. I could see it was stuffed with cash of various currencies; US dollars, Dutch Gilders, German Deutschmarks, and Sterling.

From among the banknotes he pulled a strip of clear cellophane. I could see there were about two dozen little sleeves, each containing what appeared to be a small piece of cartoon artwork featuring a big red and white spotted mushroom. He tore one off and offered it to me. I shook my head. I had smoked cannabis a few times in my life, but frankly stories about 'bad trips' had made me wary of psychedelic drugs. I simply said: "No, mate. Not my game. I am just an investor. But my friend here will be keen to try one and he will tell me about the quality – good or bad – later."

I shot Ivan a glance and he said: "Yes, I am up for that." He popped it in his mouth. We thanked Willem, who gave Ivan two or three strips of 'free samples' and I told him we would be back within a week to finalise the details of moving the money to pay for the purchase and to ship the stuff back to Britain.

As we left Willem gave me another strip of panes from his wallet and said jovially: "Here. Take this with you. It's not your scene, but maybe your friends back in England would like to sample my product. I can assure you, it is very good."

We strolled out. I was feeling relaxed. As we hailed a cab, Ivan grabbed my arm. "Get me to an all night pharmacy," he said urgently.

"Why?" I responded.

"Because I need a kilo bag of raw glucose and I need it right now. It's the only antidote to LSD. I hate the stuff, it has a bad effect on me. I only swallowed that pane so Willem wouldn't be suspicious of what we're really up to."

I told the cab driver to find an all night chemist. Pronto. It only took about 10 minutes. Ivan pelted inside and a few minutes later emerged with a big clear plastic bag of white powder. In the back of the cab he ripped it open and buried his face in it, shovelling the glucose into his mouth with his hands as fast as he could. By the time we got to our hotel he looked like he had been caught in an explosion in a flour factory. I gave the taxi man another 40 Gilders on top of the fare to help clean up his cab.

We walked into the hotel lobby and Ivan said: "Don't leave me on my own, mate, please. Come up to my room with me. I am feeling very weird already. I need someone to look after me. I don't know what's going to happen next."

His room was on the tenth floor. He flopped on to the double bed, still fully dressed, and began to snore loudly. I sat on the end of the bed, turned on the TV and discovered there was a big football match on. It was Tottenham playing Anderlecht of Belgium in the UEFA Cup final. I sat on the end of Ivan's bed, working my way through the contents of his mini bar. The match went to extra time and penalties. As the penalty shoot out started Ivan suddenly woke up, jumped off the bed, and ran to the window which he made a good effort at trying to wrench open.

I leapt after him and wrestled and pushed him away from the glass. I was worried if I didn't, in his drug delirium he would think he was a bird and fly out of the window. He was bigger and stronger than me, but somehow I managed to get him back on the bed where I sat on his legs for the next several hours to prevent him making another bid for freedom.

Ivan seemed OK the next day and wanted to stay in Holland while I needed to get back to the UK. I headed off to the airport, but before I did I put the strip of LSD in one of the envelopes bearing the Hilton hotel logo and posted it back to my office in London.

I wanted to get it back home, as a small piece of evidence my mission had not failed, and so we could photograph it. Also, I didn't want to risk passing through airport security or customs with it on me. It arrived safely, without being intercepted, at my office a few days later.

I wrote my story and it appeared prominently in the paper under the headline 'Hells Angels Plot Summer Drug Blitz'. I never saw or heard from Ivan again. I have no idea what happened to him.

Several years later I met some Dutch detectives in Amsterdam on another story. They were affable and easy to talk to (they all spoke good English) and I told them about my meeting with 'Willem' at Angel Place. One of them told me: "The guy you met was Willem Van Boxtel. He set up Angel Place. He is a very dangerous organised crime figure in Holland. He is the acknowledged boss of the Dutch Hell's Angels. He has been involved in a lot of extreme violence in Europe, up to and including gangland murders of rivals.

"You are a lucky guy. If he suspected your friend was an undercover agent for British narcotics detectives and you were an undercover journalist, you would never have been seen again until your bodies were found floating in a canal out in the tulip fields somewhere."

BOMBINGS, TERROR AND TRAGEDY

CHAPTER SIXTEEN

During the 1970s a wave of violence which had begun in Northern Ireland spilled over into mainland Britain. There was a series of bombings and shootings by the Provisional IRA (Irish Repubican Army), who believed one attack in London had more political impact than 10 in Belfast, and we all learned to live with the constant threat from the ongoing terror campaign. From the mid-1970s IRA terrorism became a huge part of my professional life and continued to be for more than 20 years. For me it really began in 1975 with the shocking killing of a 21-year-old police constable, Stephen Tibble. He had only been a member of the Metropolitan Police for six months when he was murdered by an IRA man on the run in London. The immediate assumption in Fleet Street, when the news came in, was that PC Tibble had been killed when taking part in a special operation by Scotland Yard to uncover an IRA cell operating in mainland Britain.

But by working my contacts, I soon discovered the story of his tragic killing was far more complicated than first thought. It also demonstrated the kind of random events that come together, sometimes in a matter of mere seconds, which lead to catastrophic outcomes.

PC Tibble had not in fact been part of a special operation against Irish Republican terrorists. He had not been part of any operation at all. He wasn't even on duty. The rookie officer had just been in the wrong place at the wrong time, and had made an on-the-spot decision to do something brave, and it got him killed.

Over the previous few weeks there had been a spate of burglaries in the area, particularly on the Baron's Court Estate where many of the Victorian-era homes had basements which, because the front doors were below pavement level and largely hidden from view, were a favourite target for burglars.

To try and combat the problem the local police had set up a special undercover operation to try and catch the house breakers. A number of plain clothes officers were operating in the Hammersmith area looking for anyone they thought was acting in such a way as might indicate they were 'casing the place', i.e. looking out for suitable homes to break into.

At about 9am some of them noticed a man they thought might be a housebreaker. They stopped him to question him, but as soon as they did, he took off, running like a hare, pursued by two detectives. At this precise moment Stephen Tibble, who was newly-married and lived close-by, was driving along the same street on his motorbike.

He was off duty and not in uniform, but his police instincts told him what he was seeing was a suspect being chased by police. He accelerated, overtook the running suspect and mounted the pavement. To block the escape of the running man, he dismounted and moved towards the suspect with his arms spread wide, ready to grab him.

To the horror of witnesses, the man pulled a .45 calibre revolver from under his coat and shot PC Tibble in the chest twice at very close range. The young officer fell and although he was still alive when an ambulance got him to hospital, one of the bullets had torn through his aorta, and he died from massive blood loss as surgeons tried to save him. The gunman escaped.

Calling contacts, I soon found an old friend who was now on one of the top squads at Scotland Yard. The 'buzz' had gone round the whole force that an off duty policeman had been gunned down, and there was already speculation the shooting had been carried out by an IRA man.

I told my bosses at the *Evening News*. They were impressed, because I was the first to be able to report the victim was an off duty cop. We downplayed the IRA link – on the day no one could say for sure this was the case, but overnight, after we had published our last edition of the day, strong evidence began to emerge.

The gunman was later identified as Liam Quinn, a member of the Provisional IRA, and the Anti-Terrorist Squad soon identified the flat where he had been living as part of an IRA sleeper cell. When they searched the apartment they found plastic explosives, detonator cord, timing mechanisms and other bomb-making paraphernalia. The flat was described by the police later as a 'bomb factory'.

An all points bulletin was sent out to arrest Quinn, who was actually an American citizen and not an Irishman, but he managed to slip out of the country and flee back to the USA. He was cornered, 13 years later in 1988 by the FBI, living under a false identity in San Francisco.

After a long extradition wrangle, he was eventually brought back to the UK to face justice. He went on trial at the Old Bailey in

1989, was convicted and sentenced to life with a minimum term of 30 years, and in 1999 he was released as part of the Good Friday peace arrangements. But all that was in the future.

Two days after the shooting, there was still a lot of information to track down and writing to be done about this sensational event. I was back in for another early shift when, about 9am, my boss George Hollingbery said: "Jeff, there's been a bomb at Moorgate Underground. Looks like another IRA attack. Start calling your contacts, find out what's happened." I jumped to it.

In the previous two years there had been a wave of bombings in London, all the work of the Provisional IRA. The sectarian troubles in Northern Ireland, which had begun in the late 1960s had spilled over onto the mainland. So called sleeper cells had carried out about 40 attacks.

Significantly, some of these had involved attempts to blow up trains on the Underground network.

The Stephen Tibble shooting appeared to have been a chance event, but it was a clear indicator the IRA were here, and were not going away. I called the City of London Police Control Room and an operator told me there was a major incident at Moorgate. All available police officers and other emergency services were on their way. I asked if it was an IRA attack, but the operator had no more information and hung up.

I rang a friend who was a detective in the British Transport Police who told me: "It's not a bomb, it's a crash. A tube train has overrun the buffers at the end of the tunnel and rammed a solid brick wall. There's a lot of casualties. That's all I know right now."

I went over to George, who was talking on two phones at once. I got his attention: "It's not a bomb. It's a train crash," I said.

George looked at me as if I was deluded: "We've got multiple reports of an explosion. It must be a bomb, what else can it be?"

"I've spoken to a friend in the BTP," I told him. "He says a tube train has crashed into the end of the tunnel. Lots of people hurt. The Northern Line City branch runs into Moorgate. The station is a dead end."

George continued to look doubtful. I was feeling nervous, I was still in my earliest days at the paper and this would not be a good time to wrongfoot my boss on such a big story. "Right, get down there now," he ordered. "Join the others I've already sent. Start finding witnesses, we need a better picture of what the fuck has happened."

I arrived to find the road was blocked with fire engines, ambulances, and a police cordon. There were hundreds of people milling about. I walked towards a knot of firemen hooking hoses up to hydrants. I recognised a couple of the firefighters standing by their fire engine. They were people I had played darts against in a local pub league.

They remembered me and I asked them what was going on. "It's a terrible tube train crash. It's run full-tilt into the end wall. I've not been down there myself, but some of the lads have," one said.

"There's 20 or 30 dead. Some of our crew have been down on the actual platform. They are saying the train carriages have telescoped – crushed into about half their normal length, and jammed up against the top of the tunnel. The word is it must have been going 40 or 50 miles an hour when it hit."

I looked at my watch. It was just after 11am I found a nearby public pay phone and rang the newsdesk.

"It *is* a train crash," I said: "I've just bumped into a mate, a fireman, some of his colleagues have been down there in the tunnel. He says the train has come racing into the station very fast, could be 50 miles per hour, there's lots of fatalities. The carriages have all telescoped, they've been squashed into half their length."

Seconds later I was speaking to one of the copy takers. They were equipped with headsets and typed every word as you recounted it to them, then sent it directly to the newsdesk.

Then George came back on. "Well done," he said. "Now, for your sake, let's hope this *is* a fucking train crash, and *not* an IRA bomb, as everyone else is saying. If it is the IRA, don't bother coming back here – ever! This is going to be the next edition splash. Now, go back and get some more, find some victims, you know what to do." Then he hung up on me.

By now we had at least a dozen reporters at the scene. As the day wore on it became clear there had indeed been a terrible train disaster. A six coach train, which should have coasted into the platform at about 10 miles per hour, had powered in at more than four times that speed. Its sheer kinetic energy had swept aside a long sand trap and a powerful hydraulic buffer, both of which would have stopped it at a lower speed.

The impact was so powerful the first carriage, which was of steel construction, was crushed from a length of over 52ft into an area of about 20ft. It was the worst crash ever on London's Underground network and 43 people, including the driver, 56-year-old Leslie Newson, had died. Another 74 were seriously injured, many losing limbs and suffering other life changing injuries.

The crash happened at 8.46am, at the height of the rush hour, and it was not until after 10pm that the rescue services, hampered by the narrow confines of the tunnel and the compressed wreckage, were able to extricate the last of the injured.

To this day, the reason for the disaster remains unknown. Driver Newson had been driving the route regularly for several years and was in good health. There was some alcohol in his system, probably from the night before, but experts agreed it was not enough to impair his judgement. Over the following months and years there were many attempts to explain how the disaster had happened. It emerged that in the two weeks prior to the incident Leslie Newson had twice overshot platforms at other through stations on his route.

One psychologist even suggested these incidents were him rehearsing in his own mind how he was finally planning to crash his train deliberately in a bizarre suicide. In the end it was impossible to determine whether his actions on the day were deliberate, or otherwise. One thing is certain, if he did crash his train on purpose to kill himself and by doing so killed 42 innocent passengers, he was the biggest mass killer in British criminal history.

* * *

During my first six years on Fleet Street I had been involved in reporting many IRA attacks on mainland Britain, but in most cases I was reporting 'by remote control', i.e. I was not present at or up close and personal with events.

But what happened on December 17, 1983 left its mark on me. On Saturdays we had a system at the *News of the World* where, for operational reasons, our entire staff migrated up one floor to the offices of *The Sun* where we used their newsroom. At about 1.15pm I decided to go down to our canteen to grab a cup of coffee. While there I chanced to meet a female colleague, and on our way back to *The Sun* newsroom we diverted past our own office because she wanted to retrieve something from her desk. I noticed one of our office windows was open, which I thought unusual because it was a cold day, and as I went to close it, I heard the unmistakable sound of a bomb detonating.

We had a large clock on the wall of the office. It was 1.21pm. The sound of a bomb exploding is unique. In Northern Ireland I heard many. I have also heard gas explosions, thunderclaps overhead, sonic booms, huge fireworks displays and 21 gun salutes, and I can say with certainty that nothing, nothing at all, sounds like the air-splitting crash of a bomb.

I turned to my colleague and said: "That's a bomb. Definitely a bomb." And we both ran to the stairs and dashed up two flights to *The Sun* newsroom.

By the time we got there our switchboard was already lighting up as scores of callers rang in asking if we knew where the explosion was, with a few calling to tell us it was outside Harrods in Knightsbridge.

It was the last full weekend of Christmas shopping before the holidays and I knew immediately there would be mass casualties. I sprinted to our car park, which was only 40 yards from our building.

Fleet Street was about three miles from Knightsbridge, but even driving my BMW like a lunatic, it took about 15 minutes to weave through the traffic to a point near Buckingham Palace, where I could see that jams were already building up, making it impossible to get any closer.

I dumped my car on the roadside, and ran the last three quarters of a mile towards the landmark department store. As I ran I was overtaken by probably 40 or 50 police cars, fire engines and ambulances, all going hell for leather towards Knightsbridge. As I got closer to the store I could see the road had been sealed off by the police, so I headed into the side streets to see how close I could get to Harrods.

Around the back of the store, I encountered a *Sunday Mirror* reporter I knew. We decided to see if we could get into one of the heavily damaged office buildings on the opposite side of the street.

As we did, I spotted a figure sitting on a step in a doorway. He appeared to be wearing a dark overcoat, but as I approached him I realised he was clothed in the remnants of an expensive beige camel hair coat. It looked black because it had been singed and shredded by the blast.

All his clothes were ripped and torn and as I got closer I could see his head and face were covered in blood. On the top of his head I could see a triangular piece of glass which was clearly embedded in his scalp. He was about 40.

I tried to speak to him, but he was catatonic and obviously in deep shock. I could only assume he must have been very close to the bomb when it went off, before he staggered, blinded and dazed, to the spot where I found him.

Although I did not know it then, he was an Egyptian diplomat who had been on his way to buy Christmas gifts for his grandchildren. He was one of 90 innocent shoppers, many of them visitors from abroad, who had been maimed and mangled by the blast. Five people were killed, including two police officers who were trying to evacuate the area after a warning, when the bomb exploded in a parked car. A third officer died in hospital of his injuries on Christmas Day.

I ran towards the nearest police line I could see to try and alert them to the injured man. They waved me away. I remember one saying: "You aren't injured, so fuck off and let us do our jobs."

Looking back I realise now he was angry and in shock himself knowing what I did not, that two of his colleagues had been killed outright and 14 others had been wounded, one fatally and others with life-changing injuries.

I went back to the injured man, who was still sitting on the step. I told him help was coming, even though I wasn't sure it was. He was in a bad way and did not respond.

Together with the *Sunday Mirror* journalist, we spotted an open door, which was blown in and off its hinges by the explosion. It appeared to be the offices of an advertising or marketing agency, which had been heavily damaged by the blast. The rival reporter went inside trying to climb some stairs which were blocked with a tangle of office chairs and filing cabinets.

I followed. We managed to clear a path, hoping to get a bird's eye view of the wreckage of Harrods from an upper floor. Water was cascading down from the ceilings where sprinkler systems had been ruptured. Electric conduits had also come down in a jumble of smashed office equipment. The *Mirror* guy pushed on ahead of me trying to reach a window which had been blown out of its frame by the explosion.

But as he did so I saw some electric cables hanging from a destroyed conduit in a roof void sparking as water from a broken sprinkler reached them. I grabbed him by the back of his coat and dragged him back from the imminent danger of electrocution.

Smoke was emanating from burning carpet materials which were set alight by the arcing electric cables. We both got out just in time. Five minutes later the office where we had been was alight. The fire brigade were already at the scene of the bombing and quickly dealt with the fire, but it was a salutary lesson in how the race to be the first reporter into any situation might be fatal.

Later that day, around 5pm, we got word there was a special press conference to be held at New Scotland Yard. I went, along with scores of other journalists and TV crews. We'd expected to hear the police top brass, but were all thrown slightly when Prime Minister Margaret Thatcher swept into the room. I had never seen her in the flesh before. She made the expected remarks about ruthlessly hunting down the perpetrators. Then, as she rose and turned to leave, I put up my hand, waved my pen to get her attention and, unbidden, called out: "Prime Minister. Will you be going to visit the injured in hospital?"

Her PR team accompanying her had clearly not thought of this opportunity. Mrs. Thatcher was literally going out of the door, but she turned, stepped back into the room, fixed me with her famous ice blue eyes and said: "Yes, I will most certainly be going to visit the injured in hospital."

I was never a big fan of Maggie Thatcher, but there was no denying she had a formidable presence. The next day I had the front page and four pages on the inside of the paper about how the IRA had caused Christmas carnage with a bomb packed inside a stolen car. A warning had been sent, but not in enough time for the police to organise the safe evacuation of Harrods where at least 2,000 people had been inside at the time, and hundreds more window shopping outside.

A 'side bar' to the main story was headlined "PM tells *News of the World*: 'I will visit the wounded in hospital'." It proved what I already knew – that sometimes in popular newspapers the right question at the right time can reap rewards.

CHAPTER SEVENTEEN

The Provisional IRA bombings took place over decades, and there had been a sequence leading up to a huge bomb in London. This time it was an absolute monster and brought me personal sadness when it took the life of a friend and colleague.

On the morning of Saturday April 24, 1993, a coded warning was received by the BBC saying a bomb in a lorry had been parked in Bishopsgate, near Liverpool Street, in the very centre of the famous 'Square Mile' of the City. The bomb, incorporating a main charge of an estimated one ton of 'ANFO', a military acronym for a mixture of ammonium nitrate and fuel oil, homemade explosive with a 100lb Semtex plastic explosive core, was left on a double yellow line outside number 99 Bishopsgate which was then the British headquarters of the HSBC bank. When it detonated it created a mushroom cloud of smoke visible from 20 miles away and tore a crater 15ft deep in the road. It caused unprecedented destruction to the HSBC headquarters, the NatWest Tower and Liverpool Street railway station with a repair bill estimated at £1 billion. Because the City of London is almost deserted at weekends the human cost of the attack was mercifully low.

Only one person was killed but, sadly, he was a good friend of mine. Ed Henty was a 34-year-old freelance photographer who on this day was doing a stint for the *News of the World*. I had worked alongside him many times in the past. He was easygoing, likeable and a great professional. He was happily married with two young children and he was a tenacious 'snapper'. He got to the area before the police had been properly able to organise an effective security cordon. No doubt he was hoping to get great exclusive pictures of army explosive experts defusing the device and preventing it going off.

Unfortunately for Ed, the bomb disposal people were still on their way when the truck, its deadly load hidden under several tons of tarmac, went off. Poor Ed was believed to be only 10 metres or so from the truck when it went up. After hearing he was missing, presumed dead in the mountains of rubble left by the blast, a memory struck me.

I had done a number of jobs in Northern Ireland in the previous few years. On one occasion I had been with a photographer when we were notified about an unexploded car bomb in a busy part of Belfast. We were not far away. I said: "Come on, let's go down there."

The photographer said: "No, let's wait here. You mainland types. When you hear about a bomb you all rush towards it. Us Belfast journalists wait, or go in the other direction completely. It's because people like me have seen lots of these things and, unlike you, we've seen what bombs actually do to humans."

I realised after Ed's death what wise words they were.

I had previously covered a number of so-called 'spectaculars' by the IRA in London.

On February 7, 1991, with British troops in combat in the first Gulf War in Iraq, the IRA attempted to kill British Prime Minister John Major and his entire cabinet office with a mortar bomb attack on Downing Street. They very nearly succeeded. By this time the ordnance and weapons wing of the Provisional IRA had become so sophisticated they were adept at making scratch-built mobile mortar systems using steel pipes as launch tubes and gas cylinders packed with explosives as improvised artillery rounds. The attack team acquired a reliable Ford Transit van and cut a large hole in its roof, before installing the mortar tubes, which were already loaded with bombs, into the back.

The bombs were to be launched using a cleverly-made electronic mechanism fitted with a timer. One IRA man then drove the van to Whitehall, parked the van about 180 metres from the target and escaped on the pillion of a motorbike driven by an accomplice.

It was just before 11am and inside the Cabinet Office the Prime Minister was meeting with several senior ministers and the heads of Britain's armed forces to discuss the progress of Operation Desert Storm. Because of the known security risk parking was strictly banned in Whitehall, but the timer on the bomb launcher had been set to run for only 10 minutes and although police had spotted the vehicle they were powerless to do anything.

Three missiles were launched, each weighed about 140lb and carried a 40lb plastic explosive warhead. Two overshot their target and landed in a small grass area known as Mountbatten Green. The first detonated, the second was a dud, but the third rocket-propelled bomb landed directly in the back garden of the Cabinet Office where it exploded causing serious damage to the back of the building, and smashing many windows.

Although the PM and other government figures suffered shock, they were otherwise unhurt. The IRA had failed to kill them all by a matter of a few feet. In Whitehall a preset incendiary bomb destroyed the van and any forensic evidence which might identify the attackers.

I immersed myself in the story knowing the IRA were getting

more bold and increasingly smarter and they would be back. Sure enough, they were.

This time the story happened on a Friday night in November 1991. A two-strong IRA team, one of them a young woman, travelled to St Albans, the small historic Hertfordshire city to the north of London, where they planned to bomb a theatre where a British army band were playing for an audience of about 250 innocent people. It would have been a massacre on a huge scale. But as the duo were priming their device made of 20lb of Semtex plastic explosive in a holdall in a dark shop doorway, it went off, killing them both instantly.

The next morning I spoke to a friend on the Anti-Terrorism Squad who described the incident, with an ironic laugh, as an 'own goal'. Less than six months later the IRA were back in London. With negotiations between them and the British government at an impasse, they were determined to force the issue.

The next bomb would cause a mammoth amount of damage. On April 9, 1992, there was a General Election which saw the Conservatives elected again and John Major returning to Downing Street as Prime Minister.

The next evening at 9.20pm an enormous bomb exploded in St Mary Axe in the City. In an attempt to spare innocent lives, for some time the IRA had agreed a 'code word' system to accompany telephone warnings. It was an attempt to differentiate between genuine warnings and the many hoax calls made by idiots. The coded warnings were phoned to news organisations or TV stations about imminent bombings.

These code words were supposed to be secret, but in practice most of us in the law enforcement reporting side of the business knew what they were. The weak point about the system was the bombers themselves, not being native to London or the UK generally, were often confused about where they had actually placed the bomb.

On April 10, an authentic coded warning was phoned to the Press Association in Fleet Street, saying a bomb in a van had been left in the City of London in the Bishopsgate area.

But this critical information was inaccurate. In fact it was parked about half a mile away in a different street directly outside the historic Baltic Exchange building and the offices of the insurance giant Commercial Union. As a result of the initial misinformation police were looking in the wrong place and three innocent people, one of them a 15-year-old schoolgirl, who should have been cleared from the correct area, were killed and dozens more wounded.

The bomb, in a stolen Transit van, was estimated to have a main charge weighing about a ton made from a blend once more of ammonium nitrate fertiliser, also known in army slang as 'Co-op mix', and an 'accelerator core' of about 50lbs of Semtex plastic explosive packed into scaffolding tubes. The damage to buildings was immense and estimated at a staggering £800M. The explosion was the biggest to hit mainland Britain since the German blitz in the Second World War and was estimated to have caused more financial damage to property and business than the thousands of IRA attacks in the previous 20 years. The historic and beautiful Baltic Exchange, built in 1903, was completely demolished. It was later replaced with the ultra modern skyscraper now known as The Gherkin.

I later learned that the explosion smashed an estimated 1,000 tons of window glass in surrounding areas. The following night a similar bomb planted by the IRA exploded under a huge concrete flyover at Staples Corner in Neasden, north west London, carrying the vital North Circular road over the A41 close to the Brent Cross shopping complex. Although the bridge didn't collapse onto the Midland main line railway underneath, the road was damaged enough to be closed for months causing huge disruption to one of the capital's most important transport arteries and causing millions more in losses to business.

More months passed and I lived in the certain knowledge that the IRA would continue to feature prominently in my professional life as we were no nearer a ceasefire or peace agreement.

In early 1994 I learned that the police in Gloucester were digging up the garden of a house in Cromwell Street. Human remains of several young women had been found, and a builder called Fred West and his wife Rose had been arrested. Together with several colleagues and half of Fleet Street, or so it seemed, I was catapulted towards the south west of England by my office. It looked as if I was going to be the lead reporter for the *Daily Mirror* on the worst serial killer investigation since the Yorkshire Ripper.

But, on my second day, as I was just getting a proper grip on the story, my phone rang and my news editor said: "The IRA have just mortared Heathrow Airport. You'd better get back here." I left what was to become the notorious Fred and Rose West murder trial to my colleagues and raced back to London.

Just before 6pm a volley of mortar bombs had landed at the edge of one of the main runways and on some aircraft taxiways. The bombs were very similar to the ones launched at Downing Street. Although the terrorist armourers had mastered the art of launching the mortars, they still had not perfected the way to make them detonate on impact. All four bombs were duds which failed to explode, though the disruption to the airport was enough for them to claim the attack as a success. The mortars were fired from a special launching rack fitted into the rear of a stolen Nissan hatchback car left in a car park of one of the big hotels on the perimeter of the airport.

When the mortars launched, the rocket propellant set fire to the vehicle which in turn set ablaze several other parked cars causing a huge conflagration. I was at full stretch for about 48 hours gathering information about the incident and writing it up to meet our deadlines but, sensational as the airport incident was, I really wanted to be back in Gloucester where Fred and Rose West's house and garden were yielding more and more human remains.

I was just about to head off down the M4 again and pick up the reins on what was becoming one of the biggest serial murder cases in British crime history, when a second volley of IRA mortars crashed down on Heathrow Airport. I was literally going out of the door at our offices in Canary Wharf with my overnight bag on my way to Gloucester when a phone call stopped me in my tracks and I had to divert to Scotland Yard.

There I found out that this second wave of four rocket propelled bombs, which also failed to go off, but caused enormous disruption to flights, had been launched from a deep pit dug into a field a half mile from the airport itself. An Anti-Terrorism Squad friend told me it would have taken two or three men, working with picks and shovels in the dark, an estimated two to three nights to dig the hole and install the timed mortars. Remarkably, just 800 yards from one of the world's largest airports, in an area bisected by two of Britain's busiest motorways, no one had spotted anything suspicious at all. It seemed impossible to believe. In fact, the second mortar attack was followed by a third just hours later. Now, a total of 12 bombs had hit Heathrow.

Although none of them exploded because of a technical failure, it cost airlines from all over the world millions in lost business and was hugely embarrassing to the British government and police, who were made to look slow off the mark and incompetent. It also demonstrated the IRA were becoming as technically dangerous as any other of the world's terrorist organisations. This time their bombs had failed to go off, but it was only a matter of slight adjustments. They would learn from their mistakes, and it would be to our cost.

CHAPTER EIGHTEEN

In 1994 *The Daily Mirror* relocated its offices from its landmark HQ in Holborn Circus in the very centre of London, to the regenerated Canary Wharf complex in the docklands of East London. Our new offices were on three floors of the highly prestigious 'Canada Tower' building, which at 800ft was then the tallest building in the country. The new *Daily Mirror* newsroom was on the 22nd floor, so about 400ft up.

Terrorism was still a large part of my workload and as Canary Wharf and its surrounding areas filled up with more prestigious skyscrapers housing the HQ offices of some of the world's biggest banks, deep down the thought grew in my mind that we would be the target one day, especially after the two enormous City of London bombs.

A previous attempt to bomb the Canada Tower had actually been foiled in 1992 when security guards confronted some men trying to park a truck bomb near the base of the building. Shots were fired but no one was hurt and the terrorists fled, leaving their bomb behind to be defused by the army.

By 1995 a temporary ceasefire had been declared while the British government tried to persuade the Official IRA, the political arm of the Provisional IRA, to lay down its weapons permanently. It was a complex scenario which failed because of intransigence from both sides. On Friday February 6, 1995, I was out of the office in north London trying to hunt down a story when my news editor David Leigh, a great news man and a good friend, called me. He said: "There's been a coded warning about a bomb here in Docklands. What should we do?"

Throughout the IRA campaign on the mainland, which had now been ongoing for 23 years, there had been hundreds of false warnings. The majority of these were from mischief makers, vengeance seekers, and fools. But some were genuinely the work of the IRA who knew a warning, even if there was no bomb, caused businesses huge financial losses, delayed and angered the public, and wasted the time and tied up the resources of all the emergency services. So I said to David Leigh: "Tell our people to stay put and not panic. They will be safer in our offices up in the sky than out on the street."

He replied: "I am going to tell all the non-essential staff, secretaries, etc, to evacuate." I agreed with his decision.

I said: "People will moan because you are keeping them back on a Friday night. I'm on my way in, see you in a little while." Then I laughed and said: "It's probably a false alarm anyway." About 10 minutes later I was driving down the A13 road, heading west towards the centre of London and the Canning Town flyover. I was about a mile from the office when I heard and felt the strangest sensation. My car rocked and bucked slightly and there was a rushing sound like a freight train hurtling past in the opposite direction.

A huge bomb, estimated at more than a ton and a half of explosives, had detonated at South Quay Plaza, only about 100 metres from our office. What I had felt, even more than a mile distant, was the shock wave. The exact time of the blast was 7.01pm. About four minutes later, I was on the road leading into the complex from the eastern end where I drove into our car park, which was underground and about 200 metres from the Canada Tower.

As I ran up the stairs I could hear the sound of hundreds of alarms – burglar alarms, car alarms, fire alarms, all going off together.

There was also the bizarre noise of crashing and tinkling glass as hundreds of wrecked double glazed window panels, fractured and loosened by the explosion, continued to come crashing down. A strange smell hung in the air, a sort of sweet gunpowdery scent, reminiscent of the aftermath of Guy Fawkes night when I was a child. There were no people about, and I realised most had been safely evacuated before the blast.

At the foot of my building where the reception desks were, security guards ordered me back. They were running about here and there, clearly confused and unaware of how they were supposed to react. One or two tried to block my path, but I shimmied past them. I reached our landing and hurried into our office. David Leigh spotted me. The office was covered in dust and a number of polystyrene ceiling panels had come down. He looked at me, laughed derisively, and said: "I thought you said it was probably a false alarm. You'd better get writing."

There were maybe 40 or 50 of the editorial staff in the office, subs, reporters, one or two photographers. I saw a colleague Harry Arnold, our Chief Reporter, standing by the window looking out at the damage and chaos outside. He said: "I swear to you, I was looking in this direction when it went off and I actually saw the window glass bow inwards with the blast and then bow outwards again, as if it was being sucked out. But it held. Thank God. If the glass had gone we would all have been cut to ribbons."

Harry was right. Most of the building was made of glass on steel frames, not brick. Just a few days before, I had spoken to one of the building engineers who was on our floor to examine something and he had told me our windows were built to withstand tornado force winds. He showed me how every pane, each about 12ft high and 8ft across, was backed by a shock absorbing thick rubber gasket. Thank God it had done its job.

But now we had a problem. We had a paper to get out, but Canary Wharf security and the police were telling us to evacuate immediately. There could be a second bomb.I was writing furiously. When the bomb warning was received, my colleague Adrian Shaw had been sent out to have a look around. He had driven around to South Quay where the device was said to be. He spotted a blue flatbed Ford truck and correctly surmised it was the bomb, right there. Adrian was a brilliant and experienced reporter, a very good friend with a great sense of humour. He was wise enough to know he shouldn't put himself in direct line with the bomb or he would likely be killed if it went off. He drove around the corner and watched as thousands of people piled on to buses, bicycles, or the Docklands Light Railway, before the service was suspended.

He was only about 40 metres from the bomb when it exploded. Luckily he was shielded by a large building. Even so he told me later his car was flung back several feet by the shock wave as it cannoned off various buildings. A stoic individual, taken away from us when he died a week after taking retirement, he was already 'firing from the hip' – filing copy in ad lib style by phone to the office.

When I saw him later he was clearly suffering from shock as the realisation of what a close call he had had sunk in. In the office we were coming under intense pressure from the authorities to leave over fears of a second explosion. I didn't think it was likely, but then I had thought the initial warning was a hoax, had I not?

Piers Morgan, the editor, came and spoke to me, and said he was in conversations with an air charter company to fly us to Manchester and our office in Oldham in order to get the paper out. I filed about 1,000 words in record time, based on what we knew. We didn't have much detail, didn't even know then that two people, in a shop within shouting distance of where Adrian had been parked, had been killed after being blown through two brick walls. The damage to prestige property was enormous, impossible to adequately describe.

At about 9pm the police came into our office and ordered us to leave. Anyone who refused would be arrested for obstruction. As a group of about 20 of us walked across a road bridge towards our car park I spotted something lying in the gutter. It was a piece of thick, dull, silver coloured scorched metal, about the size of the palm of my hand. I stooped to pick it up and, over two hours after the explosion, it was still almost too hot to handle. When I got to the car park I examined it with a torch from my car and showed it to colleagues. It was distorted and twisted and torn in such a way as none of us had ever seen before. It literally looked as if some supernatural force had attacked it.

We were later to find out the bomb was a classic 'Co-op' mix weapon with a main charge of about one and a half tons made from fertiliser, fuel oil, and sugar around an accelerator core of about 50lbs of Semtex explosive packed inside scaffolding tubes. The explosion, caused by the estimated total of 3,000lb of explosive, blew a hole in the ground 10ft deep and 30ft across. My guess was my 'souvenir' of a night to remember was shrapnel from one of the scaffold poles. I should have handed it in to the cops, they would have examined it and classified it as evidence, but I figured they probably would sift out all the evidence they needed.

The paper did come out the next day, a Saturday, without us having to fly to relocate temporarily to Manchester. Seventy-two hours later I went back into my office to pick up any loose ends on the story and to have a look at the devastation in daylight. In the inquest that followed it became clear that despite a series of coded warning messages from the bombers, some of them phoned in to Irish news outlets, there was confusion about the exact spot the bomb had been left. It was a familiar story. In addition, some people, me and many of my colleagues included, had chosen to ignore the warning, believing it to be a hoax.

When it detonated, the bomb, packed into a specially adapted Ford Iveco flatbed truck, was parked directly under a concrete flyover at South Quays station which carried the Docklands Light Railway over a busy main road. Although the railway bridge withstood the explosion, the devastation to real estate over a wide area was awesome. The London headquarters of the Midland bank and two other multi-story blocks were destroyed completely. The financial damage was estimated at least £170M.

One of the strange things I noticed was how some buildings close to the seat of the explosion had only suffered light damage because the blast was diverted by other structures, while others much further away, were wrecked by blast waves travelling uninterrupted through narrow corridors between larger buildings. A case in point was a McDonalds restaurant which was about a quarter of a mile from the seat of the attack, but had been virtually demolished by a part of the blast wave which travelled through a small 'slot' between larger lightly damaged buildings like a sniper's rifle bullet.

The subsequent investigation into the attack also revealed fascinating detail. The truck containing the bomb was loaded with its huge payload of explosives in Northern Ireland, then driven over to mainland Britain just two days before the attack on a regular ferry service from Larne to Stranraer in Scotland. The IRA attack team had then driven it about 500 miles along Britain's motorway network to London where it was taken to a yard rented by the terrorists in Barking, about five miles from the Docklands development. There it was fitted with a cleverly constructed 'timer power unit' (TPU) and a 'mercury tilt' anti-personnel device, which meant any attempt to defuse the weapon would have resulted in the whole thing blowing up immediately, taking any bomb disposal specialists and unwitting members of the public with it.

When the bomb was delivered to the Docklands, the operator merely had to flick a switch to set the two-hour timing device running. As well as the enormous damage to the prestige target, it was another demonstration of how technically proficient and sophisticated the IRA had become by the 1990s.

CHAPTER NINETEEN

After the Docklands bombing, political efforts in the UK, in the Republic of Ireland and internationally, particularly in the USA, were stepped up to bring about a lasting end to the 30 years of murder and destruction in Northern Ireland and beyond. The Troubles, an expression I always thought completely diminished the awful tragedy of Northern Ireland, which had cost more than 3,000 lives and caused life-changing injury, misery and financial ruin to many thousands more, looked like they were finally coming to an end.

By 1998 I thought the activities of various Irish terrorist groups, which had been a huge contributor to my professional life for so many years, were gone. How wrong I was. There are some things, often quite small and insignificant in themselves, which stay in your mind forever. In the world I inhabited professionally Saturday was the only day of the week I could be sure not to be bothered by work or calls from my office. And so it was, Saturday August 15, 1998, I was at my home in the suburbs. In the afternoon I decided to clean my car, a company Ford, which was a rare enough event in itself.

I had just finished the outside and was running a cloth over the dusty interior surfaces. The new football season had just started. I am a keen football fan, so as I cleaned, I had the radio on, tuned to BBC Radio Five Live. I was listening to the scores as they came in.

It was getting close to half-time when the sports coverage was interrupted by an urgent news bulletin. There had been a huge explosion in the normally quiet market town of Omagh, in County Tyrone, Northern Ireland. I knew the place a little. I had spent a good deal of time in Northern Ireland in the previous 25 years. Omagh was a pleasant place. Rural, attractive, friendly.

I can't remember the exact words of the news presenter, except he said that ambulances from all over the province were on their way and it was believed there had been a large number of casualties. There was no mention of deaths. But somehow I just knew what was coming. Something about the presenter's voice, the words used. Something foreboding. Call it instinct, call it a sixth sense if you like, perhaps a by-product of a life spent covering big events, told me this was going to turn out to be a momentous incident.

I realised immediately that on a fine Saturday afternoon in midsummer the centre of Omagh would have been thronging with shoppers and visitors. I tried to call my boss, Eugene Duffy, at his home in south London but got no reply. I decided to make an executive decision. I would leave immediately for Northern Ireland. I lived only a 40 minute drive from Stansted Airport. One of our photographers, Arnie Slater, I knew also lived close to Stansted. I called him, and he picked up. He'd heard the news. He agreed with my rapid assessment, we needed to get to the airport, get into Ireland, any airport in Ireland, as fast as possible.

I grabbed my pre-packed overnight bag, headed for the airport and 90 minutes later we met in the terminal at Stansted. We couldn't get on a plane to Belfast, they were all booked, but we managed to get two seats on one bound for Dublin. We made it onto the flight with seconds to spare. At Dublin we hired a car and started heading north as fast as we could. Arnie drove. I connected by phone with Eugene. He said: "Can you get to Ireland tonight?"

I said: "I am already there, and I've got Arnie Slater with me. We are heading for Omagh."

Eugene was his usual understated self: "Good lads," he said.

We arrived in Omagh at about 9pm. The centre of the town had been sealed off by the police and British army. All the side streets were deserted, everything eerily quiet. The death toll was rising and would reach 29 by the end of the week, including two pregnant women, one who was carrying twins. Their unborn babies died with them along with members of a group of Spanish tourists on holiday. Scores of people had been badly injured. Some lost limbs, some lost their eyes or their hearing.

There had been many heinous events in the previous 30 years of Northern Ireland's history, but few would argue that Omagh was the worst atrocity of them all. We found a small hotel on the edge of town where we got accommodation. It was run by a charming couple in their 60s who were clearly in shock. The woman, I do not recall her name, was crying and repeating over and over: "Who would do such a thing to the innocent people of this quiet wee town?" The palpable shock and international revulsion at the attack was amplified because after decades of grinding violence, earlier in 1998 the IRA had agreed to a ceasefire and at Easter the landmark 'Good Friday Agreement' was signed, signalling what most had believed was a final end to violence in the region.

In the morning, via various sources, including our own Ireland-based staff, who were arriving from both Belfast and Dublin, we began to piece together the events of the previous day. Although the Provisional IRA had agreed a halt to violence, a hardline break-away group calling themselves 'The Real IRA', appeared to be behind the attack.

Coded warnings had been given, but in a pattern of events we had seen many times before, the original information was inaccurate. In a series of coded phone calls from a public call box in South Armagh, close to the border with the Republic of Ireland, the target for the attack had been declared as the Omagh Courthouse. But when the car packed with 500lb of fertiliser based explosives blew up, it was parked in Market Street, in the very heart of the town, over 200 metres from the courthouse. The police, who were trying to move people to safety had inadvertently, based on the information they had been given, moved people away from the Courthouse area into the centre of town where the bomb car was actually parked.

In the wake of the attack there was speculation that those responsible had cynically and deliberately given false information about the location of the bomb in order to maximise casualties. Arnie and I were joined by a former colleague from London, Ted Oliver. Ted, a Northern Irishman by birth, was a brilliant reporter, had spent many years on Fleet Street, several of them at the *Daily Mirror* where we had become very good friends. He had recently settled back in his native land and was living in Bangor, in County Down. Ted was a very well connected man in Belfast and across Ireland. He had some news for us.

Word was, the man behind the bombing was an extremely well-known IRA man called Michael McKevitt, who had refused to fall in line with his confederates in the Provisionals when they had agreed to sign a peace treaty with the British government.

McKevitt, a man in his 40s, was an ultra hardline Republican who had taken part in scores of bombings and shootings, and planned many more. Ted said McKevitt was living in Dundalk, a town on the east coast of the Republic of Ireland, in County Louth. He had his home address. It was about an hour's drive away.

We spoke to our London office and were told: "Great. Go there now. Confront him if you can. Ask him if he did it."

It was as unvarnished as that. Knock on the door of a hardened killer and ask him if he has just killed 29 more, including women and children. So we did. Ted and Arnie and I got in my hired Mondeo and drove the 40 or so miles south over the border to Dundalk. We found McKevitt's house. It was in a pleasant, well-kept cul-de-sac in a nice part of the town. I was surprised. Over the years I had been to the worst of the IRA's enclaves in the North. The Creggan and Bogside estates in Derry, the Divis Flats and the Ballymurphy in Belfast were no go areas for outsiders, patrolled and guarded by IRA men in black balaclava hoods carrying pistols and assault rifles. They were forbidding grey places with barricades and burned out cars where it always seemed cold and rainy when I had ventured close. McKevitt's street was not like that.

In fact it was strangely reassuring to see his front garden, lined with carefully tended floral borders, rose bushes and shrubs. There were hanging baskets full of blooms around his front door. Small children, the girls in summer frocks, a boy in a replica Manchester United red shirt, played on bikes outside his front gate. It all seemed so incongruous.

We knocked. I decided to let Ted do the talking. A balding man wearing a 'Bisto' cooking apron to cover his neatly pressed shirt, opened the door. He was holding a tea towel and a dinner plate in one hand and had obviously been doing the washing up after Sunday lunch. Just like any person suspected of being a terrorist mass murderer, I thought to myself. Ted was non confrontational, but forthright. "Are you Michael McKevitt?" he asked politely.

"Yes, I am," said the man. "And who might you be?"

Ted introduced us as "Journalists. Correspondents from the *Daily Mirror*, from Belfast and London."

McKevitt asked for ID. We showed our laminated press cards. Ted got his pitch in without breaking stride: "Michael. I have to put it to you. There are people saying you were the person behind or involved in yesterday's attack in Omagh. Were you?"

I was on my guard, expecting an explosion of anger, maybe even violence. I thought it possible other IRA supporters might start pouring out of neighbouring houses like soldier ants coming to attack us. I was relieved when out of the corner of my eye I saw a marked Garda Síochána patrol car cruise by, turn around the circle at the end of the cul-de-sac, and come back slowly past us. McKevitt saw it too.

The cops had obviously been told to keep an eye on McKevitt on this day. Perhaps someone may try to kill him. The rest of the street remained sunny and quiet. McKevitt thought for a moment. Then said: "Who is saying that?"

I chipped in. "Various people we know. In Belfast, Dublin and London." McKevitt looked me up and down and said: "It says 'Crime Correspondent' on your ID. So I suppose the people saying these things are your friends in the Royal Ulster Constabulary no doubt."

I could feel the atmosphere grow tense. Then he said: "I think it's best you speak to my solicitor" and he mentioned the name of a well-known Republican legal representative based in Dublin. "Now I'll thank you to leave my doorstep and not come back." He shut the door firmly on us.

So we left. Back in my car I said to Ted: "I didn't expect him to be talkative. But you put it to him that he was behind the bombing, and he didn't deny it. We should emphasise that when we write our piece." Ted agreed. We decided to head back to Omagh. About half a mile from McKevitt's house we passed the Garda car parked at the side of the road. As we did, it fell in trail with us. I looked in my driver's mirror and told Ted the police were right behind.

"First chance you get, pull over somewhere. Let's see what they do," said Ted. After driving a short distance I spotted a lay-by, and pulled into the side of the road. Sure enough, The Garda car pulled up in front of us, then backed up tight to our vehicle, to make sure we couldn't swerve away easily.

To show peaceful intent, I switched off the engine, and Ted and I got out to greet the officers as they got out of their car. The two constables appeared to be experienced men.

"Hello gentlemen. What's your business here in Dundalk? What have you been doing in our town?" asked one of them.

I smiled in a friendly manner and said: "We are reporters from the *Daily Mirror*. And I think you know what we've been doing because we saw you drive past when we were at McKevitt's house."

The two cops smiled: "Yes, that's right. Can I ask you what you wanted with him today?" asked the second officer.

Ted replied: "We were asking him if he was involved in the terrible events in Omagh yesterday afternoon."

The cop looked thoughtful and asked: "And what did he have to say about that?"

Ted replied: "Well, he didn't say he was. But on the other hand, we gave him the chance to deny it, and he didn't do that either."

The cops nodded thoughtfully. The first cop who had asked what we were up to, said to me: "So, what was your impression of the man? What did you think of him?"

I was slightly thrown. It obviously wasn't a standard line of questioning. So I said: "He lives in a nicer place than I expected. Lots of well-tended flower beds, hanging baskets, neatly trimmed lawn. In what seems to be a respectable neighbourhood."

The first cop then said, without irony: "Ah yes. Micky loves his garden alright. Spends a lot of time and money on it."

There was a brief silence and then the other cop said: "Well, think about it. No wonder he has a nice garden. He probably gets a lot of free fertiliser." It was an unexpected remark. Gallows humour. And we all laughed. Because we all knew the major constituent part of the explosives which had devastated Omagh were made from fertiliser.

The Garda waved us off but before we left the senior of the two turned to me and asked: "Will you be going to try and talk to McKevitt again while you are here?" I replied it was quite likely.

The cop then said: "He's a dangerous man. If you do go back, call us first. We'll cover your arse, make sure nothing happens to you." I could sense there was no love lost between the Dundalk Gardaí and a man like Michael McKevitt.

We drove back to Omagh, in time to catch a press conference at the local police HQ where the RUC updated us on casualties and what they knew so far. There was some interesting information. The car used to carry the bomb was a red Vauxhall which had been stolen in Carrickmacross, in County Monaghan, in the Republic of Ireland, two days before the incident.

When it was stolen it had Republic of Ireland registration plates from County Donegal. But when it was driven to Omagh it had been fitted with a set of false Northern Ireland plates.

This information hit me with a jolt. I had come to know the little market town of Carrickmacross very well. Throughout my life I had been a keen fisherman and from the late 1970s through to the early 1990s I had visited the town to fish the lakes around it over 20 times. I had many friends there and most evenings I drank with them in the 20 or so pubs and bars in the town, which had a population of less than 4,000 people.

Over the years I had taken the time to make a few friends in the police forces on both sides of the Irish border. I made some phone calls. One was to a Garda detective who was well-informed about who was who in the IRA living around the border area. We met in a quiet bar in the countryside. He told me: "Did you hear about the practice explosion?" I had not. Nor had any other journalist I knew of.

"It was about two weeks ago. A few days before the Omagh incident. It was a big one, about the same size as the Omagh bomb. It was way up in the Cooley Mountains, in the middle of nowhere. It left a fucking enormous crater. It was about ten yards on the Northern Ireland side of the border, but it was triggered remotely from our side. The border there is just a sheep fence. Some of our people went up there to have a close look at it. The British army sent some people too. They had to be careful because it could have been a trap with the IRA ambushing them from the Republic side of the border where they are not allowed to go after them, so we gave them covering protection from our side."

He said it could only be reached by a long hike up what he described as cattle trails but said he had a colleague who knew exactly where it was, and I arranged to meet him. He pulled out an ordnance survey map and marked it with a ballpoint pen. He said: "If you go here, and park here," marking little circles on the map with his pen, "you will see the start of the trail. From the road it's a walk of about a mile. You will need good boots, it's wet, steep, and boggy. If you do go up there, be careful. There are spies everywhere in the countryside. Make sure you've got your press ID on you, in case they send someone to check you out, to make sure you aren't undercover police or army."

Apart from lilting birdsong from on high there was no sound except the rush of the wind. It was impossible to tell if we were in the Republic of Ireland or Northern Ireland. The border here seemed to be notional only. Then I noticed something on the trail. It was a lump of black slate, about the size of a paving slab, and it looked out of place. Then another and another and clods of brown peaty earth with fresh grass still growing from them. I realised these were chunks of peat and rock blown 100 yards or more by a large explosion.

And then, off to the left on the other side of the rickety wire sheep fence we saw it. A huge hole in the ground. It was probably 30 yards in diameter and about 10ft deep. I estimated that three or four tons of rock and soil had been blown out by a huge blast. You could see from the sides of the crater it was fresh, just days old. Arnie persuaded me to get down into the crater so he could use me as a human yardstick to put things in perspective. Once in the bottom I could not see over the rim. It was hard climbing in and even harder getting back out.

Back on the top of the rim I noticed a pair of wires snaking back out of the hole and disappearing for about 100 yards over the brow of a small hill. From what I had learned about IRA weaponry over the years I realised these were command wires which would have been connected to a manually operated trigger, probably using a car battery. This bomb had been different in that respect from the Omagh device which had been set off using a timer. Then we started off back down the sheep trail and the long walk back to our car.

We had been walking for about 15 minutes when the hillside silence was broken by the sound of motorcycle engines from ahead and below. The sound got louder quickly and soon three young men on powerful mud spattered scramble bikes came into view. They roared and bounced up to us, never throttling back until they were virtually on us.

One came past and slewed his bike across the trail to the rear of us. The other two blocked our path. I had no doubt who they were. These were the youth wing of the 'Real IRA' the next generation of Republican killers.

As the Irish cop had warned: "There are spies everywhere" and in a staunchly Republican area like County Louth, people noticed everything, especially strangers doing unusual things. I decided to stay as calm as I could. We weren't cops, nor undercover army.

The first rider spoke. He appeared cheery enough, but very direct: "Hullo, fellas. What are you doing up here?

I told him the truth. "We are journalists. We've come to look at the scene of the blast."

He nodded, then said: "Got any ID on you?" I handed him my press card. Arnie showed him his. The rider looked at them carefully, front and back. One of his mates was leaning forward in his saddle paying a great deal of interest to Arnie's very expensive Canon camera and special lens. For a moment I wondered if we were going to be beaten up and robbed.

"*Daily Mirror*?" said the rider's spokesman. "Is that the one owned by that Murdoch fella?" I explained that was "the other lot", our arch rivals *The Sun*. He may well have been testing me to see if I was genuine.

He handed me back my card and said: "So, what did you think? Were you impressed? It's a fucking big hole, isn't it?" I was feeling more relaxed now. There was no real reason to think they would do us any harm.

"Yes," I said. "I got down inside it," and I pointed to the mud on my trousers and boots. "It's very deep."

The motorcycle jockey looked me up and down and said: "Aye. It's a big one alright." I thought about asking him if he knew who had done it, or why. But I knew that would be unwise. "Where are you off to now?" he asked.

"Back to our hotel," I said.

His mate, who hadn't spoken before, said: "The Ballymascanlon. That's very posh. Your boss must be paying the bill." If I had any doubt who these young guns were, they had dissipated, for there were a dozen nice hotels in the area, but they knew exactly where we were lodged. They probably already knew exactly who we were before they met us. Message received.

I said: "You fellas go easy now. See ya."

Trail biker one winked at me and said: "You go carefully now, Mr. Edwards." They revved their engines and sped off the way they had come.

I looked at Arnie: "The real IRA," I said. "Full of Irish charm."

"Yes," said Arnie. "I wonder if they smile at you like that before they shoot you in the head."

I filed my story and Arnie wired his pictures and the following day we returned to London. We had ended up with about a dozen *Mirror* journalists on the Omagh story, reporters, photographers and feature writers. We provided great material and the paper presented it beautifully – thoughtfully and sensitively and at the next Press Awards, the newspaper industry's 'Oscars', we won 'Reporting Team of the Year' for our efforts.

TERROR ON THE STREETS

CHAPTER TWENTY

The IRA were not the only ones to utilise explosives. In December 1994 there was a strange and bizarre sequence of events that caught my attention. A series of small bombs, packaged in plastic video cassette boxes, were sent to the managers of six branches of Barclays Bank in various parts of West London.

The weapons were not sophisticated, but showed the maker had some engineering skills. They contained either a shotgun cartridge or an obsolete NATO issue 7.62mm rifle bullet which would be fired by a spring loaded nail, acting as a firing pin, when the package was opened. All the packages were opened on arrival by bank staff. Four of them had failed to detonate, but at two high street branches, in Hampstead and Ladbroke Grove, they had gone off and one member of staff was wounded in the eye by a piece of shrapnel.

Over the previous two decades I had built up a good knowledge of how terrorist bombs and anti-handling devices worked thanks to the scores of IRA incidents I had covered. From what I could glean from contacts, these were not in the same league of sophistication. But potentially, they were still deadly.

What was going on here? What was the sender's motive? The

packages contained no threats or demands or any words which explained what was driving the bomber. There were two other small oddities about the bomb packages. Labels stuck on the cassettes bore black and white images of men wearing hats and sunglasses in a pose reminiscent of the classic Blues Brothers movie poster of the time. They bore the words 'Welcome to the Mardi Gra Experience'. What did that mean? No one I spoke to among my contacts seemed to have any idea, And 'Mardi Gra' was spelled incorrectly. It should have had an 's' on the end of 'Gra'. Was that a deliberate mistake? Or was the sender simply illiterate?

At the time I had several Scotland Yard friends who had become very knowledgeable about crimes which fell under the heading of extortion and blackmail. Some of them had worked on the case of Rodney Whitchelo, the rogue Yard detective who had used his knowledge of the topic to try and extort money from nationally famous food companies by planting poisoned baby food and pet products on supermarket shelves in the 1980s.

Whitchelo was eventually caught and jailed, but there was a belief among certain detectives that there was a growing, unreported, problem with product contamination type extortion threats. The private view, as told to me several times in the 1990s, was that supermarkets, where most of the security directors were former senior Scotland Yard staff, had recently secretly paid off blackmailers in some circumstances.

One officer even told me where to look if I wanted to see blackmail negotiations in progress. He said: "Check the personal columns of the Saturday editions of the *Daily Telegraph* or *Times*. If you see any strangely worded messages there, chances are it will be a targeted company using that channel to communicate with blackmailers."

I was also told the key to whether a firm paid or not was in the amount of money demanded. As one contact told me at the time: "If the blackmailer asks for any sum under £100,000, the big brands and supermarkets will likely pay rather than face all the problems associated with having to take certain products out of circulation, issue warnings to the public, or risk the matter getting into the media and damaging business.

"But if it is £1M or more, at the level where major shareholders have to be told because it will affect annual profits, they will call in the police."

This was chilling stuff. It was presented to me as theoretical, but I knew, because of the positions held by those telling me these things, it must be true. So with this type of confidential background briefing in mind, I once again opened the conversation with certain people in the police and the security services when the first wave of 'Mardis Gra' attacks were targeted at Barclays, because I was forming a strong hunch this was probably an extortion plot.

After the first attacks there was a lull. Had the bomber been frightened off by something? Had he changed his mind and gone away? By then, I was following my friend's advice and buying the Saturday editions of the broadsheet newspapers, and scanning the personal adverts columns. And sure enough, one Saturday in the summer of 1995, I spotted it. A message in the personal ad section of the *Telegraph* which read: "Mardine Graham. We do not understand. We need more time. Please call." The advert finished with a phone number with a Northampton STD code.

It was a moment of clarity and revelation. 'Mardine Graham' was clearly an expansion of the name 'Mardis Gra'. And Northampton, I knew, was where the headquarters of the credit card giant

Barclaycard was situated. The words used in the message were classic extortion negotiation language. It was an invitation by Barclays, no doubt being carefully steered by Scotland Yard, for 'Mardine Graham' to make direct contact and talk.

My heart was racing as I called one of my police friends at his home. I read him the text of the ad. There was silence, then he said: "Meet me tonight, but tell no one." I didn't need to tell my friend that all of this was confidential as he told me how 'Mardis Gra' was attempting to extort a huge sum of money from the Barclays organisation. Of course, they had been warned by the blackmailer not to call the police. So I could not breathe a word to anyone, not even my own bosses.

For a few months the wave of bombs began again and intensified. Some went through the post to other branches of Barclays. Others went to random businesses, including the best known supermarket chains. My police contacts kept me abreast of events. They were trying to lure 'Mardine Graham' into a trap, but he was cautious and canny. I knew I wasn't being told everything. In the shadows, I realised there had to be some sort of conversation going on between Barclays, guided by the police, and the extortionist.

Then as mysteriously as they had begun, in the spring of 1996, the bombs in the post stopped. But then began a sequence of events that rank among the strangest in my professional career. I was very friendly with my opposite number at the *Daily Mail*, Peter Rose, who was their Crime Correspondent. Peter, who died suddenly and prematurely in 2010, was a rival but he was also a good friend. One day in the spring of 1996, I arranged to travel over to Kensington where he was based, to meet him for a lunchtime drink.

But just before I was going to leave my office in Canary Wharf, he called to say the meeting was off.

He explained he had an important officer from Scotland Yard coming to see him because the paper had received a strange letter in which the writer described planting bombs. The correspondent mentioned Barclays and even included a hand drawn diagram of one of his proposed bombs.

"What do you think, Pete?" I said. He was dismissive and said he thought it was the work of a nutcase but had felt obliged to tell the police who were now on their way. I asked if the letter bore any kind of signature.

"Yes," said Peter. "It's from someone calling himself 'Mardine Graham'." I almost leapt out of my chair. "Stay right where you are Peter," I said. "I am on my way to you right now. We need to talk, this is very important. Copy the letter before you give it to the cops. It's vital we speak, right now."

I ran downstairs to the cab rank outside our building and hailed a taxi to take me to Kensington. I met Peter in a bar close to his office. Because I trusted him completely I told him what I knew. He was flabbergasted. He knew nothing of the background.

"Look, Peter," I said, "if these were ordinary circumstances we would keep the details quiet forever. We couldn't publish and be responsible for tipping off the blackmailer with the unintended consequences which might result.

"But, by writing to you, the extortionist has himself changed the game. He is generating his own publicity. He will be expecting something in the papers now, and if he doesn't get it, what might happen next? If he is smart he may conclude the police are involved, and follow up with some new and even deadlier attack.

He could send a letter to the BBC, the Press Association, anyone to try and force a response. Whoever this person is, he has now put the ball in our court."

Peter agreed. We took the bull by the horns. Our next move was to make phone calls to the head of Public Affairs at Scotland Yard and to high level contacts I knew already had knowledge of what was going on. We both pointed out we were now in an invidious position. In normal circumstances we would have 'kept the faith' and stayed quiet. But the game had changed. Bombs were still going out, and some were exploding. Some people had been injured, others had very lucky escapes. It was impossible to predict how this might end.

The next day we found ourselves in the boardroom at Scotland Yard in a meeting with a number of very important players, including the head of the operation to catch the bomber, the top extortion specialists, and the head of 'SO11', the criminal intelligence wing.

I wasn't sure which way the meeting would go. These were all people who knew me and Peter well and knew our good reputations, but there was an undeniable feeling of tension in the room. They knew we understood the rules of the game and the meeting opened with them asking us to continue the 'radio silence' around this delicate and potentially life-threatening matter. But we explained how, from our perspective, it was 'Mardine Graham' who had changed the rules by writing to a national paper.

The police were still having difficulty with our position. They wanted the blackout to stay. Then a thought struck me. I said: "This person is trying to create publicity designed to force your hand. He doesn't understand the rules which usually bind us in these matters. I fully understand your problem, and your point of view. But consider this: you have knowledge of what this is all about, and the *Daily Mirror* and the *Daily Mail* now have full knowledge of what this is about. If none of us act, and because we have not acted, the bombs start being sent again, then surely we will all be culpable if the next bomb results in serious injury or death."

There was a long silence as my words seemed to hang in the air. Then a very senior detective nodded and said: "I had not considered it in that light. Now I think you are right. The blackmailer has taken control of the narrative. I think it is time the public, who are the ones at risk, know what's been going on."

So Peter and I returned to our respective offices and briefed our bosses. I wrote the next morning's front page 'splash' and two more pieces for a detailed spread inside. Even so, I did not share then with the *Mirror* readers everything I now knew about what was going on behind the scenes. Unbeknown to us, 'Mardine Graham' however, was not knocked out of his stride.

For a long period he did go quiet. Was it possible the publicity had caused his nerve to fail? To retreat and never come back? But after a hiatus of about 19 months, he gave us his reply. He sent out a fresh wave of booby trap bombs. But now the target had changed and the bombs were now being sent to branches of Sainsbury's supermarket. His tactics had also changed. Some of the bombs were being left in the firm's distinctive orange supermarket bags packed with grocery items in trolley racks or left at bus stops, as if by forgetful shoppers, in the hope that other customers would pick them up, open the strange package within, and be wounded by the ensuing blast. Or worse.

And it worked. At one branch in south London a shopper nearly lost a leg when she opened a package from an abandoned bag and was hit in the thigh by shotgun pellets. I could report the individual incidents, but not what was going on in the background which was a complex police plan to catch the dangerous culprit.

'Mardine Graham' was now asking for £10,000 a day from Barclays and Sainsbury's to stop attacking them. But the problem for an extortioner, in every case, is how to get their hands on the money without getting caught. The problem for the police trying to unmask and arrest the perpetrators in an extortion case is how to set up a workable scheme to provide some money, as it usually represents the only realistic way of catching them.

One of the modern ways which had been tried, not just in Britain but in the USA particularly, was to get the target organisation to provide the blackmailer with a bank card with which to withdraw money placed into a special account and accessed by a special PIN number. The devious and crooked policeman Rodney Whitchelo had used this technique in the 1980s during his campaign and had been successful at first, working on the premise that there were not enough police officers in the entire country to cover every cash machine.

But although he started by roaming far and wide from his home in Essex, Whitchelo eventually got lazy and started to reduce the distance he was prepared to travel. In the end an analysis of the pattern of his withdrawals enabled Scotland Yard to cover a limited number of ATMs in London and the Home Counties and he fell into the trap and was caught.

'Mardine Graham' made several proposals to Barclaycard to provide cards which were rejected as impractical or impossible to execute. Eventually a plan was agreed. A sum of money would be put in an account with an agreed PIN number. At the suggestion of

'Mardine Graham' a number of plastic 'rewards' cards would be given away with an edition of a well known gardening magazine which was on the shelves of every newsagent in the country every month. The reward cards would be taped to the front cover of each magazine on one agreed month – 25,000 copies in all – and be distributed to newsagents.

In reality, each of these cards would secretly be a real cash card which only the holder of the secret PIN number could use anywhere to take money from any ATM. It meant the blackmailer only had to buy a copy of the magazine, in any newsagent, from Cornwall to the Scottish Highlands, to be in possession of a means to get the money. This was a massively difficult operation for the police to set up, but they managed it.

'Mardine Graham' randomly purchased one of the gardening magazines and started withdrawing £500 per day, using cash-points apparently chosen at random. But the police had set up a technical operation whereby they could track the withdrawals from every cash dispenser in the country.

And like bent cop Whitchelo, 'Mardine Graham' eventually slipped up and fell into the trap. Late one evening in April 1998 he made a withdrawal from a bank in Whitton, near Twickenham. When he put in the special PIN number into the keypad, an alarm rang on a computer in the Control Room at Scotland Yard which pinpointed the bank. As part of the operation, hundreds of plain clothes police in unmarked cars were patrolling London and the south east of England. One team were only a few yards from the bank when they received an alert the man they had been hunting for four years was at the cashpoint and in the act of trying to withdraw money.

The cops swooped and arrested 60-year-old Edgar Pearce as he stuffed a wedge of new £20 notes into his pocket, together with the gardening magazine reward card. I was driving to my office the next morning when I received a call from a colleague who told me: "They've arrested the Mardis Gra bomber."

I was amazed. "Where did you hear that?" I asked. The woman told me she had been dating an ex-Marine Commando who had been renting a room in a house in Chiswick from a man called Ed Pearce. Her boyfriend had called her to say he'd just been released by the police who had broken down his front door and arrested him at 3am that morning as a suspected accomplice in the extortion plot.

The former marine was completely innocent and allowed to go within a few hours. I called the man now in charge of the case, Detective Superintendent Jeff Rees at his office in Scotland Yard and when he answered I said: "You must be a happy man. I understand you've nicked the Mardi Gra bomber." Rees, who was originally from South Wales and thus known affectionately to all as 'Rees the Police', laughed and said "You must have psychic powers!"

So he wouldn't worry about unauthorised leaks, I told him how I knew. He said: "I'm a detective and I don't believe in coincidence, but that's the best one I've ever come across." It definitely was.

In the next few hours I learned that when the police raided Pearce's home in Chiswick, West London they uncovered an entire bomb making factory. The contents included six completed butane gas bombs, six pipe bombs under construction, a number of homemade trigger devices, hundreds of shotgun cartridges, 50 rounds of army issue rifle ammunition, a loaded revolver, crossbows, and a stack of video cassette boxes.

After more than two years of having to hold off, I was able to tell the whole story in the pages of the *Daily Mirror*.

When it was tallied up, Edgar Pearce, with some help from his brother Ron, had sent out 32 bombs in his four year campaign.

He was charged with attempting to blackmail Barclays and Sainsbury's, threats to kill, explosives and firearm crimes. He was jailed the following year for a total of 224 years.

CHAPTER TWENTY-ONE

The day the World Trade Centre in New York was brought down by Al Qaeda terrorists using hijacked jet liners I was in an Italian restaurant near Waterloo station, in London, with an old friend of mine who was a Scotland Yard detective. We had just finished lunch and were about to settle the bill when he received a text message from his son. It merely said: "Have you heard the news, Dad?"

Alan, whose son was an avid Chelsea fan, read the message out to me and said whimsically: "I expect Chelsea have sacked their manager Claudio Ranieri." We both laughed, then left the restaurant and went in different directions. I went into the station and down the escalators to the Jubilee Line for the five stop hop back to my office at Canary Wharf, which normally took about 10 or 12 minutes. Everything seemed normal.

The deep escalators at Canary Wharf carried me up to a pedestrian square lined with shops and bars and then to a flight of wide stairs leading up to the road outside Canada Tower. As I exited the tube station I was met by what looked like a human torrent of people coming towards me down the stairs. Hundreds of women and men were streaming away from the complex.

I seemed to be the only one going in the other direction. Something was up. This was the middle of the day, not the evening rush hour. My assumption, based on previous incidents I'd witnessed was it was a bomb scare. I entered the building, used my electronic pass to clear the security barriers and took the express lift to the newsroom.

As usual, there were probably about 100 people working in our huge open news HQ, which spanned two sides of the building facing south and west. Across the newsroom we had six or seven big screen TVs placed strategically, either on ceiling mounts or on spare desks. Large groups of people were gathered round some of them which was unusual. What was going on?

My eyes were drawn to the nearest showing the Manhattan skyline and a huge pall of smoke streaming from one of the World Trade Centre towers. As I approached the newsdesk one of our news executives shouted to me. "A plane has hit the tower in New York. It may be terrorism. We need your input into this, right away." The office had been trying to call me, but I had been incommunicado deep underground. I got to my desk. Several colleagues were gathered round the nearest TV.

I was taking my jacket off when there was an audible gasp from some of my colleagues as, live in real time, a second Boeing ploughed into the other tower in a huge explosion of orange flame. Now we knew for sure it was not an accident, this was extreme terrorism. I knew instinctively I would be part of another huge team effort. Although it was America which was under attack, my role would be to write about the very real security implications for the UK.

I started calling friends I had in Counter-Terrorism policing. No one was picking up. Were they all transfixed in front of TV screens as we were? I noticed signs of nervousness with some of my colleagues. Here we were, halfway up one of the latest and most symbolic landmark buildings in London.

If the terrorists had actually hijacked four passenger jets in America, were they also simultaneously doing the same in Europe?

What might happen next? The anxiety for some was made worse by the fact that Canary Wharf, which stood in a bend in the River Thames at the north end of the Isle of Dogs, was right alongside one of the most frequently used flightpaths into Heathrow Airport.

Every day, a procession of huge Boeings and Airbus airliners flew past our windows, less than a mile distant and almost at eyeball level with the pilots as they descended the last 15 miles along the River Thames corridor.

To make the fear worse, we were only three miles from the end of the runway of the busy City Airport further out in East London. Jets departing to the west from the City Airport appeared to head directly for us as they climbed before veering off to safely pass us.

Our executive team picked up on the worries showing in some of the staff and, as with the Canary Wharf bomb seven years before, told all non-essential staff they could evacuate if they wished. I don't remember anyone leaving. My reporting role that day and evening was largely peripheral. Our staff reporters in the USA did a phenomenal job. In the aftermath of New York it was clear everything had changed. Now everyone was asking, could it happen here?

For many months I had been telling colleagues at the *Mirror* it not only could, but it would. Because this was the message I was getting from the highest levels in British policing. I was told over and again, 'It's not a question of if, it's when'. So after September 2001, when I sat down either informally, or formally with top people in Counter-Terrorism, instead of the IRA, the talk was now about a mysterious Saudi-born individual called Usama Bin Laden – better known these days as Osama – and an organisation called Al Qaeda.

His name cropped up so often my contacts started referring to him with the short form 'UBL' and the organisation he headed simply as 'AQ'. Except, I was warned, it wasn't an organisation as such. AQ was an umbrella term for a number of allied organisations in Pakistan, in Afghanistan, in Iran, Iraq, and Syria, who followed a doctrine.

One of my closest contacts described it to me as: "Not so much an organisation in the usual sense of the word, more of a collective state of mind." And I was assured, AQ-inspired people were here in the UK, right now. In the suburbs of Birmingham, Bradford, Manchester, Luton and London. There was evidence emerging of plotting by jihadist groups and fundraising. My contact pointed to the fact that there had recently been an upsurge in 'crash for cash' traffic accidents on the M1 motorway, which went directly past Luton, and said there was intelligence to say much of the money being swindled from insurers by this means was going to fund Al Qaeda and allied organisations. I had another contact, an ex-policeman turned insurance loss adjuster, who told me he had been temporarily held hostage and threatened with violence while investigating insurance fraud in Luton and had reported the episode to the Special Branch because he suspected he had been dealing with jihadists.

I had written and attempted to get published stories on the subject over the previous year or so, but it was often hard for specialist reporters like me to get our stories published, especially if they were about some theoretical rather than demonstrable threat to national security. Contacts I had in the police and MI5 were briefing me, and a few like me, that their counterparts in America were saying it was only a matter of time before something big happened in the UK.

The ideal example came nine months prior to the New York attacks. I had a prize contact in the field of counter-terrorism but he did not work for Scotland Yard or the British secret services. Yves was a French secret service agent who worked for the DGSE (Direction Generale de la Securite Exterieure), the French equivalent of the CIA.

Yves was based in London where he was often called on to liaise with M15 and MI6, because terrorism, especially that emanating from the Middle East, was a global issue. We were introduced sometime in 1998 by a mutual friend who worked for Scotland Yard's Special Branch.

I have no doubt Yves saw me as someone he might be able to use, as well as me seeing him as someone who might be useful. We used to meet sometimes for coffee or beer in Soho. He was full of interesting takes on world events, and how things might impact the world going forward, but at first there was nothing very useful.

Then, one day at the end of 2000, the *Daily Mail* ran a story about an Afghan asylum seeker, an Imam with 12 children, who had been given a council house in Birmingham and was receiving hundreds of pounds a week in benefits. It was a fairly typical *Daily Mail* story.

But a couple of days later I got a call from Yves asking to meet me. He pushed a copy of the *Daily Mail* story in front of me, asked if I had read it, and then said: "They have missed the most important part of the story. This man is not merely a social security scrounger. He is an international terrorist." Now he really had my attention.

He explained how the man was not an Afghan, he was an Algerian and a leading member of the Algerian terrorist organisation, the GIA, who had been wreaking havoc in their home country for several years. A ferocious civil war had been raging in Algeria, a former French colony, for most of the 1990s. There had been gruesome atrocities and the death toll was estimated at over 100,000. I could see why the French were so interested.

The Algerian war of independence in the 1950s and 1960s had wreaked terrible violence, which had been inflicted on French citizens and soldiers and involved terror attacks, mainly in Paris. No doubt they were concerned about a new terror campaign on the French mainland.

Yves added that the name given to the man was not his true identity, but one of several aliases he used. Then as a piece de resistance, he produced a copy of a document that had clearly come from French secret service files. It listed the man's real identity, the details of the Saudia Airlines flight he had arrived on earlier in the year at Gatwick from Jeddah, the identities of two family members he had travelled with, plus the details of the forged passports they had been using, including photocopies of the documents showing serial numbers and other bogus details.

The report also contained a summary of why the French believed this man was now in England. It was for 'liaison' between the Algerian-based GIA and Al Qaeda representatives resident in the UK. The conclusion was that this was an early sign of the creation of an international network of Islamist terrorists.

I had no doubt whatsoever this information was true, I knew Yves was the real deal. Details of false passports, especially photocopies of original documents, were first class proof. I told Yves his information was for us, dynamite. But I would still have to 'stand up' the story, especially when it came to satisfying the *Mirror's* in-house legal team. "Not a problem," said Yves. "Go to the Algerian Embassy here in London. They will confirm everything."

Then he wrote a name down on a piece of paper and said: "Go and see this man. He will help you." I called the man Yves had suggested. He invited me to the Consulate which was then in Holland Park in West London. I was shown into a conference room. There then followed a strange series of meetings at which I was introduced to the Ambassador, then to other dignitaries, and their Head of Security in London.

I told them why I wanted to see them. They did not seem too keen to confirm anything, only to know how it was that I had this information. I, of course, could not reveal that. But from their reactions, I could tell my information was clearly correct.

Interestingly, when I suggested, if the information was wrong they could say so, they didn't deny it. The meeting ended with them refusing to confirm or deny any part of my information. But I was asked to return in a few days. When I did I was shown into a small room where a diplomat I had not met before pulled a cardboard file from a cabinet and showed me a number of horrific pictures of victims of torture said to have been carried out by the GIA.

I was asked if I wanted to visit Algeria "to see what the GIA do". I did not. My research showed the GIA had specifically targeted journalists – 70 had been assassinated. I didn't want to be added to the list. They still didn't confirm my information that one of their most feared enemies was now living undercover in Birmingham. I could see I was caught in a sort of diplomatic game of hide and seek. A few days later I returned to the embassy for a third meeting, which was similar to the second.

I withdrew to think about what else I could do. Then I got a call from a high-ranking Algerian diplomat asking me to return once more. I was ushered into a cabinet room by several officials. This time I was told they would confirm my story, provided I made a solemn undertaking not to attribute anything I reported to them.

I had actually offered them this at the first meeting, but thought they had failed to grasp the point I was making. Back to my office I went, and I told my line managers I had this brilliant story. Most of them weren't impressed but Eugene, my head of news, showed real interest.

"The problem is, the powers that be don't really get it," he said. "They don't understand why Al Qaeda is a threat to this country, as well as a global threat." I should have known.

But eventually an opportunity opened up and my story went front page and across two pages inside. Response to it in the office was muted, but a number of my counter-terrorism contacts called to congratulate me. For over 30 years of my career before 2001, I would estimate half of my working life had been dominated by reporting terrorism. Ninety per cent of that had been driven by the politics of the island of Ireland.

But I had also been called on to report on politically-driven shootings of Israelis, Iraqis, Sri Lankans, Chechens, Turkish Kurds, Afghans, and others, in London and elsewhere in the UK.

But it was the allied invasion, first of Afghanistan post 9/11, and then of Iraq in 2003 to finally overthrow Saddam Hussein, which was to be the catalyst for Britain's biggest terrorist outrage.

CHAPTER TWENTY-TWO

In early 2003 a supposed plot to kill thousands of innocent people using the poison ricin on the London Underground was uncovered. There were raids in London, Bournemouth and Manchester, where in January a young police officer, Detective Constable Stephen Oake was horrifically stabbed to death by one suspect, during a counter-terrorism search operation.

In the end, despite a lot of media spin by the police and government sources, no real evidence of a poison plot was found. Certainly no evidence that ricin had actually been manufactured, let alone planted. At trial the cases all fell apart and many critics said the plot had been largely drummed up by the government to justify the invasion of Iraq. Whatever the truth of the matter, it would be fair to describe the overriding atmosphere at the time as highly-charged, or febrile.

In January 2004 I received an intriguing piece of information from one of my security service contacts. It was absolutely confidential and I could not act on it but, nonetheless, I was pleased to be informed. MI5 and Scotland Yard's Counter-Terrorism team had uncovered a plot to set off a series of huge homemade bombs in London.

Around a dozen suspects, all young British Muslims said to be inspired by Al Qaeda, were under round the clock surveillance. But most interesting of all, the group had acquired over half a ton of ammonium nitrate fertiliser, a key component in powerful homemade explosives. They were storing it in a storage unit they were renting near Southall, in West London.

To make sure the terrorists could not get a jump ahead of the authorities, detectives had secretly entered the lock-up in the dead of night and removed several high capacity 'Hippo' type builder's bags containing some 1,300lbs of fertiliser. Because they were still building a case against their suspects they replaced them with identical bags of a harmless material identical in appearance to ammonium nitrate granules which was described to me as 'cat litter' – and actually may well have been exactly that.

Eventually 'Operation Crevice' sprang their trap. Several men were arrested in Crawley, Luton, Ilford and elsewhere and a large biscuit tin of aluminium powder, another vital component in making the type of bomb they intended to use, was discovered. The police found evidence the group intended to target the Bluewater Shopping Centre in Kent, the Ministry of Sound nightclub in London, and several synagogues in the capital.

It wasn't until three years later in March 2007, when the trials of five of the group concluded with life prison sentences that I was able to report the whole story about how the police had actually neutralised the plot by stealing the explosives and replacing them with a harmless substitute. But by then, another group of young men had brought death and destruction to London on an unprecedented scale.

The morning of July 7, 2005 started like any other for me. In suburban Essex where I lived at the time, I got in my car just before 9am and started to drive the 15 miles to my office at Canary Wharf, a journey which normally took about 40 minutes in the rush hour.

I was listening to BBC Radio 5 news. I was a regular contributor to the station at this time and knew several of the presenters. I can't remember the time exactly, but I had only been driving for two or three minutes when a presenter broke the normal running order of the show to announce there was a problem on the London Underground which was severely disrupting services on the Circle, District, Metropolitan and Hammersmith and City lines around Aldgate.

The information said Transport for London, the body who controlled the Underground network, was describing the cause of the problem as a 'power surge'. I had grown up with railwaymen in my family and thus understood a lot about railway operations. My first thought was it must be a very big power surge indeed to knock out four busy lines simultaneously.

It may just have been instinct, but I sensed something much more serious had happened. The response from TFL didn't sound right to me somehow. I knew the London Underground rail network very well and knew all three lines shared the same tracks in some areas, Aldgate being one of them.

I remember thinking that if all four routes were stopped, it had to be something really serious. I pulled over into a lay-by and called a long time friend of mine, a detective in the British Transport Police, based in London. He answered and immediately I could tell something was up. He sounded rushed and under pressure.

"What's going on at Aldgate?" Before I had even got out the last syllable he said quickly: "It's a bomb, a big one. There may be two. Lots of casualties. I am driving there now. Call me later." And he was gone.

I called my news editor Anthony Harwood and told him what I'd just learned. He was unsure. He said: "But Transport for London are saying it's just a power surge."

"I know," I responded, "but I have just spoken to a contact who says it is a bomb. He's in a position to know. And he's sure." I understood Anthony's hesitation, he had a busy news schedule to staff already that day, but said: "Please, listen to me. Get everyone available heading for the area. If my information is right the whole network will shut down imminently. London will gridlock and we won't be able to get anyone anywhere." I was also thinking that with our HQ on the Isle of Dogs, staff heading into the office would be miles from where they needed to be and unable to get into the centre of town.

I implored him: "If I am wrong, you can always reel them back in, or redeploy them." Anthony decided to act on my advice and by the time I got to the office it was apparent there had been a major terror attack.

Three bombs had already gone off on packed tube trains, at 8.50am at Aldgate in the east on the edge of the City, a minute later at 8.51am to the west at Edgware Road and, worst of all, to the north on the Piccadilly Line near Russell Square, where the narrow and deep tunnel meant the blast was completely contained in the train, inflicting terrible damage on scores of people. News was also coming in that a fourth bomb had gone off on a double decker bus at Tavistock Square.

By now it was becoming apparent these were suicide bombs. I kept looking at the distribution of the explosions and noticing how all the routes affected had a connection to the main line terminus at St Pancras. The Circle line ran directly underneath. Two bombs had exploded on the Circle. Had two of the bombers got on at St Pancras, one travelling in either direction? And the Piccadilly ran past the same complex, underneath the closely connected Kings Cross terminus.

St Pancras was the London end of the old Midland Railway connecting to Leicester, Nottingham and Sheffield. It was also served by the intensive Thameslink commuter service from Bedford to

Brighton, and going north from St Pancras it was just 10 stops and 35 minutes to Luton. The warnings I had been given by friends in the security services that 'Luton is a hot bed of radical Islam' and that the famous motor manufacturing town now harboured many Al Qaeda supporters, kept going through my mind.

Later that evening there was a press conference at Scotland Yard. I asked police chiefs if they thought the terrorists had come in from Luton. The formal answer at that stage was they did not know. But the next day, as a result of piecing together CCTV footage it became clear the four bombers who had carried their weapons in rucksacks had indeed got on at Luton. And a car which remained uncollected at Luton station car park was found to contain another bomb.

The next day I attended another police press conference when Scotland Yard revealed CCTV images clearly showing the four bombers, with their deadly backpacks, boarding the train at Luton, getting off at St Pancras, then walking through the network of pedestrian tunnels to the Circle Line and the Piccadilly Line.

In fact, only one of the bombers lived close to Luton, about eight miles away near Leighton Buzzard, but the attackers had clearly rehearsed and planned their actions carefully in advance.

The events of that day led to the deaths of 52 people and injuries, many life-changing, to hundreds more.

Then, exactly two weeks after the first bomb attacks, on July 21, a second group of Al Qaeda inspired attackers set out to create an even more horrific wave of terror on the London Transport network. Five men set off from a base in West London, each carrying a bomb in a backpack.

Three boarded various underground lines, and a fourth planned to blow up a bus. A fifth man lost his nerve and dumped his bomb on waste land near Wormwood Scrubs prison at Shepherds Bush. At around midday the four more determined attackers attempted to simultaneously set off their bombs on the underground network at the Oval, Shepherds Bush, and Warren Street Stations and on a double decker bus in Hackney.

But this time their bomb-making skills failed them. The weapons only partially detonated, causing no casualties and little damage. For me it was a second round of frenetic work as together with about 20 colleagues we did our best to pull together all the known information and write it into a comprehensible piece of work covering nine pages of the *Daily Mirror*. Once again, it demonstrated how vulnerable we in Britain were to this kind of guerilla warfare. I went home at about midnight thinking things could not get any more extraordinary. How wrong I was.

Knowing that several suspects for the latest transport attacks were on the run in the face of an enormous police hunt, I went back to work on the morning of the July 22 early, arriving at Canary Wharf at about 8am. I knew I was going to have another full-on day, but I could not have ever anticipated what was going to happen next.

At about 9.30am, I decided to head for Scotland Yard.

Opposite New Scotland Yard, which then stood in Broadway, stood the headquarters of London Transport, under which was St James' Park station, plus a few small shops and cafes. These cafes were used every day by detectives from the Yard who preferred them for a cup of tea and a bacon sandwich to their own in-house canteen.

It was a good place to grab my own breakfast in the hope of bumping into a friend or two who might drop a gem of background intelligence or a good story on me. As I travelled to the

Yard I got a call from the office to say there had been an incident at Stockwell tube station and the police had shot a man dead, actually on board an Underground train.

This was another sensational twist. There was an immediate assumption that the shooting victim was either another bomber, or one of the suspects from the day's previous failed attacks.

As I arrived I spotted one of my police friends, a counter-terrorism man I had come to know well. He had just gone out to grab a takeaway coffee. I stopped him and said: "Good news, eh? I just heard. Your people have just shot dead a terrorist at Stockwell. Well done. Was he one of the suspects for yesterday?"

This man was a well-educated and thoughtful individual, careful always about what he said to me. He looked around as if to make sure we were not being observed, stepped in a little closer so we couldn't be overheard, and said: "No. We have not shot a terrorist. It's a total fuck up."

I was momentarily confused. He said: "Jeff. We've shot the wrong guy. He's not a suspect, he's just some innocent guy going about his business. It's a disaster. Believe me."

Then he put his finger to his lips in a 'hush' gesture and, coffee in hand, he vanished back into Scotland Yard. I called my office. "The police have shot the wrong man at Stockwell. It's a fuck up. They've shot someone innocent." At the other end of the phone I could tell there was disbelief. I said again: "They've shot the wrong man. Trust me on this. My information is impeccable. I'm on my way back." I hailed a taxi.

When I got back a couple of execs button-holed me. The line still running from formal sources, some of it Government Minister level to my Parliamentary office colleagues, was the police had killed a terrorist. One said: "Look at this piece from our own reporter at Stockwell. He's spoken to a member of the station staff. He says he saw the terrorist vault over the ticket barriers and run down the escalator. Then he saw pursuing cops do the same thing."

I said: "That's what the reporter *thinks* he saw. Not what he *actually* saw. Give me a little while to get to the bottom of everything."

I started calling people who I thought might know what had happened at Stockwell. I quickly found someone prepared to, unofficially and anonymously, give me the heads up.

I told him about the station witness and he said: "There was a surveillance operation in progress on a man thought to be associated with yesterday's bomb attacks. There was a long and complicated 'follow off' going on. The surveillance team were not armed. The suspect was on a bus and got off at Stockwell. He had a bag. The surveillance people thought it might be a bomb. They called for firearms teams to intercept him. But the firearms teams had to approach without sirens and lights because they didn't want to spook a suspected suicide bomber, in case he detonated his bomb right there and then. So they struggled to get through the heavy traffic and were a few seconds behind events as they unfolded.

"Your witness who saw a 'terrorist' vaulting the ticket barrier at Stockwell saw nothing of the sort. What he saw was a surveillance cop in plain clothes vaulting the barrier trying to catch up with the suspect going down the escalators. Then your witness saw several more cops, running flat out, vault the barriers and run down the escalators a few seconds later."

"Do you know what happened on the platform?" I asked.

"Yes. The surveillance officers ran onto the platform just as a train came in. Our 'suspect' got on the train and sat down. The surveillance guy grabbed him and pinned his arms to his sides so he couldn't detonate a bomb. It's a standard technique they practice in training. The firearms team came piling on to the train, took one look, and blew the suspect's head off. The surveillance officer was covered in blood and brain matter. Apparently he looked at the gun team and said: 'What the fuck did you do that for? I had him under control'."

This was a stunning conversation. "How do you know he's the wrong guy?" It was an obvious question. "He's got ID on him. He's an innocent bloke, an electrical engineer, on his way to work. It's fucking terrible. I don't know what we are going to say as an organisation."

Then a last question: "There are CCTV cameras on the platform, correct? So at least it's all on video?"

There was a silence. "You know what we say. Never assume anything," said my friend. "There are cameras, yes. But it looks like they were temporarily out of action this morning. So no footage."

"Fuck," I said: "You know how that's going to play, don't you." It was a statement, not a question. People will say the police deleted the film."

"Yes," said my friend "They will. It's not a nice world. Especially if you are an honest citizen going about your lawful business and we rock up and kill you."

And that's exactly how it played over the next 48 hours. The innocent victim was a young Brazilian electrician, Jean Charles de Menezes. He had been wrongly identified by a police surveillance unit.

Before I went home that night, very late as usual, I managed to speak to another contact who was part of the Metropolitan Police Armed Response group, who operated a number of 'ARV's (Armed Response Vehicle) out of a covert base in Stepney in the heart of the East End, where there was also an underground police shooting range. The officers involved in the shooting were based there.

My friend knew the gun team personally and he had been at the Stepney base when they got back from the scene at Stockwell. He was in a sombre frame of mind and at home when I spoke to him late in the evening, he said: "When they came back in they were in shock. One of them was covered in the victim's blood. He was in tears. You cannot overstate how terrible this is for everyone involved. An innocent man is dead and the officers who shot him know now he wasn't a terrorist and they are utterly distraught.

"No one wants to have to shoot another person, even in the line of duty, even if it is completely unavoidable. It would be bad enough if the person killed had been a terrorist about to blow up innocent people. But to learn straight after it's all a terrible mistake has utterly devastated everyone involved. Lives have been altered irrevocably for everyone who was there."

I could still have got some of these powerful quotes into the story. But after thinking things over for a few minutes I decided not to. I was concerned my friend might be identified by his words and then face a disciplinary hearing for speaking out of turn. I decided I was not going to risk putting a man, who was already in anguish for his close colleagues, in danger of his words rebounding on him.

I am glad I did. I had done it many times in my career and looking back and reflecting, there were very few times I would have done it differently.

CONMEN AND HITMEN

CHAPTER TWENTY-THREE

Over the years I had interesting colleagues and inevitably some interesting and hair-raising jobs too. One of the first I tackled after joining the *News of the World* began when two former members of the British Army's Parachute Regiment approached me with a strange-sounding saga. They had seen an advert in the 'personal' columns of the *Daily Telegraph* newspaper asking for any 'former special forces or similar military background' types who would be up for an 'interesting assignment'. Via a box number they had been put in touch with a man called Charles Merrill Mount. He told them he was divorced with two children. According to him, he had been awarded custody of the children, but his wife had snatched them and was now living with them at a house in an up-market part of Dublin.

Charles Merrill Mount was no ordinary man. He was a British-born American citizen who liked to play the part of an aristocratic English Lord. He was also a brilliant and acclaimed artist, a world-renowned specialist and biographer of the American portrait painter John Singer Sargent and a wealthy member of New York's elite society. Meeting with him in London, he told the former soldiers he was on his way to Dublin to snatch back his children. Telling them the job would be relatively easy and that he just needed some 'back up' to ensure things went smoothly, he offered them £2,000 each to accompany him. It was a good payday for a pair of out of work former British soldiers.

A rendezvous had been arranged at a nice Dublin hotel where Merrill Mount had booked an expensive suite. But when the ex-British squaddies arrived, their task master opened a briefcase and produced a pair of brand new and fully loaded .38 calibre Colt Python revolvers which he handed to them, adding casually the guns were just in case they encountered any 'opposition'.

The two soldiers fled the scene, without their promised money, and came straight to the *News of the World* and me and told me their story. I headed immediately to Dublin where I called on Mrs Merrill Mount, who knew nothing about the plot to kidnap her children at gunpoint, and was unsurprisingly very distressed.

On my advice she called the police – for all we knew her ex-husband was still in Ireland, intent on kidnap, and packing two fully-loaded handguns. The Garda Síochána, taken aback by this outlandish and sinister story, took me into custody for several hours at Rathmines Garda station, while they got me to explain what I was doing on their territory. By the time we were finished, Merrill Mount had made it to the airport and was already jetting back to the USA.

Released by the Dublin cops and back in London, I did some research and discovered Charles Merrill Mount was actually a back street boy from Brooklyn whose real name was Sherman Suchow. He liked to pretend he was an English aristocrat. I thought he was an out and out con man and a thief, and so it proved. I wrote a front page story, which we headlined 'I Want You to Kidnap my Kids'.

The next week several leading American newspapers, including the *Washington Post*, and a leading US TV channel, contacted me wanting to develop the story. I also got a furious call from Merrill Mount himself who, in the same breath, threatened to sue me, and to shoot me too. I was unconcerned that he would do the former, a little more worried about the latter as I knew he was somewhere in the world with a pair of loaded Colt revolvers.

A few weeks later I got a call from a detective in Thames Valley police, in Reading, asking if I knew where Merrill Mount was. It turned out, several months before, Merrill Mount had hired a new Ford Granada from a company in that area, put down a deposit using a dud cheque, and neither he nor the car, which had been hired for one week, had been seen since. So my hunch about him being a con man was right. A few years later, after I had left the *News of the World*, I read, quite by chance, an article describing how he had been arrested by the FBI in Washington for trying to sell about 200 historic documents concerning the American Civil War which he had stolen from the National Archives.

The FBI described the documents as 'priceless' but for the purposes of justice they were given a value of $100,000. Unfortunately for Merrill Mount, the bogus English aristocrat, the buyer was an undercover federal agent. He got seven years in jail and died in 1996.

CHAPTER TWENTY-FOUR

Sometimes life as a journalist throws up a strange series of connections, which are not always immediately clear. Such was the case in 1994. I met up with one of my well-placed friends from within Scotland Yard. We went to a wine bar near Tower Bridge, and after a few drinks we moved on to a well-known fish restaurant. This detective was a very straight talking individual, but intelligent, shrewd and insightful. I knew he felt comfortable in his dealings with me, aware I was always careful never to professionally compromise any of my friends in a world of intrigue, both inside and outside Scotland Yard.

As the evening wore on we talked about football, cricket, mutual friends and acquaintances, cars, and the price of beer, and then he said: "Have you ever heard of a little place in Scotland called Tomintoul?"

I replied that being a fan of single malt Scotch whisky I had heard of the tiny Scottish town. So I said: "It's in the Cairngorm mountains. The Highlands. Near the valley of the River Spey. There is a very famous whisky distillery there."

And he laughed and said: "Well, we've got a really interesting job centred there right now. One of our own people, a civil servant, a very senior accountant, has embezzled several million pounds from our own coffers. He's been doing it for months, probably years. He has been up in Tomintoul and spent the money he has stolen from us buying up real estate. He's bought the post office, the fire station, a hotel, a big house – he's even bought himself a heraldic title. He calls himself 'The Laird of Tomintoul'. It's all being kept under wraps by us at the moment. But it's all true."

I asked my contact for the man's name and he replied: "Anthony Williams."

I was incredulous, but I trusted my contact completely.

"How did he divert all that money, and no one notice?" My friend shrugged and smiled. "Ah. Therein lies the real problem. The money has been stolen from a top secret fund for paying a special informant. Williams and one of our Assistant Commissioners are the only people who know about it, and are allowed to sign off the bank transfers. Williams is authorised to sign, no problem. But it looks like he's become very adept at forging the signature of the Assistant Commissioner."

So, somehow Williams had been able to transfer vast chunks of the police's own money into a bank account of his own – without anybody noticing.

"What do you mean 'a top secret special informant'?" I ventured. "What type of informant is so fucking good, you are giving him MILLIONS of quid?"

My friend looked into his wine glass, then at me. "I have no idea. Even I am not allowed to know who this informant is or what he does for us. No one I know knows who it is. Security around this informant is so tight, there seems to be only three people in the organisation who know who he is. One of them must be the Commissioner of the Metropolitan Police himself, the second is the assistant chief responsible for the covert funds, and the third is Williams, who is the thief."

The last key point I had been able to ascertain was the case was now subject of a very covert inquiry by the Yard's own Fraud

Squad. Williams had been arrested and questioned under caution and released on bail while under investigation.

Charges were sure to follow which meant we had to get in quick, because criminal charges would severely curtail what I could write in advance of a criminal trial. It was now late at night. I went home but hardly slept with excitement. The next morning I called my Head of News, Eugene Duffy, at his home in Kent at 7am and told him what I'd discovered.

We had a reporter based in Aberdeen, and by the time I got into our office in Canary Wharf about two hours later, he was arriving in Tomintoul and knocking on doors. Our reporter, Jonathan Russell had been told to find out everything he could about the new 'Highland Chieftain', but without disclosing the real reason he was asking. We wanted to make sure we had the story exclusively to us.

Jonathan went to Tomintoul and in reporter terms, he 'cleaned up'. Everywhere he went he found locals who knew the "well-spoken Englishman who has been buying up the whole town".

Thus I was able to break the story of Anthony Williams, mild mannered, middle class accountant, thief and pretend Scottish aristocrat.

We carried a front page splash saying "£3 Million Missing at the Yard" which turned out to be £2M on the conservative side, the actual figure being closer to £5M. Together with Jonathan Russell I had four more pages on the story on the inside. A couple of weeks later Williams was charged with theft and false accounting.

When I met with my detective friend again, he said: "The money Williams stole? I've found out what the fund was for. It was set up to pay a secret IRA informant. The money was given to us by the Home Secretary. This person was probably the first and most important Irish terrorist informant we have ever had. No wonder it's been such a closely guarded secret."

And we could both see it had provided the perfect opportunity for a clever man like Williams to capitalise. Because in effect he was stealing money from a fund that officially didn't exist and would be denied.

"Any idea what this informant has given the Counter-Terrorism people? He must be very near the top of the organisation to be worth making him a multi-millionaire."

My friend took a slurp of his pint of Guinness. "Not a clue, my friend. Don't know who, don't know what." Then he smiled and said: "And if I did know and I told you, I would be signing your death warrant, because I would have to kill you straight away to prevent you telling anyone else."

"That important, eh?" I said, asking another direct question.

"Yup," said my friend. "It's that important."

I have often wondered since who that informant was. There couldn't have been anyone else in police history who received seven figures in reward cash, a lottery win in effect. It's 30 years or so now since peace broke out in Northern Ireland, and subsequent events have revealed the IRA and other terror organisations were riddled with informers. I can only think the person who received that money must have been very close to the high command and a man considered so dedicated to the cause to be beyond suspicion.

The crooked accountant was later tried and sent to prison for nine years. He served about three years of that term, a model prisoner no less, and when he was released he became a London bus driver, and that was the last I ever heard of him. I loved the story about Williams. One of the reasons was, at the time I shared a desk with our Royal Correspondent, Jane Kerr.

We were on good terms, she was a nice woman and good colleague, but our jobs were very different and we were also very different character types. One day, a few weeks prior to breaking the 'Laird of Tomintoul' story she said, in an off the cuff jibe: "You are not interested in any story where someone hasn't died."

On the day we front paged the Williams' theft story I pointedly dropped a copy of the paper on the desk in front of her. "Look Jane," I said, "an exclusive splash and inside spreads. And nobody has died. Or even been slightly injured."

CHAPTER TWENTY-FIVE

In November 1983 a big political scandal broke in the media. Cecil Parkinson, a senior minister in Margaret Thatcher's Cabinet, was exposed for having a long affair with his secretary Sara Keays. Parkinson was married and, to the outside world, conveyed the impression of being a solid family man adhering to his party's stance on good old fashioned family values.

After 12 years of illicit liaisons, Sara became pregnant. Parkinson wanted her to terminate the pregnancy, fearing, correctly, if the news came out his career in politics would be severely damaged. The satirical magazine *Private Eye* broke the story just before the Conservative Party's annual conference. The next day the scandal was front page news on every Fleet Street daily paper.

A few weeks later I got a phone call from one of my police contacts in south London. He told me he had a very good story. I suggested a meeting as soon as possible. Normally this would have been in one of several pubs we frequented, but this time my friend was uncharacteristically nervous. Under no circumstances did he want to risk being seen with me. Instead, he suggested, in a scene reminiscent of something from a spy novel, we meet at midnight under a darkened backstreet railway arch near London Bridge.

This seemed a bit melodramatic, but I agreed. Usually our meetings were very sociable. This was different. As I waited in the gloom under the deserted bridge I saw a figure approaching. It was him. As he drew level with me he simply said "hello mate" then produced an A4 envelope from under his coat. In one swift move he thrust it into my hand and said: "Stick that under your coat. You'll like what's in there."

I swiftly transferred the envelope to an inside pocket. My friend said: "Don't call me for a couple of weeks," and then he vanished back into the darkness.

I hurried back to my car and drove home. Once indoors I opened the envelope. There were three or four pages, stapled together. I could see they were photocopies of a Scotland Yard crime report, dated a couple of days beforehand. And I could see this was newspaper dynamite.

It was the report of a break-in at a house belonging to the sister of Sara Keays and where Sara had been staying while a cottage she had bought near Bristol was being renovated. At the time of the burglary she had been away in the West Country with her sister and brother-in-law. It was clear from comments written by detectives about the crime that they believed the burglary was far from run of the mill.

The house had been thoroughly searched from top to bottom, yet despite being packed with valuables, nothing obvious had been stolen. Ms Keays had installed two filing cabinets at the house and these appeared to have been rifled through, as did several other boxes of her private correspondence. There were notes attached to the crime report from officers suggesting they thought that due to the thoroughness of the search – even the speakers of a hi-fi system had been taken apart to see what was inside – the crime might have been carried out by security services 'spooks'. One officer had even noted; 'possible M15 involvement?' on the file.

Sara had told the police she thought some of the hundreds of documents she kept at the house, including some private diaries were missing. Evidence was already emerging that an angry Cecil

Parkinson, a man once tipped as a future Prime Minister, had set out on a campaign to smear and discredit her. The suggestion was clear, this burglary had been ordered from the highest level of The Establishment, possibly even signed off by Margaret Thatcher herself. I had a stunning exclusive. My news editor Bob Warren was ecstatic. I wrote up the story with every scrap of detail I had. It would be this week's front page splash in the *News of the World*

Then on the Saturday morning before publication, I arrived at work to discover that early that day, November 26, a gang of armed robbers had raided the Brink's-Mat security warehouse at Heathrow Airport and stolen three tons of gold bullion valued at an astonishing £26M. It was the biggest robbery in British crime history, knocking the 1963 Great Train Robbery off the top spot it had held for 20 years. And it had fallen perfectly in my lap in our timeframe.

I feverishly wrote up that story as more and more information came in. About 5pm, Bob Warren came over to me and said: "The Editor has decided to split the front page. The Brink's-Mat robbery will be on the left hand side, and your Sarah Keays burglary exclusive on the other. You will have the entire front under your bylines and several pages inside too."

"It's extraordinary," added Bob." I can't remember another time when one reporter has had the whole of the front page with two enormous stories."

An hour later, the printers – represented by a hugely powerful union – walked out, and that week's *News of the World* was not published. I didn't know whether to laugh or cry or do both. In the end Bob and I went to the pub and got drunk as skunks. I had long learned that as a reporter, there were always going to be disappointments. But that was the biggest let down I ever experienced.

CHAPTER TWENTY-SIX

There were many other strange and bizarre episodes in my career at the *News of the World*. One occurred when a man called John Durrant arrived at our front office and asked to see me. As *News of the World* staffers, 'Front Door' jobs, as we knew them, were the bane of our lives. A paper with a near five million circulation attracted every kind of strange person, many of them it has to be said, chronically deluded or psychiatrically disturbed.

I lost count of the number of old ladies who owned knitting supply shops in Surrey who turned up wanting to tell us how the Russians were using surveillance satellites to tap into their thoughts. But you had to at least give these people a few minutes of your time, because every now and then, somebody actually did have a belting story to tell. John Durrant was one of them.

He turned up at our offices, unannounced on a Saturday lunchtime and told the reception desk he wanted to talk to the crime specialist on the paper.

I went downstairs to the front office, quiet on a Saturday, to see who this cold caller was. There, I encountered a slightly built, but fit and wiry looking ex-paratrooper aged about 45 with close cropped salt and pepper hair. He told me straight off his name was John Durrant and he was just out of prison.

I couldn't put my finger on it, but there was something about this man which made me feel he could be dangerous. So I sat down with him and asked him to tell me what he'd been doing since he left the army. He was perfectly frank. Since quitting the military, with an honourable discharge, he had made a living and a jail reputation for himself, by breaking into country houses at night, tying up the people who lived there, and then stealing their valuables.

He was very direct about this and admitted it with an air of pride. He made no bones about it at all. It was this lifestyle which had led to him being caught and jailed more than once, and it was prison where he had just come from, after being released from his latest stretch.

Durrant didn't want to be seen talking to me publicly, so I took him inside to our canteen and bought him a cup of tea and a bacon sandwich. He then told me the following story; because he had been near the end of his sentence in Bristol's Horfield Prison, he had been moved to Ley Hill prison near Bristol, which was a Category C low security jail. I knew this was normal practice.

In Ley Hill he had become friendly with a man called Richard Hardy, who had been a dentist, but had taken to raping female patients at his practice in Nottingham, in his dentist's chair, after he had sedated them.

This had earned Hardy a well deserved 12-year sentence. While he was in jail, his wife had had the temerity to divorce him and move in with another man – who just so happened to be another dentist. Now Hardy wanted to have them both murdered.

He was an educated and cultured man, but lacking in the necessary skills to be a killer. However, in jail he had rubbed shoulders with every kind of low life, including Durrant who he regarded as a 'proper criminal' who could arrange things like that. But as Durrant pointed out to me, rough and tough and criminal as he was, he drew the line at killing innocent women. "So," I said, anticipating him, "you want to take me to meet Hardy and for me to pretend to be a contract killer. Yes?"

Durrant laughed out loud and said: "No. Fuck off. You look much too nice. Haven't you got anyone who looks, well… proper horrible?" And at that moment Martin Turner strolled into the canteen. Now Martin, one of my reporter colleagues, was, deep down, actually a nice bloke. But he always seemed to have a permanent scowl on his swarthy face, even when he was happy, and his trademark outfit was a calf length black leather trench coat which he'd had handmade while on assignment in Argentina. It gave him the look of an unemployed Gestapo officer.

"Him," said Durrant, pointing at Martin. "Is he a mate of yours? He'd be perfect." So I called Martin over, introduced him, and got him involved. To cut a long story short, the following week, the three of us drove in the dead of night to a lane near Ley Hill jail near Bristol where Martin and Durrant disappeared into the darkness for a pre-arranged assignation at the perimeter fence of the prison with Hardy.

Martin was carrying a concealed 'Nagra' make tape recorder. At the time the Nagra – at the *News of the World*, we had two or three – was the most 'state of the art' miniature tape machine in the world, used not just by undercover hacks like us, but by the CIA, MI5 and other spy agencies.

The pair returned an hour later. Hardy had refused to say outright he wanted Martin to kill his ex-wife, because he was a bit too canny. But when I listened to the tape recording, it was clear from the nature of the conversation he was looking to hire a hitman and prepared to pay about £3,000 to have his ex-wife, and her new man, 'terminated'.

It was always our intention to involve the police because we really couldn't be sure what was going on: Hardy could be negotiating with other contract killers that we didn't know about. There could have been another murder plot already in action – and I reasoned we couldn't take that chance. But the next move Martin and I made was to visit Hardy's ex-wife and her new husband at their home in Worcestershire, warn them, and tell them what we had found out. Perhaps unsurprisingly, they were terrified and immediately called their local police. We waited with them for detectives to arrive.

Because the offence of 'solicitation to murder' had been committed at Ley Hill jail, the job was handed over by the West Mercia force to the Avon and Somerset CID. Two officers came to see me and Martin in London.

But in the interim Durrant had vanished. And that's where it got a bit tricky. Because, a few days later, one of the Bristol detectives said to me: "Tell me what Durrant told you about his situation?"

When I replied: "He told me he had been recently released from prison," the CID man laughed and said: "I think he's been a bit slippery with you there. A bit economical with the truth. He hasn't been discharged, he's actually escaped. He's over the side from jail, he's on the run."

So we had been driving around for several days with a prison escaper in the rear of my car, a man with a dangerous record for violent crime. And to make things even worse, now we didn't even know where our key witness was. But a few days later the Bristol detectives rang me again and asked me to come to Kensington police station in London, adding cheerily: "We've got a bloke here who wants to say 'hello'." It was of course Durrant, who'd been arrested in London for attempting to break into a jeweller's shop in the dead of night.

He had been caught red-handed and was now being returned to jail. I went to Kensington where the two West Country detectives greeted me and took me to an interview room. Five minutes later Durrant was led in. Because he was now considered an escape risk he was handcuffed by the wrist to a policeman. He looked crestfallen.

"Sorry," he said. "I've fucked up." He certainly had. But the police were confident that with my evidence and that of Martin Turner, they still had a good case. And their view was Hardy was the sort who was obsessed at getting at his ex-wife and would keep trying unless he was stopped. So the cops arrested him, and charged him with solicitation to murder, a very serious crime. He appeared for trial a few months later at Bristol Crown Court.

He was represented by the very charismatic barrister Paul Chadd, QC. Martin and I had to give evidence, on oath, from the witness box, and to boil things down, Mr. Chadd ripped us up for lavatory paper under cross examination. He effectively portrayed the whole affair as entrapment by me, Martin and the wicked *News of the World* as a whole. Even though that was not what had happened at all.

Because it would be 'prejudicial' to his defence, the jury were not allowed to know the nature of the dreadful crimes which had got Hardy sent to prison in the first place. In the witness stand he came across as a hapless, but well-educated, drop out, who had been framed by a career criminal and two horrible unprincipled reporters.

I knew we were well beaten. The jury took less than half a day to declare Hardy 'not guilty' and he walked free, at least from that case. He still had several years to serve on the rape sentence the jury had not been allowed to know about, and was returned from the court to a jail cell. Martin and I walked away licking our wounds, and decided to put it down to experience. And I thought that was that. But I was completely wrong.

About 18 months later I was contacted out of the blue by a stranger. Paul Cassidy was a small time but persistent drug dealer from Northampton who had just been released from Bedford jail. He had an interesting story to tell. While in jail, he told me over pints of lager in a Northampton pub, he had shared a cell with Richard Hardy.

Despite him being found not guilty of soliciting to have his wife murdered, the Home Office had decided to move him from Ley Hill to a more secure prison for the rest of his sentence. But the move from Bristol to Bedford had done nothing to curb his enthusiasm for having people murdered. I assumed Cassidy had read the account of how Hardy had tried to hire us to commit murder on his behalf. To my surprise he knew nothing of Hardy's previous attempt to recruit a hitman, or of how the *News of the World* had already tangled with him.

But sure enough, as it turned out, the rapist dentist was at it again. This time he had homed in on Cassidy as the sort of professional criminal who might be able to find him a contract killer. Again, Hardy's judge of character had been wanting. Like Durrant before him, Cassidy was a full time criminal, but he drew the line at the cold blooded murder of a young woman. I asked Cassidy why, as he didn't know what had gone on before between Hardy and the *News of the World*, he had contacted me in particular and he said:

"Well, Hardy has given me a list of people he wants murdered. And you are one of them."

As far as I was aware, this was the first and only time I was to be the subject of a murder plot. In fact Hardy had given Cassidy a list of about a dozen names, still starting with his ex-wife and her new partner, But now including me, John Durrant and Martin Turner, and several other people we didn't know, who he wanted to either meet a grisly end or be maimed for life.

I thought the situation over carefully. Where was Hardy now? According to Cassidy he had just been released and was living back with his parents in his native Sutton Coldfield, near Birmingham. I decided we would draw Hardy onto another sting – only this time there would be no mistake. Obviously I could not involve Martin Turner again, but needing to scope the seriousness of the threat I introduced Cassidy to another brilliant undercover reporter, Gerry Brown.

On appearance Gerry looked like he might really be a ruthless hitman. Glasgow born, he was burly and muscular with a scarred face that looked like it had been rearranged in a bottle fight. The truth was, as Gerry had once told me in confidence, the scars on his face were the result, years before, of servicing his own high powered Norton Commando motorbike and then forgetting to tighten the front wheel retaining nuts properly.

The crash on his first test run resulted in a broken jaw, smashed nose, and about 50 stitches in his chin and forehead. Nonetheless, with his broken face, he looked the part alright. It was enough to fool Hardy when he was introduced by Cassidy at a subsequent meeting.

To this day I am not sure what happened next, but I had a call from a senior detective from Northampton demanding a meeting. The next day at Northants police HQ, together with Gerry Brown, I was surprised to find myself meeting all the 'top brass' from the local force. It turned out that staff at the hotel where we were staying had seen us coming and going in a selection of hired vehicles, including a battered Ford Transit van, and decided we were a gang of criminals about to pull a big job in the locality.

They had contacted the police who had put us under surveillance, which included gaining entry to our rooms. I realised this when one of the cops said: "OK, who spilled the super glue on the table?" The answer was me. I had spilled the glue while fixing a loose connection on one of our covert tape machines. But it was obvious there was only one way they could have known.

I thought they were going to scotch our plan, but after we explained what had gone on, including the previous shenanigans at Bristol, they very gamely agreed to let us go ahead, but only as long as they could introduce their own undercover man to work alongside me and Gerry. We were not in a position to say 'no', and this suited our plan well, so they introduced us to a tough looking undercover detective called John Furness. Gerry set up a meeting between him, Furness and Hardy. Hardy was delighted, he was now getting what he thought was two hit men for the price of one.

He offered them £5,000 each to kill his wife, her new partner, and me. Furness and Brown had subsequent meetings with Hardy, which were secretly recorded, until the undercover cop was satisfied the former dentist had said enough, several times, to warrant a new charge of Solicitation to Murder and to cause Grievous Bodily Harm to other people on his hate list.

He was arrested and charged once again. This time he was put on trial at Oxford Crown Court. Again, he pleaded not guilty and once more he was represented by the very capable barrister who had defended him in the previous trial at Bristol, Paul Chadd.

But this time things were different. In order to defend Hardy a second time, Mr Chadd decided it was necessary to tell the jury all about the history of the case. Once again, I had to testify from the witness box, under oath, and counsel for both the prosecution and the defence were given permission by the judge to ask me about my previous dealings with Hardy's attempts to find a hitman to kill his ex-wife.

It was absolutely crucial for the new jury to hear. And unlike the jury at Bristol, they did not have the wool pulled over their eyes. They found him guilty.

When Hardy was giving evidence under cross examination I noticed that several times he used phrases that indicated he might belong to a Freemasons Lodge. I am not and never have been a Freemason, but one of the cops listening to his evidence later confirmed my suspicions. When the jury came back with their guilty verdicts, Hardy leapt to his feet in the dock and shouted to the judge: "In the name of the Great Architect of the Universe, I am innocent of these charges." The Great Architect of the Universe is how Freemasons refer to God.

As Hardy made his outburst a cop sitting near me whispered to me: "Fucking hell. He's playing the Freemasons card!" The judge sentenced Hardy to three years in jail. As we all stood to leave, the detective grabbed my arm and said: "There you go. It fucking works. He should have got at least eight years for those crimes!"

As I left the courtroom I was approached by the beaming defence barrister Paul Chadd. He stuck out his right hand and shook mine, then said: "So then, Mr Edwards, it's a draw, one all." Then he laughed and said: "What say you? Shall we make it best of three?"

I like to think it was out of mutual professional respect and mutual contempt for the legal process we went to the pub next door and enjoyed several large gin and tonics together,

In the meantime I had lost touch with John Durrant, the ex-paratrooper and country house burglar who had started off the whole sequence of events, but on seeing the story of Hardy's conviction he rang me up. Over the next few years, usually out of the blue, he would call me.

Every time he did, it was always something extreme, outlandish sounding even. I am quite sure he was a smart and dangerous criminal, but I am also convinced he was round the bend. His subsequent behaviour did nothing to dissuade me. I had not at first realised how right wing he was until he called me and said he was living near Leighton Buzzard and had opened a factory manufacturing replica Nazi uniforms. Not my cup of tea at all.

Then several years later, after I joined the *Daily Mirror*, he rang and said: "I've just been in Albania. They've got thousands of boxes of small arms ammunition left behind by the Germans after the Second World War. And lots of Nazi uniforms and guns and other stuff." I had heard about this hidden hoard of German war material before, and believed it to be true.

He continued: "I've met some Albanian gangsters and I am trying to do a deal with them to ship a lot of it to Germany. Do you want to come over and see it?" Again, I declined. Albania, I knew, was then a dangerous country for outsiders. But he sent me a fax with a full list of the military hardware he had located and the message concluded: "I am using the ONLY fax machine in Albania."

This was 1993. Under communist control for decades, Albania was still regarded as a mysterious 'closed' country where anyone from the UK or the rest of Europe was banned from entry and would immediately be locked up.

Yet there he was. I have no doubt, with his own brand of cocky criminal swagger, he had just walked in and introduced himself to people of his own ilk. But then things took a very sinister turn. Again, out of the blue, a phone call. Not from him, but from his wife Sandy, who I had never met. "John's in trouble," she said: "Can you go and see him?"

"Where is he?" I asked.

"Germany," came the reply.

"What kind of trouble?"

"He's been charged with murder. They say he's shot a man. He needs your help."

She gave me the number of a lawyer representing him in Germany who was friendly and told me the police had found the body of an arms dealer called Eberhardt Broll dead in a forest. He had been shot in the head several times..

Durrant had been arrested and police had found a gun in his possession. The bullets used in the murder matched the gun and it looked bad for the English ex-soldier. I asked the lawyer: "Does this have anything to do with a large shipment of rifle and machine gun bullets from Albania?"

The lawyer was shocked. "You know about this?" he asked.

At the time the war in the Balkans was raging and the lawyer explained to me how Durrant and Broll had conspired to import the ammunition, over one million rounds of it, from Albania and then export it via Germany to one of the warring parties. The whole operation was dangerously illegal from start to finish. Somewhere along the way the two men had fallen out and Durrant had shot his business partner dead.

I flew over to Germany to see him. Unlike the British prison system I was not allowed to visit him unaccompanied. A German prison officer was present as we talked. This didn't prevent Durrant, who I suppose thought the guard would not understand what we were saying, asking me to visit and bribe witnesses against him, and to help smuggle in metal files which he might be able to use in an escape bid.

I listened intently and just nodded and responded, "Uh-huh, right" and "OK, I'll think it over" to every illegal request. I was totally non-committal, the last thing I wanted was to be arrested in Germany as part of some hare-brained conspiracy. But as I was being escorted out of the jail again, the guard, in perfect English, said: "I hope, Mr Edwards, you are not giving any consideration to assisting Mr Durrant with his requests. It would be a very serious matter for you."

I looked at him and, in the internationally recognised sign language, tapped the side of my head with my forefinger, looked towards the room we had just vacated and rolled my eyes. The guard smiled in acknowledgement and I shook his hand and said: "No. Not a chance." A few weeks later Durrant went on trial, was convicted, and sentenced to life imprisonment. I thought I had heard the last of him, but no.

Several years later I received a phone call from Leicester prison. It was Durrant. He had been transferred back from Germany to serve his sentence in the UK.

He was direct as usual and asked me for a favour. Could I just nip over to Albania on his behalf? In his own words, while he had been there he had made some Albanian friends, who just happened to be serious gangsters.

Together with his new mates they had raided the central bank of Albania and made off with most of the nation's gold reserves. His share of the bullion, he explained, was hidden in the mountains near the capital, Tirana. If he gave me the precise location, could I go over and get it for him and bring it back and deliver it to his wife?

I am quite sure it was true, he had been involved in a huge robbery, and I am quite sure he was serious in his request. But as I hardly knew him, and as I had two young children to take care of, I decided being found dead with my throat cut in a ditch in remote Albania, was not an attractive prospect.

So I made an excuse and declined. I never heard from him again.

CONVERSATIONS WITH KILLERS

CHAPTER TWENTY-SEVEN

I visited people in jail often, almost always at the request of the prisoner. I have been a visitor inside at least 20 of Britain's jails, ranging from tough Category Triple A Maximum Security prisons like London's Belmarsh, Whitemoor in Cambridgeshire and Frankland in County Durham, to more easy-going Category D jails like HMP Ford in Sussex.

The range of criminals I have interviewed behind bars was varied, but murderers were undoubtedly the biggest single category. I have sat down with cold and callous hitmen like John 'Bruce' Childs to sexually-driven sociopaths and serial killers..

It is safe to say most of the jail visits I made were strange and memorable for one reason or another. But none were stranger than the encounters I had with a man who was arguably Britain's best known villain of modern times, Reggie Kray. The story of Reg Kray and his twin brother Ron has been told over and over in the 55 years since they were jailed for murder.

There have been at least 15 books, two movies, and countless TV documentaries made about them and their history of murder and violence. Many years after their deaths there continues to be a huge public fascination with them. So in 1996 when I received a message saying Reg Kray wished to grant me an audience, I was not going to say no.

The message came from an East London solicitor who represented Reg. I went to see him at his office in Ilford where he explained the situation to me. His client, Mr Kray, had become upset with recent stories which had appeared in some newspapers, which seemed to suggest the closest thing Britain had ever had to a mafia don, might be gay.

Such matters were no longer even considered to be newsworthy – with certain exceptions. One of those exceptions being the Kray twins. Now it turned out that Reg Kray had, while in jail, become an avid reader of the *Daily Mirror*. He had noticed my byline and, as the lawyer put it, his client 'Mr Kray' thought I was the ideal chap to put the record straight.

Normally my prison visits were arranged by the prisoner in question sending me a 'Visiting Order'. This formal document, better known simply as a 'V.O.' was issued by the Home Office and was supposed to be scrutinised by the Prison Service, as part of a vetting procedure to make sure no journalists got into the prisons unchaperoned.

But in practice no 'V.O.' I was sent was ever challenged, even though I always filled out the forms with my correct name and business address. The most cursory check would have revealed I was one of those reporters government departments supposedly feared most. But frankly, I don't think the Home Office really gave a damn. Anyway, the Kray situation was different. Instead of going in as a routine visitor I was going to go to Maidstone Prison, where Reg Kray was held, on what was referred to as 'a brief's visit'. In other words I would be going in with his solicitor and everyone would think I was part of his legal team.

It also meant our visit would be in a private room without the background noise of unruly children and weeping mothers that were the usual soundtrack in a prison visiting area. Arriving at Maidstone Prison with the lawyer, we were shown by a prison officer to a small meeting room with a table and four chairs and bare of any other furniture. After a wait of a few minutes, a door opened and Reg Kray stepped in. He was slighter, in both height and build than I had expected him to be, and looked older.

He wore a pressed blue shirt and jeans and his hair was neatly combed back, but he had that pallid, almost translucent, skin tone so usual in long term prisoners denied access to the open air by their circumstances. His well kept appearance was enhanced by a pair of reading glasses with gold wire rimmed frames and lenses which were tinted with a pale blue or violet tinge.

I had expected him to be on his own, but he was accompanied by another man, much younger and of striking appearance. He was well over 6ft tall, muscular and with shoulder-length dyed blonde hair. He was 22, one third of Reg Kray's years and looked like a surfer. I can clearly remember thinking he looked like an extra from the TV show *Baywatch*, which was a big hit at the time.

Kray shook hands with his solicitor and then, when formally introduced, shook hands with me. He was very polite, very formal. It was a much more limp handshake than I had expected from a former boxer with such a fierce reputation. He cleared his throat and introduced me to the man with him.

"This is Bradley," he said. "We go everywhere together. Don't we, Bradley?" Bradley nodded agreement. "Bradley is my best friend," said Kray. "We share a cell, we do everything together, we're very close. Isn't that right, Bradley?" Bradley, who I learned was an armed robber from East London serving a nine year term, nodded again.

"Right," said Kray. "The first thing I want to ask you, Mr Edwards, is, do I have your goodwill?" I wasn't quite sure what he meant but I answered with an affirmative.

"Good," said Kray. "Now you might be aware Mr Edwards, certain stories have recently appeared in some newspapers that seem to suggest, how can I put this?, that I might be, in plain terms, what we call in the East End where I am from, a 'poof'."

I nodded and told him I had seen the stories adding that I thought stories like those might be very hurtful to him.

"Yes," said Kray "They have hurt my feelings. But much worse than that, they've hurt Bradley's feelings too. Isn't that right, Bradley?"

Bradley nodded.

I decided to be very diplomatic with my first question: "Why would Bradley be hurt by those stories, Reg? His name is not even mentioned in them."

Kray looked at me as if I had lost my reason. "No, he's not. But when those stories hurt me, they hurt Bradley too, don't they, Bradley? You have to understand, Mr Edwards. Bradley and I are very, very close." Then to emphasise the point he said to Bradley: "Show Mr Edwards your bracelet Bradley."

Bradley rolled up the right sleeve of his prison issue shirt, to reveal a gold chain bracelet with a plate which had something engraved on it.

"It says 'Goombah, My Son'," offered Kray. "Do you know what that means?" I shook my head. "It's Yiddish, Mr Edwards, and it means we are very close friends. I gave him that bracelet, I had it made specially, it's 18 carat gold."

"And look," said Kray, rolling up his own right shirt sleeve and revealing an identical gold bracelet. "He gave me this at the same time I gave him his. It's got the same thing written on it." He thrust it under my nose.

"Very nice," I said. "So you exchanged identical bracelets at the same time?"

"Yes," said Kray, "because we wanted to show how much we meant to each other."

"So," I said, "you and Bradley have exchanged friendship bracelets. His and his bracelets, in fact." I sat back in my hard wooden prison chair and nodded thoughtfully. I scribbled some notes into my pad. I wanted to say I was confused, but thought better of it. I wasn't sure what Bradley's take was on all this. He was keeping his own counsel and saying nothing. If this wasn't a prison romance, what was it? What was in it for Bradley? Status? Category A kudos?

There were questions I was dying to ask, but wasn't sure what would happen if I did. Kray broke the silence: "So, what I'd like you to do is write a story making it clear I am not gay. Can you do that? Do I have your goodwill?"

"Yes, Reg, you have my goodwill. And I'll definitely write a story." Then I plucked up my courage and asked a question: "The thing is, Reg. If I write a story in which you state firmly that you are not a homosexual, some people might think you are protesting too much. Can you see the risk in that?"

Kray looked at me as if I was completely uncomprehending of his view of the world. He leant forward towards me across the table and very deliberately and slowly said: "No, son. I don't think that."

Our meeting ended, we shook hands and before we parted he asked me once more: "Do I have your goodwill?"

I replied it was an absolute given. I went back to my office and told my boss Eugene Duffy about the encounter. "Brilliant," he said. "Write up every word."

There was no other way to spin it. I wrote about Bradley the hunky surfer dude, the 'his and his' bracelets, the 'very close' friendship, and more. It would leave any rational person in little doubt there was something gay going on in Reg Kray's life. A few days later we ran my story. The headline, which I was not responsible for, read 'Reg Kray. I'm not Gay'.

I thought Reg Kray would be furious. A few days after the article was published, prominently on page five, Kray's lawyer called me again and said his client wished to have a second meeting. Together with the lawyer I went back to Maidstone Prison on another brief's visit. It was no less bizarre than the first meeting.

Shown into an interview room close to some workshops by prison staff we waited and waited, and waited some more. Eventually, after we had been delayed about 40 minutes, the lawyer asked a prison officer what the hold up was. The PO disappeared for a while and when he returned he explained that Reg and Bradley had had an argument. Bradley didn't want to meet us again, but Reg did, but not without Bradley. The lawyer said to the jailer: "Can you sort it out for us? We can't wait indefinitely."

The jailer vanished again and returned ten minutes later and said: "I am sorry gentlemen, but it appears your client and his friend have had what I would describe as a 'domestic argument'.

They are in the workshops. But they are now not speaking to each other." It seemed to be an impasse.

My lawyer contact then said to the PO: "Can you tell Mr Kray we will wait for another 15 minutes, but no longer." I agreed with him. The jailer disappeared out of the door again, but 10 minutes later he appeared back at the door with Reg Kray.

The gangster was smartly turned out as usual but looked subdued. He shook our hands again, and was his usual correct and formal self, but said: "I am here on my own, but I don't want to be interviewed without Bradley. Unfortunately he is refusing to come to this meeting and we've had an argument."

Then he looked at me and said: "Thank you for the goodwill you have shown me and thank you for putting things straight in your article and making it clear I am not a poof as some people have suggested."

Then he got up and left the room. I remember thinking at that moment that Reg Kray was one of the strangest and most obviously gay men I had ever encountered.

I didn't meet Reg Kray again and he died from Hepatitis B in October 2000 in hospital in Norfolk, a few weeks after being given a compassionate release from a jail near Thetford. He was 66.

Bradley Allerdyce was released from jail and later admitted to the BBC he had been in a sexual relationship with Reg Kray. In 2005 he received a life sentence for helping to murder a man who was attacked with a variety of weapons including a hunting knife, a sharpened screwdriver, a metal bar and a cosh.

CHAPTER TWENTY-EIGHT

I had several other jail encounters with notorious men. On a visit to Whitemoor I visited an organised crime character, Roy Garner, who had been jailed for cocaine running and wanted to make allegations of corruption against the police. He was unable to back his claims with any evidence whatsoever, but while I was there he introduced me to Dennis Nilsen, who had murdered at least 12 young men between 1978 and 1983.

I had covered part of Nilsen's trial which heard grisly details of how he had lured young gay men, mostly homeless drifters, back to his flat in north London. Then after getting them drunk he had strangled or smothered them to death, and in some cases slept with their corpses until the smell of putrefaction got so bad he was forced to act. Some of his victims' remains were burned on a garden bonfire, others were dismembered in his bath, then boiled up in saucepans on his kitchen stove and flushed down the lavatory, piece by piece. He may have gone on to murder many more but his method of disposal of human flesh blocked the drains outside his home and he was exposed.

After rotting flesh was confirmed to be human he was arrested by a detective, Scotland Yard's Peter Jay, who introduced himself with some of the most memorable words ever spoken by an arresting officer: "Good morning, Mr Nilsen. I have come to talk to you about your drains."

At the time he was jailed I was completely baffled by a justice system that, after hearing repeated descriptions about all the aspects of his killings, declared Nilsen sane and of sound mind and thus suitable to spend the rest of his life in the ordinary prison system and not in a secure psychiatric hospital – Broadmoor being the most well known example.

At that time in my career I had covered many murder trials at the Old Bailey and other crown courts and had seen people who appeared completely of sound mind packed off to a mental hospital, where their condition was treated by psychiatrists. This sometimes even ran parallel with cases of killers who were quite obviously seriously deranged, yet ended up in jail and got no help whatsoever.

I found Nilsen, who I kept in touch with through visits and phone calls for several years, completely non-threatening and benign, but he was so obviously, in plain terms, round the bend. The best example of this was his paranoia about how the authorities at Whitemoor, one of Britain's new 'supermax' prisons built in the 1980s, were "out to get him". In one phone call he said to me: "I have been counting the cornflakes in my breakfast portions every morning and keeping records."

Yes, Nilsen had been counting his cornflakes for months. He told me: "Listen to this. In the period April last year to April this year, the average daily portion of Kellogg's Cornflakes I received was 246. But the previous year the average was 258! What more proof do you need that they are persecuting me?"

Nilsen had 'taught' himself music in prison. As a long term inmate he had been allowed to acquire a battery-powered keyboard. He made recordings of his compositions and sent the cassettes to me to review. I didn't wish to laugh at him but his 'music' sounded like the sort of disjointed organ renditions heard coming from the home of TV comedy shows like *The Addams Family* or *The Munsters*. The hideous sounds were made worse in that the batteries in his keyboard were usually failing when he made the recordings he sent me. He explained how the prison authorities in Whitemoor strictly controlled the number of batteries he was allowed, even after they were worn out and dead, because of the 'black market' trade in the heavier 'C' and 'D' types, which when packed into a sock, made an easily improvised cosh.

The Home Office cracked down on our correspondence in the late 1990s, intercepting the mail between us. I was told, informally, by a senior prison officer that the Home Office thought corresponding with a journalist was 'affecting Nilsen's mental health', but frankly I think government wonks just wanted to stop him telling me about the shortcomings of the prison system. He died in hospital in York in 2018 after being taken ill in nearby Full Sutton jail where he had been transferred from Whitemoor a few years earlier.

***

Bruce Childs was also a serial killer, but in a different category altogether. He was a professional hitman who, together with his partner in crime, Henry MacKenney, known to his friends as 'Big H' because of his enormous frame, got into the habit of murdering people. Most terrible of all, one of their victims was a schoolboy aged 10.

The story of their killing spree came out almost by accident. In 1978, together with a man called Terry Pinfold, they carried out a spectacular armed robbery. After hijacking a security van, they tied up the guards, put on their uniforms and visited three banks in Hertfordshire where the crew were scheduled to collect large sums of money. They got away with nearly £500,000, but due to a couple of slip-ups, they were tracked down by the Flying Squad and arrested.

In that era Scotland Yard's 'supergrass' system was at its peak. Many men held for armed robbery would cut a deal with the police, to admit to the robberies they had done and go to court as prosecution witnesses against their former comrades and put them in jail.

For this breach of the criminal code, many big time villains were given a huge discount, sometimes as much as 75%, on the usual sentence for such serious crimes, by Crown Court judges. Childs, a man who already had convictions for robbery, didn't want to go to jail for close to 20 years, the expected 'tariff' for gun crime in the 1970s. So when Flying Squad officers were interviewing him about the Hertfordshire robberies, Childs asked if he could get a deal if he confessed to some other serious crimes, and grassed on his mates.

The cops said yes, but they were not expecting what he was about to reveal. Instead of confessing to more armed robberies, Childs told incredulous police he had killed six people and got rid of the bodies. Five of them had been killed for cash.

The first to die was a man called Terry Eve.

In 1974 Childs and MacKenney were renting a small business unit in Goodmayes in East London, where MacKenney, who was an expert scuba diver and a talented engineer, was manufacturing a new design of oxygen valve for the diving industry.

Also renting a unit in the same complex was 32 year-old Eve, who had a thriving business making soft toys, earning him the nickname 'Teddy Bear'. Childs and MacKenney decided if Eve could be made to 'disappear' they could take over his business and make lots of money.

So they asked him to come to their office late at night where they battered him to death with hammers and an iron pipe. Eve's killing was the catalyst for their second murder. He had employed a small time criminal and ex-professional wrestler called Robert Brown in his toy business.

While Childs and MacKenney were cleaning up the crime scene from their attack on Eve, the hapless Brown walked in on them. McKenney wanted to kill him there and then but Childs talked him out of it. However 'Big H' later insisted Brown knew too much, was a risk to them, and needed to be 'eliminated' .

But there was a problem. While the two killers vacillated, Brown, who was 28, got arrested and jailed for a warehouse burglary. MacKenney was frustrated, but a few weeks later Brown escaped from Chelmsford jail. The man he went to for help was MacKenney.

He directed him to go to Childs' flat in Bow, assuring Brown a safe house was being arranged for him to lie low. But the ex-wrestler had been set-up. At the flat MacKenney walked in and shot Brown three times with a silenced pistol. But instead of dying instantly Brown fought back. There was an epic battle during which MacKenney hit him over the head with a fireman's axe and Childs stabbed him repeatedly with a diver's knife. Still Brown would not die, until finally Childs came at him and drove a Samurai sword through his heart. While confessing to police later, Childs described Brown as "near impossible" to kill. He told the police, "He had three bullets in him and still he came at us like a wounded Grizzly Bear."

The next victim was 31-year-old haulage contractor George Brett.

This was a paid-for contract killing. Two years before, Brett had been in a fight with a scrap metal merchant and knocked out his teeth with an iron bar. The scrap man allegedly paid Childs and MacKenney to kill his rival.

Brett was lured to their workshop on a pretext. Suspecting he might be being set up, Brett took his 10-year-old son Terry with him as 'insurance' believing no one would harm him with the child present. He was wrong. When they got to the workshop, MacKenney shot them both dead with a silenced sub machine gun. Childs then cut up the bodies and disposed of them.

The fifth victim was small-time villain Freddie Sherwood, who was 48. He had crossed another East London criminal who paid MacKenney and Childs £4,000 to lure him to a meeting where he was shot dead.

Their sixth and final murder was carried out not for cash, but for lust.

Ronnie Andrews was a 38-year-old roofing contractor. Unbeknown to him his wife was having a secret love affair with MacKenney. He decided to kill Andrews who was lured to a meeting and then shot through the head with a .38 calibre pistol.

Although all the victims were reported to police by loved ones as missing persons, none of the cases up to that point were investigated as murders because their bodies had never been discovered. By police reasoning of the time, it meant there was no evidence they had been killed.

Now the police were both shocked and intrigued by what Childs was saying. What had happened to the bodies? Childs told a chilling story. They had all been taken to a council flat he rented in Dolphin House in Bow, East London, where they had been dismembered with butcher's knives in the bath. He had then planned to grind down their remains using an industrial meat mincing machine he had bought for £25 after it was advertised in the magazine *Exchange and Mart*.

But the plan had not worked because the domestic electric supply in the flat was insufficiently powerful to run the motor of the machine. So instead, he had used butcher's knives to dismember and slice up the corpses in the bath and then burned them to ash in a tiny fire grate. It had taken him days to complete the job.

When he explained how he had disposed of his victims, the police did not at first believe him. The fire grate in an East End council flat was only about a foot square. So detectives went to the meat market and bought an entire pig's carcass, which weighed about 175lbs. They cut it into chunks, and using only small amounts of coal to get a fire going, they attempted to burn it.

To their astonishment they discovered it worked, although it took teams of officers about four days, with the fire burning day and night, to get rid of the entire carcass and involved dozens of trips to the rubbish chute with buckets of ash.

When neighbours of Childs' flat were interviewed in house to house inquiries, several mentioned what they had taken to be the constant smell of what they thought was roast pork percolating through the walls at the times Childs was incinerating his victims. When he was asked what he had done to get rid of the ash and bits of bone which refused to burn away completely, he told officers he had made numerous trips out in his car and tipped buckets of ash down street drains in the dead of night. But in confessing to the police and hoping to get leniency for grassing on MacKenney and Pinfold, Childs had made a serious error of judgement.

No judge in the land had the leeway to grant a reduced sentence to a serial murderer. He went on trial at the Old Bailey along with MacKenney, where they were convicted of all the murders and given multiple life sentences. However, there was another murder which many people thought he had carried out, but which he had not confessed to.

After MacKenney and Childs shot dead and got rid of the body of their sixth victim, Ronnie Andrews – a man who had to die because MacKenney fancied his wife – they drove his American Chevrolet Impala car to East Anglia to get rid of it. They drove nearly 100 miles from East London to the area north of Kings Lynn on the Norfolk, Lincolnshire border. There, in the heart of the misty fens, in the dead of night, they rolled the car into the River Nene, close to where it flows out into the sea via The Wash. The car sunk into the depths and vanished. Months later, when the water level fell a couple of feet, an angler spotted it and the police winched it out.

It was traced to Ronnie Andrews, but he could not be found. By that time he had been reported as missing by his family and when his submerged car was found, police concluded he had probably committed suicide by drowning, and because the windows of the Chevy were open when it was recovered, it was assumed his body had simply floated off somewhere. It wasn't until Childs told his story to the police, months later, detectives were able to fully understand the sequence of events.

In 1979 Childs went on trial at the Old Bailey charged with six counts of murder. He pleaded guilty to them all and was jailed for life. The following year MacKenney went on trial charged with the same murders. He pleaded not guilty, claiming Childs had acted alone, but after a 40 day trial the jury convicted him of four of the killings; George, Brett, Sherwood and Andrews and he too was jailed for life. I was present on the 'Press Bench' when both men got their just desserts.

But there had been another strange and terrible event close to where the pair had disposed of Ronnie Andrews' car. At Sutton Bridge, a village in Lincolnshire where a road bridge spanned the river forming the border between Norfolk and Lincolnshire, there was a small motor garage and petrol station called Sutton Bridge Motors. A rarity in that era, the petrol station was open all night. At 2am on Easter Monday, 1979, the forecourt attendant Gordon Snowden was found murdered behind the counter. He had been battered to death with a heavy blunt weapon which was never found. The motive was robbery. The first thing police noticed was the cash till was missing.

The garage was only a few minutes drive, less than five miles, from where Ronnie Andrews' car was pushed into the river which flowed past just yards from the fuel pumps. When Childs confessed to being involved in the Andrews murder and told police about how his car was dumped in the River Nene, he never mentioned the murder of the petrol station manager. He was vague about exactly when he had been in the area of Sutton Bridge.

But by cross checking when Andrews had last been seen alive, to when his car was found submerged, the Scotland Yard squad were able to deduce it must have been very close to Easter 1979. Lincolnshire police investigating the Snowden case, which officially still remains unsolved, also never made the connection to the trip to the fens by the two London killers to get rid of the Chevrolet.

In 1998 I was contacted by a woman called Sandra Watson who lived in Hull. She had led an unremarkable life until she met and married a man who was an armed robber. When he was caught and jailed she visited him often in prison. As a result, although she had left school with no qualifications and worked in a Humberside caravan factory, she had started going to night school to study criminology. Her marriage had ended, but she'd gone on with her studies.

Of her own volition, she had started reading about notorious murders and writing to several convicted killers in jail and asking for interviews. Only one of the murderers had replied. His name was Bruce Childs. By the time she contacted me she had actually made a long trip to see him several times. I visited her at her home in Hull, and she asked me if I would like to go with her to visit Childs who was in Long Lartin jail, near Evesham, in Worcestershire.

By the time I went to visit him there with Sandra, Childs had been in jail for over 20 years. He knew he would never be released and had come to terms with the prospect. Security at Long Lartin, which had a reputation for being a tough regime, was some of the strictest I had ever encountered. At that time the prison also had a reputation for being the place where the Home Office tended to transfer prisoners who were considered to be difficult – which usually meant out and out troublemakers. Childs definitely fell into that category. He had been in a number of violent incidents, including some where prison staff had been attacked and injured with improvised weapons, in both Wormwood Scrubs and Parkhurst.

When Sandra and I arrived we were shown to a special visiting room where there were no other prisoners or visitors. Childs, a wiry balding man with darting blue eyes, was already waiting for us at a small wooden table which was bolted to the floor so it couldn't be picked up and used as a weapon. All the chairs in the room were bolted down the same way. The only other people in the room were five burly prison officers who sat around a table on a raised stage at the end of the room, reading newspapers or playing cards.

Childs, who was 62 by then, stood up and shook my hand. He nodded towards the group of guards at the end of the room.

"Know why they're here?" he asked. I shook my head. He leant forward slightly in his chair and said: "It's 'cos they are worried I am planning to kidnap you and take you hostage. They need to be ready to move in right quick."

I looked nervous. He burst out laughing. "Nah, don't worry mate. I'm not going to kidnap you, not this time anyway." He winked at Sandra: "I'm just in a playful mood."

I relaxed. A bit. Then Childs said: "Right. Buy me a Mars Bar," and he pointed to a dispensing machine in the corner loaded with crisps and chocolate bars, "and then we can talk." He wolfed it down in about three bites. Childs loved Mars Bars, and in a 90-minute meeting with him I had to buy him four, just to keep the conversation going.

We got down to business and he told me, straight out, that he had decided to confess to several more murders he'd not told the cops about when he was arrested in 1979. As he described the first four, he was either deliberately vague, his memory had faded, or he was just plain lying. I probed him carefully on each one, but no matter how hard I tried he could neither remember times, dates, places, or anything useful. He didn't know the names of any of his victims either, because in every case they had been strangers who, he said, had annoyed him, usually late at night, when he was a bit drunk and wasn't quite sure where he was.

So he killed them, usually with a big knife he habitually carried in his jacket. He was very matter of fact. But what I really did notice was, the one thing he really could remember and describe vividly, was the actual act of murder.

Childs seemed to light up, to become fully animated and excited, when he described plunging a knife into a stranger's heart, or in one case, pumping bullets from a gun into his victim's body. As he talked he would get to his feet and act out each stab thrust and as he did, a sort of maniacal grin spread over his face, and his voice rose an octave or two.

I knew he wasn't merely acting that part. But I was quickly forming the view he was lying, probably to impress Sandra who he undoubtedly had taken a shine to. However, we then came on to just one other murder, and this one really did interest me. It was the Sutton Bridge case. The brutal killing of garageman Gordon Snowden.

There was something very different about his countenance and the detail with which he described the event. He asked me: "Are you familiar with how Harry and me murdered Ronnie Andrews? And how we got rid of his car?"

"Yes," I replied. "I was at your trial, and have since read more about it."

"Good. Well, on the night we dumped the car, Harry chose the spot because it was an area he had been to in the past. We needed a place where the road ran right next to the river. Although it was a long way from East London, Harry knew it and said it was perfect. Now obviously, going all that way to dispose of a car in the back of beyond, we needed another car to get us back home again. So I followed him. I was in a Vauxhall Viva which I was using as a run about at the time.

"So after we pushed the Chevy down the bank, into the water, which was hard, because it was a big heavy car, and we had to make sure it sank completely. Harry and I got in my car to drive back to London. But because we had gone much further than I had expected, we were running low on fuel. So Harry said: 'That's OK, I know there's a garage up the road a few miles, we can get some there.' I thought he meant we'd siphon some out of another car on the forecourt or something. But when we got there the place was open. So we got the attendant to put some petrol in for us. When we went in to pay. I saw the till and I thought 'middle of nowhere, middle of the night, I'm having that'.

"I kept a heavy metal bar, a big case opener, under the seat of my car, so I got that, threatened the attendant with it and told him to open the till. But he couldn't because it was a brand new machine, one of the latest ones that was electric, not mechanical. He was an old boy and I think I'd properly put the wind up him, and he got flustered trying to open it quickly.

"Being me, a violent man by nature, I thought he was just pissing me about, so I hit him round the head with the bar, and he went down like a sack of spuds, spark out.

"I didn't know at that moment I had killed him, but obviously there was no chance of getting him to open it now, so I just nicked the whole thing, shoved it in the boot of my car and drove it back to London. We broke it open later, There was only a few fivers in it, I can't remember how much exactly, but I think it was less than 50 quid."

I asked Bruce what he had done with the iron bar and he said he had thrown it out of the window of his car in the darkness on the journey home. "What about the till? What did you do with that?" I asked.

"After we broke it open, I chucked it in the Thames near Bow Creek, where the River Lea runs in, the tidal bit."

"When did you find out you had killed the garage attendant?"

Childs thought for a bit then said: "There was a little bit about it in the morning papers a couple of days later. And when it said it was at Sutton Bridge, well, I knew it was the bloke I'd hit."

I asked him how he felt when he realised he'd killed a man. His response was memorable: "I'd already been involved in killing six others. So one more wasn't going to make any difference either way, was it?" Then he thought for a moment and said; "But I never meant to kill him. I hit him because he was fucking me about, but I overdid it. But like I said, I am a violent man, always have been. All the other people I killed were villains or people you'd not have much sympathy for. But the garage bloke was just a poor family man, a grandpa trying to earn a few pounds to make life a bit easier."

Later he added another reason why he had killed him, saying he and 'Big H' were worried the garage man would remember them if the sunken car was found and the police started asking questions. It was about eliminating any possible witnesses.

I thought Childs was applying what I term 'gangster logic' at this point. In other words, in his world, better to say you killed a man to stop him giving evidence against you than admit you had murdered a nice and defenceless old timer during a botched robbery for a measly few pounds. It was the one and only time I heard Childs show any regret or contrition for his crimes. He was very hardcore. And his account of the death of Gordon Snowden remains the one story he told me at Long Lartin which I thought was very probably true.

The timing, coinciding with the disposal very nearby of the Chevy, fitted perfectly. The logic of needing another car to follow MacKenney to the fens was perfect. And who else would MacKenney have taken as back up at that time if it wasn't his partner in murder Bruce Childs? And in the middle of the night, would a man with a lust for armed robbery and murder pass up the easy opportunity to steal the takings from an all night petrol station, protected only by a silver haired grandfather?

In addition, his description of the cash till, details of which were not made public, were accurate. It was one of the latest electronic models, when most others in thousands of shops and petrol garages were still older mechanical versions. I wrote up the story. It was headlined: "I have killed five more". It was accurate in as much as that was what he had said, but I didn't really believe four of the cases had ever happened. There wasn't a shred of evidence to back up his story. But with the filling station murder, on the balance of probabilities, it had a kind of symmetry and I think it is very likely he did it.

In 1998 it was the only unsolved murder in Lincolnshire. Two detectives came to see me from Lincoln police HQ and we had several hours of conversation. They asked me whether I thought Childs had done it. I said: "Well, we certainly know he is capable of murder. No doubt about that. And many of the facts go far beyond coincidence and do match."

They agreed. But after careful consideration they decided not charge him with the murder of Gordon Snowden. A confession without supporting evidence, forensic, witness, or an artefact which could be linked to the scene, was without value. There was quite an irony in this matter, I thought. Bruce Childs had spent much of his life as a criminal trying to prevent police proving he had committed serious crimes. Now he wanted to confess to a notorious unsolved murder, and he himself couldn't provide sufficient evidence to prove he HAD done it .

EPILOGUE

The world keeps turning and news keeps occurring. Every second of every day.

Even though after nearly five decades at the sharp end of news reporting I am out of it, I am still an avid follower. There are various expressions used to describe retired news hacks, most of them profane. 'Events Junkies' and 'Headline Jockeys' are two acceptable ones that come to mind. I am still one of those. Nowadays I read fewer papers, but I listen to and watch constantly broadcast news. Today, as I write this I have the choice of 20 or so news channels on my TV, about the same on my radio. I don't bother much with social media, but when I do it opens up hundreds more avenues.

When I began my professional life in the summer of 1967 there were only three channels on TV and only about five on radio, and two of them were 'pirate' music stations called 'Radio Caroline' and 'Radio London' which were based on old cargo ships anchored out in the North Sea to avoid prosecution by the British authorities.

So, what is news? That's a debate that has gone on in every beer-soaked bar used by journalists since the days of Charles Dickens. I still can't put a definition on it and frankly there were many times that every single publication I worked for ran articles that I read, scratched my head, and thought, "Why on earth do we think this is newsworthy?" I guess it is all in the eye of the beholder, or in my case, one of the 30 or so editors I was working for at the time.

As far as I am concerned, news, real news, needs to be 'revelatory'. A really good story needs to be telling the reader, viewer or listener something they absolutely did not know before. Preferably something that impacts their lives directly, or stops and makes them think.

Perhaps the best definition I can recall of 'news' came from a colleague who described it as: "Something someone significant, somewhere, does not want to be revealed."

I can't do better than that.

I know I was lucky in very many ways. Lucky, because I got an unexpected break which led me into journalism. I wanted to be a sport reporter, but had to learn the news business first.

Lucky because I was living and working in East London, where there was so much going on that any reporter with even a modicum of ability couldn't really go wrong.

Lucky, because instead of having to have a degree, as I would have to have today, all I had was a handful of O-Level exam passes. I was thrown in at the veritable deep end. It was immersion training. I learnt by doing the job.

Lucky because I worked for a series of dedicated news professionals who really knew their stuff and were full of good advice and cheerful encouragement.

Lucky, because I got a break to go and work in the hard knock but exciting world of Fleet Street when it was the epicentre of the news universe, and thus in some ways, the centre of the whole world.

Lucky, because I was well paid. From what I learn, today's journalists earn literally a third in real terms of what they received when I was at my peak.

Lucky because, again, partly by accident, I became a crime specialist, which opened up an unparalleled range of chances to report powerful stories.

And lucky because through enthusiasm combined with my own personality, I was able to persuade people to tell me things I really was not supposed to know, which I could then turn into the big revelatory stories my bosses demanded.

I was fortunate in other ways too. I grew up professionally in an era when police officers were allowed to speak to people 'from the press' inside and outside of work, in a way which they would not be allowed to do now.

Today almost every contact a police officer has with a journalist has to be authorised, recorded and logged.

I grew up in an era when local papers were the cornerstones of local communities, as important as the town hall, the various churches, and the hospitals.

Today three of the four local papers where I cut my teeth have vanished completely and one can only be found online.

Two of the daily regional papers I staffed for, including the once mighty *London Evening News*, have gone altogether. So have dozens more across the nation. When I was a child, London had three evening newspapers. Now it has none.

Of the national titles I worked for that sold millions of copies a day, only two remain.

Would I still encourage any youngster to become a journalist? Yes, I would. Few jobs offer the opportunity to experience so much, even to travel the world, and to have so much fun with so many good people.

ACKNOWLEDGEMENTS

I worked for 26 different editors in my career on Fleet Street and five others in my early years on local papers. I worked for more news editors and 'Heads of News' than I can possibly remember.

Some were excellent, some were indifferent, a couple were simply dreadful in every way conceivable.

Many of them, probably half of that total, are no longer with us. I did learn a lot from many of them and I like to think I got along with most of them. Not easy in a business so pressured and driven by the need to succeed. There were several who were key and I will always remember and be thankful to.

Tom Duncan at the *Newham Recorder* was pivotal. He had enough confidence in me to take me on when I was barely 21, and he taught me a lot in a very short time. He was the first to realise my potential as a crime and law enforcement specialist and appoint me to that specific role, which the paper, a very influential one at a time when local papers were actually important pillars of the communities they served, had never had one before.

Likewise George Hollingbery at the *London Evening News*, who gave me my first chance on Fleet Street, and who was always a source of sound advice.

At the *Sunday People*, Richard Stott and Phil Hall, both of whom had been terrific reporters before they took the helm, understood instinctively what I was about professionally and let me operate without interference.

Likewise, at the *Daily Mirror*, I would like to thank Colin Myler, Piers Morgan, Richard Wallace, Conor Hanna, and the late and much missed Eugene Duffy for having enough belief in me to allow me the freedom and latitude to operate in an often complex, nuanced and much misunderstood environment with little or no unnecessary interference.

I should also say that I have worked with a cast of literally hundreds of reporters and photographers, many of whom were outstandingly good professionals, and outstandingly good friends and colleagues.

The job of being a news reporter is a great leveller. I worked with equal ease with men and women who were from all four parts of the United Kingdom, the Republic of Ireland, Australia, New Zealand, Canada, the USA, and more.

They were from every faith and drawn from every part of society. I worked with women colleagues who had been to Cheltenham Ladies College and men who had left school at 16 in places as far apart as Stepney, Sunderland, Sheffield and St Austell and had worked their way up from the humblest of beginnings.

Part of the joy of working in a busy newsroom, even on the frequent days when events we were reporting were grim, was the irrepressible resilience of those around me, which manifested everyday in a blizzard of witty remarks, backchat, and often raucous humour. Sometimes it was a form of defence, but mostly it was just spontaneous.

As one esteemed colleague, a defence reporter who had experienced near death under fire with our soldiers several times in Iraq and Afghanistan: "If you can't see the funny side of this job , then you shouldn't be in it at all."

As for my many friends in policing, who have willingly and happily given me assistance and allowed me to see, hear and know so many things I should not have been able to – there are simply too many to mention by name.

I have been trusted and received excellent help and advice from a very disparate group of characters – mostly men, but some influential women too – and for that I will always be most grateful.

They not only allowed me a window onto their strange and mysterious world, where things were very often not what they at first seemed to be, they also taught me integrity, discretion, and the ability, very often, to see life from someone else's perspective.

From them I not only learned interesting things I could write about, they also taught me many life lessons. I like to believe that the person I am today (whoever that is) was shaped significantly by the men and women I met and became friends with in policing.

To all of them I offer my most sincere thanks.